PROTO-SLAVIC AND OLD BULGARIAN SOUND CHANGES

Boryana Velcheva

Translated, edited, and typeset by
Ernest A. Scatton

Slavica Publishers, Inc.

Slavica publishes a wide variety of textbooks and scholarly books on the languages, people, literatures, cultures, history, etc. of the USSR and Eastern Europe. For a complete catalog of books and journals from Slavica, with prices and ordering information, write to:

Slavica Publishers, Inc.
PO Box 14388
Columbus, Ohio 43214

ISBN: 0-89357-189-X

Original title: Праславянски и старобългарски фонологически изменения. Copyright © 1980 by Boryana Aleksandrova Velcheva. All rights reserved.

Translation copyright © 1988 by Ernest A. Scatton. All rights reserved.

Printed in the United States of America.

In memory of my brother

Nikola Velčev

Table of Contents

Introduction	7
Chapter 1	25
I. Preliminary Remarks	25
II. Persistent Changes	27
Chapter 2: Assimilatory Fronting	31
I. Progressive Palatalization of Velars	31
II. The First Regressive Palatalization of Velars	34
III. -as Becomes -us	38
IV. Vocalic Fronting	38
V. aj and a:j Become e:	40
VI. The Second Regressive Palatalization of Velars	41
Chapter 3: The Elimination of Closed Syllables	46
I. Clusters Containing Anterior Consonants	46
II. Early Changes of l and N	48
III. Regressive Assimilation for Height	51
IV. Regressive Assimilation for Height: Vowels	51
V. Word-Final Changes	59
VI. Regressive Assimilation of Consonants for Height; Dental Palatalizations	68
VII. Delayed Release Consonants and Clusters with Strident Consonants	78
VIII. Dental Epenthesis and Its Relation to Liquid Metathesis	85
Chapter 4: Reorganization of the Vocalic System	88
I. Prothetic j and w	89
II. The Evolution of ü:	99
III. ы and the Evolution of the Vocalic System	102
IV. The Development of Nonhigh Lax Vowels: a → o	105
V. Low Tense Vowels	106
VI. High Lax Vowels	123
A. The Yers	123
B. Nasal Vowels	148
Conclusion	168
Works Cited	174

Translator's Note

In translating *Proto-Slavic and Old Bulgarian Sound Changes*, I applied the following conventions for transcription and transliteration. Old and Middle Bulgarian examples are given as cited in the original — in cyrillic and glagolitic. Attested examples from modern languages are italicized, cyrillic transliterated. Bold-faced transcription is generally used for all other examples, including sample derivations, and underlying and intermediate representations. All examples follow the original as closely as possible, and Velčeva's transcription symbols (1.2) are used with minor exceptions (page 30, note 1). Cyrillic place-names and bibliographic references are transliterated according to the so-called "scholarly system"; Bulgarian ъ is transliterated as â, in keeping with the practice of the Bulgarian Academy of Sciences.

The translation was composed with SoftCraft's FancyFont. I am grateful to David Birnbaum of Harvard University for the cyrillic and glagolitic fonts and for numerous diacritics. I am also grateful to Linda Scatton for her invaluable assistance in editing the translation.

INTRODUCTION

I. Goals and Methods

1.1. This investigation attempts to provide a basis for the systematic study of the historical dialectology of Old and Middle Bulgarian through the reconstruction of the earliest underlying phonological system common to all Bulgarian dialects. Whatever revisions it eventually requires, a reconstruction of this sort — the result of applying rigorous analytical methods — is of unquestionable priority.

In recent years linguists describing the dialects of Bulgarian have made significant progress. Now it is up to those concerned with the history of the language to make a concerted effort to establish the chronology and form of the changes which have occurred in them. It has become increasingly clear that dialect descriptions must be based on strictly determined historical foundations. For example, we must attribute concrete linguistic value to symbols such as ѥ, ѧ, ѫ, ѧ, ъ, and ь, which at the present time are widely used in attempts to establish the original forms underlying the modern dialects.

Investigators of the historical dialectology of Bulgarian may concentrate on one of three basic concerns:

1. historical reconstruction based upon analysis of modern structures;

2. investigations of New Bulgarian dialect differences recognizable in written records dating from the seventeenth, eighteenth, and nineteenth centuries; comparison of these to the modern facts; and the identification of historical processes and tendencies;

3. analysis of the written records of Old Bulgarian and comparison of the results with data from later periods.

Regardless of the system we choose to study, it is absolutely essential to compare it with Old Bulgarian, on one hand, and with the modern linguistic situation, on the other.

Only in the future will historians of Bulgarian be able to undertake the task of associating systematically related features of the written records with specific modern dialects. [1] In addition, the investigation of each and every dialect will require identifying and tracing all changes which have made it, as a dialect system, part of the Bulgarian language. As prerequisites for research of this sort, we must have:

1. *Full and systematic data on modern Bulgarian.* We can make little use of the fact that features A, B, and C occur in a given *group* of dialects. Rather, we need to know if, in a particular dialect, feature A co-occurs with B and C, or with only one or the other of them; or if, in actuality, B and C are characteristic of some neighboring dialect. Dialect maps and atlases, grammars of individual dialects, and full dialect dictionaries are very useful; differential dictionaries and combined descriptions of several similar, neighboring dialects are much less so.

2. *Complete and systematic philological data on the two alphabets and the written records of Old Bulgarian.* We still need to study the distribution of graphic and orthographic features, the evolution of orthographic systems, the mixing of the norms which arose in various literary centers, the literary centers themselves, the "psychology" of scribal errors, and much more. Linguistic claims can be made only on the basis of well specified *sets* of features whose connection is more or less probable with respect to origin, time, and place.

The written records of Old and Middle Bulgarian have been extensively studied as data for the history of the Bulgarian language and its dialects (e.g., Miletič 1886, 1896; Conev 1905, 1906, 1914, 1919; Ščepkin 1899, 1906; Kul'bakin 1907; von Arnim 1930; Il'inskij 1912; Bernštejn 1948; Mirčev and Kodov 1965). However, an independent, systematic investigation of Bulgarian historical dialectology — including consideration of problems, goals, and methodology — has yet to appear. [2]

Previous studies of the language of written monuments have provided indispensable data for the study of the history of Bulgarian dialects. At the same time, however, they have raised many questions which earlier analytical methods have been unable to answer satisfactorily. These include, for example, the question of exactly where the texts originated — a question closely related to establishing the organization, distribution, and subsequent developments of the original dialects (Velčeva 1964).

Existing studies of the written records do not consistently indicate whether they are concerned with locating a *text* or a *manuscript*. Nor is it always apparent what is actually under consideration, the system underlying the graphic and orthographic characteristics of a given manuscript or the system serving as the norm for its scribe. It may not even be clear if the study is dealing with the dialect of one or several scribes. And, most important, there exist virtually no attempts to determine which features are *systematically* related in a given manuscript. In general, most existing studies describe isolated, individual features. Because the manuscripts passed from hand to hand and came to contain layers of different systems, traces of systems, and divergences from systems, attempts to establish where such isolated features originated are futile. Future investigations will first have to reconstruct the old orthographic systems found in the written records and then, if possible, relate these systems to specific dialects. Perhaps the best example of research of this sort is von Arnim's study of *Psalterium Sinaiticum* (1930).

At present, the investigation of glagolitic records holds the most promise. The graphic and orthographic systems of glagolitic are fewer than those of cyrillic; their chronology is better understood; we know where the creators of the glagolitic alphabet came from. The present study is based primarily on glagolitic records dating from the tenth and eleventh centuries. Cyrillic texts are used only as supplementary material. The philological study of Old Bulgarian cyrillic records in general and the development of cyrillic graphic and orthographic systems in particular remain important subjects for future research.

The present work was preceded by a number of philological and paleographic studies which attempted to shed light on various controversial and troublesome aspects of the development of glagolitic: the composition of the original glagolitic alphabet, the classification of glagolitic written records, the written shape and vocalization of certain glagolitic letters, the evolution of the shapes of glagolitic letters, the development of glagolitic orthography, and the utilization of abecedariums as sources of historical data (Velčeva 1966, 1966a, 1968, 1973, 1977). These studies are related to some of the rich and highly polemical research on these topics over the last twenty years: e.g., Mareš 1956, 1964, 1971; Tkadlčík 1956, 1964, 1971; Hamm 1970; Nedeljković 1965, 1971; Pavlović 1957; Vrana 1963, 1964; Mošin 1973; Lunt 1957, 1959, 1974; Auty

1963; Samilov 1968; Kolesov 1973; Gâlâbov 1963, 1974; Ilčev 1969, 1972, 1973; Dobrev 1969.

The variations observed in glagolitic records lead to a series of questions. In sets of alternating forms, such as the following, which is the older or oldest: жѣба or жаба, пишѧ or пишѫ, тоуждь, цюждь or цоуждь, ѣгнѧ or агнѧ? What shape do the common underlying forms of Slavic take? How did they arise? What place do specific changes occupy in the general development of Slavic dialects and in the individual developments of Bulgarian dialects? Which features are common to all Bulgarian dialects, and when did they appear? Which dialect differences are the oldest? To answer these questions — even tentatively — we must trace the development of the system of Old Bulgarian, beginning with the oldest Proto-Slavic sound changes, in order (1) to establish the nature and chronology of a number of important changes and (2) to specify more precisely the earliest common underlying forms of the phonetic features reflected in Old Bulgarian.

The present study does not pretend to be a full phonological history of Proto-Slavic, much less a comparative grammar of the Slavic languages. It seeks only to establish the basis for the subsequent differentiation of Bulgarian dialects. Nevertheless, to the extent that issues of Proto-Slavic are considered, we attempt to solve certain problems concerning the organization of the data. We must bear in mind Toporov's (1959) concerns and suggestions for the historical study of Proto-Slavic. [3] Toporov contends that previous work in this area has merely related Proto-Slavic to Indo-European on one hand and to the individual Slavic languages on the other, while depriving Proto-Slavic "of its own history." Consequently we must (1) create a theory which explains the known facts, (2) reconstruct Proto-Slavic on the basis of the individual Slavic languages, (3) keep in mind that Old Bulgarian is not Common Slavic, (4) take into account the findings of Indo-European linguistics, (5) attempt to establish the *relative* (not *absolute*) chronology of linguistic changes [4], (6) apply the principle of choosing "the simplest theory covering the greatest number of facts — all other things being equal" (Toporov 1959:25), (7) look for general lines of development in separate events, for "the methodological value of finding (or constructing) tendencies of this sort is that they explain facts which otherwise remain isolated" (Toporov 1959:26).

Because of the need to consider the mutual relationships among problems frequently discussed in the past, the present study tries to be maximally economical and general. References, examples, and quotations are kept to a minimum. For additional information, readers may turn to a number of important recent studies of Proto-Slavic phonology: Lekov 1960, 1968; Bernštejn 1961, 1974; Filin 1962, 1973; Shevelov 1964; Stieber 1969; Furdal 1961; Birnbaum 1966. The latter two contain extensive bibliographies of works devoted to the dialects of Proto-Slavic. Diels 1932 offers rich material regarding Old Bulgarian manuscripts.

Problems of phonological theory are not taken up here. Nevertheless, in attempting to arrive at a profitable "working" methodology for historical analysis, we adopt a view of language close to the views of Reformatskij 1963 and Halle 1962. Theoretical positions taken from them include:

1. "Neither the linguistic sign nor language as a whole is conceivable without 'contemptible' phonetics. But in this regard we must understand phonetics in a new way, not as the nineteenth century understood it" (Reformatskij 1963:107).

2. Linguistic descriptions do not require three separate levels of phonological representation (morphophonemic, phonemic, and phonetic), but only two: morphophonemic (Reformatskij's *phonemic*; systematic phonemic) and phonetic (systematic phonetic).

3. It is essential for phonological analysis to specify these two levels of representation. According to Reformatskij (1963:109), their relationship is given by the formula *phoneme — allophone*, e.g., /k/ — [k] → [k']; or *phoneme — variation — allophone*, e.g.:

$$/k'/ \left\{ \begin{matrix} [k] & \to & [k'] \\ [k'] & \to & [č] \end{matrix} \right\}$$

According to Halle, the two levels of phonological representation are related by ordered rules. First, /k/ — [k] → [k'] under certain circumstances; then [k'] → [č] under others. In so far as rules represent linguistic phenomena as processes, Halle's approach is more applicable to historical investigations.

INTRODUCTION

Historical grammar is taken to be the history of changes in the grammar of a given language; historical phonology is part of historical grammar. The phonology of a language is that component of its grammar which contains rules relating morphophonological and phonetic structure; these rules are referred to as phonological. For example, the Bulgarian alternation *ródove* ~ *róden* ~ *rót* is subject to a grammatical (in this case phonological) rule which devoices word-final nonsonorant consonants:

$$[-\text{sonorant}] \rightarrow [-\text{voice}] \mathbin{/\mkern-2mu/} \text{———}\#$$

The phonological component of the grammar — the phonological rules — link the two levels of phonological representation, the *morphophonemic*, in which the phonological system appears in an abstract form, and the *phonetic*, in which sounds take concrete shapes. On the other hand, phonological rules specify the linguistically relevant phonetic or phonological features which play a role in the sound system of a given language and at the same time reflect the invariance present on the phonetic level.

From the historical point of view, the morphophonemic level of representation often corresponds to older, underlying structure, while historical changes appear as phonological rules, which, at each successive stage of development, provide the link to underlying structure. In this way, the descriptive method itself becomes a theory of sound change.

The underlying forms used in this study are based on etymological forms proposed by Indo-Europeanists, especially Meillet, Brückner, St. Mladenov, Georgiev, Mareš, and Stang. In unclear cases or when these sources disagree, we choose forms which agree with the reconstruction of Proto-Slavic proposed here.

At a certain point changes in the phonological component of the grammar may lead to changes in morphophonemic structure and to reorganization of the phonological system. The question of "restructuring" has been the subject of lively debate among American linguists (e.g., P. Kiparsky 1965, King 1969, Vennemann 1974). The evolution of Proto-Slavic offers an opportunity to clarify a number of theoretical issues by revealing different stages in individual processes:

1. Innovations which have no effect on morphophonemic structure. These include innovations which take place under specific phonological circumstances and are predictable in terms of phonological environments; they are of two types:

a. innovations which do not involve changes in the inventory of the system's distinctive features (e.g., vocalic changes in Proto-Slavic prior to the elimination of diphthongs);

b. changes which lead to the introduction of new contrasts (e.g., the velar palatalizations, which gave rise to new oppositions of distinctive features; changes of this sort represent the phonologization of a given feature; consider, for example, the appearance of contrast of [±strident] in consonants or the appearance of the feature *labial* in vowels after the elimination of diphthongs).

2. The loss or appearance of correlations leading to subsequent innovations which radically restructure the phonological system (Jakobson et al. 1928).

Restructuring — changes in morphophonemic structure — represents a qualitatively new stage in the evolution of a phonological system. For example, Proto-Slavic velars could not occur before nonback nonconsonantal segments — front vowels and j; in this environment they became nonvelar (i.e., nonback) and strident. As a result of the first palatalization, the alternations k ~ č, g ~ ž, x ~ š arose: могж ~ можеши, пекж ~ печеши, грѣхъ ~ грѣшьнъ. At a certain stage of development the alternation *velar* ~ *alveopalatal* was environmentally conditioned and could be expressed as a rule. After the change of ѣ to a after soft consonants or j, which dates from the time of the palatalization of dentals or shortly thereafter, conditions arose for changes in the morphophonemic inventory of the language and for the "lexicalization" of groups such as ča (часъ) and l'a (волю). In this way, at certain stages of development, phonological changes may give rise to new underlying morphophonemic forms, which themselves serve as the basis for subsequent changes.

Morphological factors frequently play a role in changes of morphophonemic structure. This is observed quite commonly in generalizations of suffixal and inflectional morphemes. Consider the replacement of c (from the progressive palatalization) by k —

one of the earliest examples of restructuring in Proto-Slavic morphemes (Avanesov 1968). Similarly, the occurrence of a in the nominative singular of ja-stems and the genitive singular of jo-stems may be explained as generalization: here ѣ was replaced very early by a from hard a- and o-stems (cf., мѧжа for мѧжѣ, доуша for доушѣ, отьца for отьць).

The approach taken in this study is most effective when reconstructing old changes with the help of strictly formalized rules, which leads to maximum precision, explanation, and objectivity. Throughout the study distinctive features — rather than phonemes — are taken to be the minimal contrastive units. [5]

In historical grammar in general and historical phonology in particular, changes are described in two ways: (1) as the addition of new rules to the grammar and (2) as simplifications or generalizations of existing rules. [6] For their part, rules may be "persistent," i.e., apply over an extended period of time whenever the appropriate conditions arise; or they apply only a single time. The essence of historical phonology is that new rules correspond to sound changes (Halle 1962, P. Kiparsky 1965), while rule simplification is related to so-called generalization, analogy, and hypercorrection — processes based on grammatical generalization. In this regard recall Paul's terms (1960) "Lautwandel und abweichende Neuerzeugung."

Dialect differences in a given language are related to common underlying forms reconstructed for a given stage of historical development. Differences themselves are due to differences in the rules of the dialects' grammars: their number, their form, or the order in which they apply. [7] For example, a number of features characteristic of Eastern Bulgarian dialects (e.g., the *jat-shift* and vowel reduction) may be attributed to rules which are absent from the grammars of other Bulgarian dialects or which occur with different degrees of generality. On the other hand, we can explain the contrast **vnuka** ~ **unuka** as the result of the application of the same two general rules in different orders. The underlying form of both examples would be **wъnuka** (with prothetic w before high back nonlabial vowel; 5.1). The relevant rules applying to this form are the loss of weak yers and the elimination of w (→v before vowel and u before consonant). Let us assume that these rules apply in different orders in the two dialects under consideration:

Dialect 1		Dialect 2	
	wъnuka		wъnuka
1. loss of yer:	wnuka	1. loss of w:	vъnuka
2. loss of w:	unuka	2. loss of yer:	vnuka

Two previous phonological studies carried out within the framework of generative grammar are of special interest for Bulgarian readers: the sixth edition of Lunt's *Old Church Slavonic Grammar* (1974) and Scatton's *Bulgarian Phonology* (1975). The present work is distinguished from them by its historical approach. However, a number of the observations and rules proposed here are similar or identical to ones found there. In this regard, our study has somewhat more in common with Scatton's work than with Lunt's. [8]

II. Phonetic Features

1.2. We use the inventory of phonetic features discussed in detail by Chomsky and Halle 1968:176 and 293-329. Accordingly we distinguish the following major classes of speech sounds:

	obstruents	m	n	ŋ	r	l	vowels	glides
consonantal	+	+	+	+	+	+	−	−
vocalic	−	−	−	−	+	+	+	−
sonorant	−	+	+	+	+	+	+	+
syllabic	−	±	±	±	±	±	+	− [9]

Consonantal segments are specified for point of articulation as:

	labial	dental	alveo-palatal	palatal	velar	labio-velar
high	−	−	+	+	+	+
back	−	−	−	−	+	+
anterior	+	+	−	−	−	−
labial	+	−	−	−	−	+
coronal	−	+	+	−	−	−

Additional features include: *nasal, voiced, continuous*, and *strident* (for f, v, and the sibilants). The affricates c, č, ӡ, ӡ̌ are specified [+delayed release]; this feature is also used to specify the long stops tː, tʼː, and dʼː (table 1).

In this classificatory system, soft (palatalized) consonants are specified by the pair of features [+high, -back]. Hard consonants are [-high, -back] or [+high, +back], that is generally [αhigh, αback] (Scatton 1975:8).

The full vocalic inventory necessary to describe the chronologically and territorially different systems considered here is [10]:

	i	ɪ	ü	y	ə	u	ʊ	e	ɛ	ъ	ʌ	o	ɔ	ä	a	ô
high	+	+	+	+	+	+	+	-	-	-	-	-	-	-	-	-
low	-	-	-	-	-	-	-	-	-	-	-	-	-	+	+	+
back	-	-	-	+	+	+	+	-	-	+	+	+	+	-	+	+
tense	+	-	+	+	-	+	-	+	-	+	-	+	-	+	+	+
labial	-	-	+	-	-	+	+	-	-	-	-	+	+	-	-	+

For the earliest period in the development of Bulgarian, vowels are usually represented by the following symbols:

[i] : и, iː, i   [ɛ] : є, ӓ, ě
[ɪ] : ь, ĭ, i   [ъ] : ъ, ə
[ü] : ю, ü   [ʌ] : o, ŏ, ă, ə, ъ
[y] : ы, y, uː, yː   [o] : o, ŏ, ă
[ə] : ъ, u, ŭ   [ɔ] : o, ă, ŏ
[u] : oy, u, ů   [ä] : ѣ, ê, eː, äː, æ
[ʊ] : ъ, ŭ, u   [a] : a, aː, oː
[e] : є, eː

In the modern dialects, the lax vowels [ɪ], [ə], [ʊ], [ɛ], [ʌ], [ɔ] occur in unstressed syllables (Scatton 1975:17).

In the interests of readability and typography, discussions of Proto-Slavic here employ the letters customarily used in Slavic studies. The feature specifications of segments are those appropriate for the concrete examples under consideration at a given point.

	j	w	r	l	ł	p	b	v	m	t	t:	d	d:	n	s	z	ʒ	c	č	š	ž	ǯ	k	k'	g	g'	x	ŋ
vocalic	−	−	+	+	+	−	−	−	−	−	−	−	−	−	−	−	−	−	−	−	−	−	−	−	−	−	−	−
consonantal	−	−	+	+	+	+	+	+	+	+	+	+	+	+	+	+	+	+	+	+	+	+	+	+	+	+	+	+
sonorant	+	+	+	+	+	−	−	−	+	−	−	−	−	+	−	−	−	−	−	−	−	−	−	−	−	−	−	+
high	+	+	−	−	+	−	−	−	−	−	−	−	−	−	−	−	−	−	−	−	−	−	+	+	+	+	+	−
back	−	+	−	−	+	−	−	−	−	−	−	−	−	−	−	−	−	−	−	−	−	−	−	−	−	−	+	+
anterior	−	−	−	+	+	+	+	+	+	+	+	+	+	+	+	+	−	+	−	+	−	−	−	−	−	−	−	−
coronal	−	−	+	+	−	−	−	−	−	+	+	+	+	+	+	+	+	+	+	+	+	+	−	−	−	−	−	−
labial	−	−	−	−	−	+	+	+	+	−	−	−	−	−	−	−	−	−	−	−	−	−	−	−	−	−	−	−
voiced	+	+	+	+	−	−	+	+	+	−	−	+	+	+	−	+	+	−	−	−	+	+	−	−	+	+	−	+
continuant	−	−	−	−	−	−	−	+	−	−	−	−	−	−	+	+	+	−	−	+	+	−	−	−	−	−	+	−
nasal	−	−	−	−	−	−	−	−	+	−	−	−	−	+	−	−	−	−	−	−	−	−	−	−	−	−	−	+
strident	−	−	−	−	−	−	−	−	−	−	−	−	−	−	+	+	+	+	+	+	+	+	−	−	−	−	−	−
delayed release	−	−	−	−	−	−	−	−	−	−	−	−	−	−	−	−	−	+	+	−	−	+	−	−	−	−	−	−

Table 1

III. Notational conventions

1.3. The following notational conventions and abbreviations are commonly used throughout this book:

  C : consonant   V: vowel
  G : glide   N: nasal consonant
  + : morpheme boundary #: word boundary

  ∼ : constraint; alternation

  $\emptyset \to x$: x is inserted
  $x \to \emptyset$: x is deleted
  $x \to y$: x becomes y

  $x \to y \mathbin{/\mkern-2mu/} \underline{} A$: x becomes y before A
         (xA→yA)
  $x \to y \mathbin{/\mkern-2mu/} A \underline{}$: x becomes y after A
         (Ax→Ay)
  $x \to y \mathbin{/\mkern-2mu/} A $: x becomes y before or after A
         (xA→yA, Ax→Ay)
  $x \to y \mathbin{/\mkern-2mu/} A \underline{} B$: x becomes y between A and B
         (AxB→AyB)

  x (y) : x or xy

  $\left\{ \begin{array}{c} x \\ y \end{array} \right\}$: x or y

  <x> : if x is present

  / ... / : morphophonemic representation
  [...] : phonetic representation

  C_1 : one or more consonants or glides

  $C_\emptyset$: none or one or more nonsyllabic segments

  $C_\emptyset V$: syllable

The conjoined presence or absence of features is indicated by Greek letter variables: α, β, γ; for example:

[αx, αy] : [+x, +y] or [−x, −y]
[αx, −αy] : [+x, −y] or [−x, +y].

IV. Abbreviations

acc	accusative	pal	palatal
ant	anterior	pers	person
aor	aorist	pl	plural
cont	continuant	pres	present
cons	consonantal	prog	progressive
cor	coronal	prn	pronoun
dent	dental	PSl	Proto-Slavic
del	delayed release	regr	regressive
dial	dialect(al)	Russ	Russian
gen	genitive	SC	Serbo-Croatian
Got	Gothic	sg	singular
IE	Indo-European	son	sonorant
inst	instrumental	strd	strident
lab	labial	strs	stress
loc	locative	syll	syllabic
masc	masculine	tns	tense
nas	nasal	vcd	voiced
NB	New Bulgarian	vel	velar
nom	nominative	voc	vocalic
OB	Old Bulgarian		

Notes

1. The first steps — specifying the chronology and the locations of many changes — have already been taken; see Conev 1919, St. Mladenov 1929, and especially Mirčev 1958.
2. In this respect Bulgarian linguistics lags behind Soviet linguistics; see Gorškova 1972 for references to the basic literature of Russian historical dialectology.
3. The comparative Slavic grammars of Lekov 1960 and 1968, Bernštejn 1961 and 1974, Shevelov 1964, and Stieber 1969 appeared after Toporov's article.
4. In this connection, Toporov (1959:16) asserts that "for the history of Proto-Slavic it is not significant whether one particular change preceded another in general, but only whether it preceded another which depended upon it or was in some way connected to it."
5. For discussion of the advantages of this approach see Jakobson, Fant, Halle 1955, Revzin 1964, and Lekomceva 1966.
6. Numerous studies of grammatical rules have appeared in the recent past; see, for example, Halle 1962, P. Kiparsky 1965, 1972, and 1973, Chomsky and Halle 1968, King 1969 and 1973.
7. For detailed defense of this theoretical position see Keyser 1963, Saporta 1965, and King 1969.
8. During visits to the University of Washington-Seattle, Harvard, and MIT, I was able to discuss many of the problems considered here with Morris Halle, Horace Lunt, Paul Kiparsky, James Augerot, Michael Brame, Ernest Scatton, Robert Ewen, and others. To all of them and to my reviewer, Miroslav Janakiev, I am deeply indebted.
9. Syllabic m̥, n̥, r̥, l̥ are reconstructed for Proto-Indo-European, and syllabic r̥, l̥ for stages in the development of several Slavic dialects.
10. This matrix is based on Chomsky and Halle 1968, Halle and Stevens 1969, Perkell 1971, P. Kiparsky 1974, and Keyser 1973.

Primary Sources

Abcd: *Abecedarium Bulgaricum* (Paris abecedarium). See, e.g., V. Jagić, "Glagoličeskoe pis'mo," *Enciklopedija slavjanskoj filologii*, vol. 3, p. 235, table 7, no. 16 (also plate 7, no. 16), SPb.: Imp. akademija nauk, 1911.
Ass: *Codex Assemanianus*, Vatican Library, Cod. slav. 3. J. Vajs and J. Kurz, *Evangeliarium Assemani*, 2 vols., Prague: Československá akad. věd, 1929-55.
Banduri abecedarium: (a) A. Banduri, *Animadversiones in Constantini Porphyrogeniti libros de thematibus et de administrando imperio*, pag. 115 [64]. In *Imperium orientalle*, vol. 2, Paris, 1711. (Also: *Byzantinae historiae scriptores, Graece et Latine*, 24, Venice, 1729.) (b) I. Sreznevskij, *Drevnie glagoličeskie pamjatniki*, SPb.: Imp. akademija nauk, 1866, 26-28. (c) J. Vrana, "O postanku i karakteru staroslovjenskih azbukvara i azbučnih molitava," *Filologija* [Zagreb] 4 (1963), 191-204.
BDA: *Bâlgarski dialekten atlas*. 4 vols., S.: BAN, 1964-81.
BojE: *Bojana Gospel*, Lenin National Library, Moscow, Grigorovič collection, no. 8, M., 1690.
BojP: *Bojana Palimpsest*. Iv. Dobrev, *Glagoličeskijat tekst na Bojanskija palimpsest: starobâlgarski pametnik ot kraja na XI vek*, S.: BAN, 1972 [glagolitic text in the *Bojana Gospel*].
Bol: *Bologna Psalter*, University Library, Bologna, no. 2499. (a) V. Jagić, *Psalterium bononiense*, Vienna: A. Holzhausen, 1907; (b) Iv. Dujčev, *Bolonski psaltir: Bâlgarski pametnik ot XIII vek*, S.: BAN, 1968 [photo-reproduction].
Čergeg prayers: L. Miletič, "Sedmigradskite bâlgari," *Sbornik za narodni umotvorenija, nauka i knižnina* 13, S.: Dâržavna pečatnica, 1896, 153-256. Also L. Miletič, *Sedmigradskite bâlgari i texnijat ezik*, Spisanie na Bâlgarskata akademija na naukite, 33, S.: P. Gluškov, 1926.
Cloz: *Glagolita Clozianus*, (a) City Museum, Trident, no. 2476 and (b) Ferdinand Museum, Innsbruck. (a) V. Vondrák, *Glagolita Clozův*, Prague: Česká akad., 1893; (b) A. Dostál, *Clozianus*, Prague: Československá akad. věd, 1959.
DE: *Dobromir Gospel*, (a) National Public Library, Leningrad, Q p I 55; (b) St. Catherine's Monastery, Mt. Sinai, no. 43. (a) M. Altbauer, *Dobromirovo evangelie: kirilski pametnik ot XII vek*, Skopje: Makedonska akademija na naukite i umetnostite,

1973 [photo-reproduction]; (b) B. Velčeva, *Dobromirovo evangelie: bâlgarski pametnik ot načaloto na XII vek*, S.: BAN, 1975.

En: *Eninski Epistle*, Cyril and Methodius National Library, Sofia, no. 1144. K. Mirčev and Xr. Kodov, *Eninski apostol: starobâlgarski pametnik ot XI vek*, S.: BAN, 1965.

Euch: *Euchologium Sinaiticum*, (a) St. Catherine's Monastery, Mt. Sinai; (b) National Public Library, Leningrad, Glag. 3. R. Nahtigal, *Euchologium Sinaiticum*, 2 vols., Ljubljana: Akademija znanosti i umetnosti, 1941-42.

GP: *Grigorovič Parimeinik*, Lenin National Library, Moscow, Grigorovič Collection, no. 2, M., 1685. R. Brandt, *Grigorovičev parimejnik v sličenii s drugimi parimejnikami*, 1-2, M., 1894.

Hil: *Hilendar Fragments*, Gor'kij National Scientific Library, Odessa, P 1/533. (a) S. Kul'bakin, *Xilandarskie listki: Otryvok kirillovskoj pis'mennosti IX veka*, Pamjatniki staroslavjanskogo jazyka 1, no. 1, SPb.: Imp. akademija nauk, 1900; (b) A. Minčeva, "Xilandarski listove," *Starobâlgarski kirilski otkâsleci*, S.: BAN, 1978, 24-39.

KE: *Kjustendil Gospel*. B. Conev, "Kjustendilsko četveroevangelie: srednobâlgarski prototip na VI pravopisna škola," *Periodičesko spisanie na Bâlgarskoto knižovno družestvo* 66 (1905), 536-61.

KF: *Kiev Fragments*, Central Academy Library, Kiev. Iv. Ohijenko [Ilarion, Metropolitan of Winnipeg and All Canada], *Nayvažnišči pam'jatky cerkovno-slov'jans'koji movy. Častyna 1: Pam'jatki staro-slov'jans'ki X-XI vikiv*, Studiji do ukrajins'koji hramatyky, 5. Warsaw: Drukarnja Synodal'na, 1929, 310-23.

MacFol: *Macedonian Cyrillic Folium*, Academy Library, Leningrad, no. 24 4 16. (a) G. Il'inskij, *Makedonskij listok: Otryvok neizvestnogo pamjatnika kirillovskoj pis'mennosti XI-XII v.*, Pamjatniki staroslavjanskogo jazyka 1, no. 5, SPb.: Imp. akademija nauk, 1906; (b) A. Minčeva, "Makedonski kirilski list," *Starobâlgarski kirilski otkâsleci*, S.: BAN, 1978, 76-114.

Mar: *Codex Marianus*, Lenin National Library, Moscow, Grigorovič Collection, no. 6, M., 1689; V. Jagić, *Pamjatnik glagoličeskoj pis'mennosti: Mariinskoe evangelie*, SPb., 1883.

Munich abecedarium: (a) N. Trubetzkoy, "Das 'Münchener slawische Abededarium,'" *Byzantinoslavica* 2 (1930), 29- 31; (b) N. Durnovo, "Das Münchener Abecedarium," Ibid., 32-41.

OchrE: *Ochrid Epistle*, Lenin National Library, Moscow, Grigorovič Collection, no. 13, M., 1695. S. Kul'bakin, *Oxridskaja rukopis' apostola konca XII veka*, Bâlgarski starini 3 (1907). S.: Dâržavna pečatnica.

OchrFol: *Ochrid Folia* (*Ochrid Gospel*), Odessa University Library, no. 24. G. Il'inskij, *Oxridskie glagoličeskie listki*, Pamjatniki staroslavjanskogo jazyka 3, no. 2, P.: Rossijskaja gosudarstvennaja akademičeskaja tipografija, 1915.

OstE: *Ostromir Gospel*, National Public Library, Leningrad. A. Vostokov, *Ostromirovo evangelie 1056-1057 goda*, M.: Akademija nauk, 1843. Reprinted: Wiesbaden: Harrassowitz, 1964.

Pir: *Pirdop Epistle*, Cyril and Methodius National Library, Sofia, no. 497.

Ril: *Rila Folia*, Rila Monastery and the Academy Library, Leningrad. Iv. Gošev, *Rilski glagoličeski listove*, S.: BAN, 1956.

Sav: *Savvina Kniga*, Central National Archive, Moscow, f. 381, no. 14. V. Ščepkin, *Savvina kniga*, Pamjatniki staroslavjanskogo jazyka 1, no. 2, SPb.: Imp. akademija nauk, 1903.

SPs: *Psalterium Sinaiticum*, St. Catherine's Monastery, Mt. Sinai. (a) S. Sever'janov, *Sinajskaja psaltyr'*: *Glagoličeskij pamjatnik XI veka*, Pamjatniki staroslavjanskogo jazyka 4, P.: Rossijskaja gosudarstvennaja akademičeskaja tipografija, 1922; (b) M. Altbauer, *Psalterium Sinaiticum: An 11th Century Glagolitic Manuscript from St. Catherine's Monastery, Mt. Sinai*, Skopje: Macedonian Academy of Arts and Sciences, 1971.

SlepA: *Slepče Apostol*, preserved in Leningrad, Moscow, Kiev, and Plovdiv. G. Il'inskij, *Slepčenskij apostol XII veka*, M.: Tip. G. Lissnera i D. Sobko, 1912.

SlepT: *Slepče Triod*, National Public Library, Leningrad, no. F I 75.

Stam: *Stamat Gospel*, National Public Library, Leningrad, Arx. Obšč., no. 338. (a) I. Sreznevskij, *Svedenija i zametki o neizvestnyx i malo izvestnyx pamjatnikax*, Sbornik otdelenija russkogo jazyka i slovesnosti 20, no. 4, SPb.: Imp. akademija nauk, 1880 [1879], 40-49 (fol. 1-12); (b) B. Velčeva, "Kâm ustanovjavaneto na srednobâlgarskite pravopisni tipove (Stamatovo četveroevangelie ot XIII vek)," *Izvestija na Instituta za bâlgarski ezik* 17 (1969), 280-86 (fol. 12b-15b).

Supr: *Codex Suprasliensis*, (a) National Library, Warsaw; (b) University Library, Ljubljana; (c) National Public Library, Leningrad, no. Q p. I 72. S. Sever'janov, *Suprasl'skaja rukopis'*, Pamjatniki staroslavjanskogo jazyka 2, SPb.: Imp. akademija nauk, 1904.

Trojan tale: Tale of the Trojan War in the Vatican copy of the Chronicle of Constantine Manasses of 1344-45. Cod. Vat. Slav. 2. J. Bogdan, *Cronica lui Constantin Manasses*, Bucharest: Socec, 1922. Reprinted: *Die slavische Manasses-Chronik nach der Ausgabe von Joan Bogdan*, Munich: Fink, 1966.

Und: *Undol'skij Fragments*, Lenin National Library, Moscow, the Undol'skij Collection, no. 961. (a) E. Karskij, *Listki Undol'skogo: Otryvok kirillovskogo evangelija XI-go veka*, Pamjatniki staroslavjanskogo jazyka 1, no. 3, SPb.: Imp. akademija nauk, 1904; (b) A. Minčeva, "Listove na Undolski," *Starobâlgarski kirilski otkâsleci*, S.: BAN, 1978, 18-24.

Vladislav inscription: I. Zaimov, *Bitolski nadpis na Ivan Vladislav, samodâržec bâlgarski: starobâlgarski pametnik ot 1015-1016 godina*, S.: BAN, 1970.

Zo: *Codex Zographensis*, National Public Library, Leningrad, Glag. 1. V. Jagić, *Quattuor evangeliorum Codex Glagoliticus olim Zographensis nunc Petropolitanus*, Berlin: Weidmann, 1879.

ZogrFol: *Zograph Folia*, Zograph Monastery. P. A. Lavrov and A. Vaillant, "Les Règles de saint-Basile en vieux-slave: les Feuillets du Zograph," *Revue des études slaves* 10 (1930), nos. 1-2, 5-35.

CHAPTER ONE

I. Preliminary Remarks

2.1. What is the shape of the earliest Proto-Slavic phonological system, which serves in turn as the point of departure for the study of historical change? Previous work has established that three features were distinctive for vowels in this system: *high*, *back*, and *tense (long)*. Serious objections — supported by our analysis — have been raised to the presence of an opposition with respect to the feature *labial* (Vaillant 1950:15, Mareš 1956, Georgiev 1964 and 1969, Georgiev et al. 1968, Shevelov 1964, Stieber 1969). We assume that from the time of the first velar palatalization to the elimination of diphthongs, *rounding (labial)* was not phonologically relevant in vowels. Vowels were opposed as *high (closed)* vs. *nonhigh*, *back* vs. *nonback*, and *tense (long)* vs. *nontense (short)*. The high vowels of Proto-Slavic were reflexes of IE i:/i and u:/u; the nonhigh vowels of IE e:/e, o:/o, and a:/a.

The vowels of Proto-Slavic have been transcribed in a number of ways. For example, ъ has been given as ŭ, y̆, ъ̆; y as u:, y:, ы; ь as ĭ, ь; ě as e:, ä, æ, ê, ě; o as o, ă. During this early period, for which phonetic transcription is hardly possible, the significance of these diverse spellings is more graphic than phonological — given, of course, some agreement as to the features which they represent. One of the most appropriate transcriptions is Mareš's (1956), which uses y:/y, ä:/ä, and a:/a. However, y is not entirely satisfactory for the high back nonround vowel because this symbol is used for the front glide j.

In this work we conventionally use i:/i, u:/u, e:/e, and a:/a for Proto-Slavic, with the stipulation that u: and u represent high back vowels that are *unmarked* for the feature *labial*. e:, e, a:, and a are nonhigh vowels — unmarked for the feature *low* due to the absence of mid vowels. When considering the restructuring of the vocalic system, we use æ [1], a, ʌ, o, ɛ, e to distinguish mid ʌ, o, ɛ, and e from low æ and a.

We use a:/a, u:/u, and a:/a for Proto-Slavic in order (1) to make clear their connection with Indo-European, (2) to preserve tradition (at least to some extent), (3) to keep the inventory of symbols simple, and (4) to avoid entirely — at least for this early period — any semblance of phonetic transcription.

Our analysis of Proto-Slavic phonological changes is therefore based on the following underlying (morphophonemic) system of vocalic oppositions:

		[−back]	[+back]
[+high]	[+tense]	iː	uː
	[−tense]	i	u
[−high]	[−tense]	e	a
	[+tense]	eː	aː

It is more difficult to reconstruct the phonological features of other sonorants: consonants and glides. The liquids are particularly problematical. Assuming that earlier syllabic consonants had disappeared by this time, we propose the following tentative inventory: /r/, /l/, /m/, /n/, /j/, /w/ (see Introduction, table 1 for feature specifications).

For Proto-Slavic prior to the velar palatalizations we posit the following obstruents:

	p	b	t	d	s'	z	s	š	k	g
high	−	−	−	−	+	−	−	+	+	+
back	−	−	−	−	−	−	−	−	+	+
anterior	+	+	+	+	+	+	+	−	−	−
coronal	−	−	+	+	?	+	+	?	−	−
labial	+	+	−	−	−	−	−	−	−	−
voiced	−	+	−	+	−	+	−	−	−	+
continuant	−	−	−	−	+	+	+	+	−	−
strident	−	−	−	−	+	+	+	+	−	−
delayed release	−	−	−	−	−	−	−	−	−	−

It is clear that prior to the palatalization of velars and, consequently, before the appearance of affricates, the features *strident* and *delayed release* were apparently redundant. In addition, *coronal* and *labial* were complementary with respect to one another, and one of them was probably nondistinctive. Obviously the system is asymmetrical. The central consonants (i.e., those that are nonanterior and nonback) are represented by a single segment, š. Oppositions with respect to *high* and *voiced* are similarly asymmetrical. Thus, one would expect changes leading to the introduction of new consonantal segments and new oppositions. The velar palatalizations, in fact, introduced dorsal consonants (nonanterior and nonback), affricates (strident, delayed release, continuant), and new fricatives (continuant, strident, delayed release). Many of the new consonants were palatalized (high and nonback). The number of voiced consonants also increased.

II. Persistent Changes

2.2. Sound changes are considered here in the order in which our analysis suggests they took place. In many respects the proposed order, as well as the formulations of the changes themselves, contradicts what has been generally accepted in Slavic linguistics. Inasmuch as many of the problems we consider are controversial, we rely, first and foremost, on the results of our analysis, examined in light of data drawn from written records and modern dialects. Those of our findings which are new are justified less by accepted or widely held opinions explaining various Proto-Slavic or Old Bulgarian linguistic facts, than by the total *system* of interdependent rules expressing putative sound changes — rules based on the analysis of the widest possible range of relevant linguistic material.

In all probability, the order of the rules which we propose coincides generally with the order in which the respective sound changes took place. In isolated instances (e.g., the velar palatalizations — especially the progressive palatalization — and changes applying to word-final segments), the order in which the rules apply contradicts evidence indicating their absolute historical chronology. In such cases we assume that generalizations and reinterpretations led to the *reordering* of rules. (See King 1973 and 1969:51-58 for discussion of similar developments in Germanic.) This issue is not given special attention here; it could form the subject of a separate study.

A number of rules apply repeatedly, rather than only once. So-called "persistent rules" (Shibatani 1973:102) represent, in fact, phonetic constraints valid for an extended period of time. Several persistent rules are relevant for the present study.

A. Consider the constraint against the occurrence of two neighboring syllabic segments:

$$\sim [+\text{syllabic}] \; [+\text{syllabic}]$$

In Proto-Slavic and Old Bulgarian this constraint is responsible for the avoidance of contiguous high and nonhigh vowels: under such circumstances the high vowel becomes a glide (cf. the diphthongs aj, ja, ej, je, wa, aw, ew, we). For example radi:a:N → radja:N (OB рождя). This distribution suggests the rule:

$$(A) \begin{bmatrix} -\text{cons} \\ +\text{high} \end{bmatrix} \rightarrow [\,-\text{vocalic}\,] \; // \; \begin{bmatrix} +\text{voc} \\ -\text{high} \end{bmatrix}$$

(A nonconsonantal segment is nonvocalic contiguous to a nonhigh vowel.)

A similar change — high vowel to glide — is observed in modern Bulgarian, where nonstressed (short) high vowels (u, ə, i) become glides (w, ə̯, j) contiguous to nonhigh vowels; for example /nóžici/ → [nóici] → [nójci], /oréxi/ → [uréi] → [uréj], /ímam/ → [íəm] → [íə̯m], /d'ádo/ → [d'áu] → [d'aw].

B. Regressive assimilation for *voice* in obstruent clusters and the devoicing of word-final obstruents are persistent changes; e.g., /magti/ → makti, OB мошти, /padti/ → patti, OB пасти. [2]

C. The three velar palatalizations and the dental palatalizations involve a rule which requires every soft consonant to become strident (hushing or hissing); for example pek'et- → OB печетъ. Towards the end of the Proto-Slavic period, this rule ceased to apply — at least in Bulgarian — and the existence of nonstrident soft (high and nonback) consonants became possible. The Proto-Slavic rule is:

$$(C) \begin{bmatrix} +\text{high} \\ -\text{back} \end{bmatrix} \rightarrow [\,+\text{strident}\,]$$

The application of this rule is still observed rarely in the modern dialects; consider the *new* change of k' → č', g' → ǯ', x' → š' in the dialect of Razlog (e.g., zek' → zeč', nix' → niš'; see Stojkov 1971).

D. In Proto-Slavic and Old Bulgarian we observe the persistent avoidance of the labial glide w contiguous to labial consonants or vowels and the avoidance of the front glide j contiguous to nonback high vowels and consonants (i:, i, or soft consonants). This general tendency appears in several different changes (4.5, 4.11, 8.8).

E. Finally, we note another tendency in the development of consonants: high dentals and labials ("semi-soft" consonants), apparently unstable, become either soft or hard:

$$\sim \begin{bmatrix} +\text{anterior} \\ +\text{high} \end{bmatrix}$$

This constraint requires additional study. There is reason to believe that in the history of Bulgarian dialects, according to a loose, unevenly applied rule, [+high] may be preserved if the consonant becomes [-anterior] (i.e., alveopalatal or palatal). So, for example, bifocal consonants (e.g., m', b', p', s', z', c') may function as nonanterior with respect to following segments.

The change of high consonants to nonanterior appears in the dental palatalizations as well as before back vowels during the restructuring of the vocalic system in Bulgarian dialects. Today it can be observed before front vowels in many eastern and southern dialects. Traditionally this development has been viewed as the loss of the distinction between *positional* and *phonological* softness.

If the consonant does not become nonanterior (i.e., does not become alveopalatal or palatal), it is hardened — becomes nonhigh. Perhaps this explains the hardening of c', s', and ǯ' in late Proto-Slavic. A tentative formulation of this rule is:

(E) $\begin{bmatrix} +\text{anterior} \\ +\text{high} \end{bmatrix} \rightarrow \begin{cases} \begin{bmatrix} +\text{anterior} \\ -\text{high} \end{bmatrix} \\ \begin{bmatrix} -\text{anterior} \\ +\text{high} \end{bmatrix} \end{cases}$

(A soft dental or labial consonant has two possible developments: it hardens — becomes nonback — or it becomes alveopalatal or palatal [nonanterior], eventually bifocal.)

Notes

1. Translator's note: Here and elsewhere the original uses ä; it has been replaced throughout by æ for typographical purposes. Similarly, : is used instead of ¯ to mark length.
2. Regarding the development of Bulgarian v and consonants contiguous to it, see Tilkov 1974 and Scatton 1975.

CHAPTER TWO

Assimilatory Fronting

3.0. In order to assess the widely held view that the correlation of hard and soft consonants existed in Proto-Slavic (Kalnyn 1961, Popova 1962) and the question of possible existence of synharmonic consonant-vowel groups — which various scholars place at various points in the history of Proto-Slavic[1] — it would be useful to provide a brief survey of the early sound changes of Proto-Slavic, particularly velar palatalizations and vowel shifts.

A general tendency towards assimilation to *nonback* unites the following changes:

1. the progressive assimilation of velars (the so-called third palatalization),
2. the first regressive palatalization of velars,
3. the fronting of vowels following soft consonants or j,
4. the change of aj to e:,
5. the second regressive palatalization of velars,
6. the onset of the change of w to v.

In all these changes, a back vowel, a consonant, or a glide becomes nonback (front) under the influence of a contiguous nonback segment.[2] The feature *high* is also relevant for the general tendency: it is encountered in each of the changes — either in various phases of their development or in their conditioning environments.

I. Progressive Palatalization of Velars

3.1. The relative chronology of the three velar palatalizations has been a critical problem for all who have studied the phonological development of Proto-Slavic. The nature and chronology of the so-called third palatalization (also known as the progressive or Baudouin palatalization) constitute crucial issues in analyzing the relationships among the three changes. Four general solutions have been proposed:[3]

1. the progressive palatalization is part of the second palatalization;

2. the progressive palatalization is indeed the third and last of the series;

3. the progressive palatalization is actually the second, occurring prior to the one ordinarily referred to as the second (the most popular view in the recent past);

4. the progressive palatalization is actually the first.

Resolving the controversy surrounding the timing of the third palatalization requires the precise formulation of the effects of the change, which in turn leads to several additional questions. Exactly which velars were subject to the change, g and k, or g, k, *and* x? After which segments did the change take place? Did it occur before all vowels, or only before the nonhigh back vowels a: and a (o), or before j followed by a back vowel (as Ekblom 1935, 1937, 1951 has repeatedly tried to prove)?

Recent studies (e.g., Mareš 1956 and 1959, Machek 1958, Channon 1972, Shevelov 1964, Lunt 1974) have established conclusively that the progressive palatalization preceded the second palatalization and the elimination of diphthongs. There is also strong evidence for the following claims:

1. The progressive palatalization applied after i(N) and occasionally after r̥, l̥ (or ir, il).

2. Machek has demonstrated that the progressive palatalization applied to g and k. There is no incontrovertible evidence of the change of x to s, a fact which suggests that the progressive palatalization took place *before* the first palatalization, that is, at a time when only two velars, g and k, existed.

3. If we accept the prevailing view that the progressive palatalization took place only before nonhigh back vowels, we may place it *before* the first regressive palatalization without encountering problems.[4] While not agreeing with Channon's claim that k', g', and x' were intermediate stages in all three palatalizations, we may nevertheless accept the relative chronology which he proposes:

      1. the progressive (Baudouin) palatalization
      2. the first regressive palatalization
      3. the second regressive palatalization

The form of the change itself suggests additional evidence for the early occurrence of the progressive palatalization: it clearly resembles the unquestionably early change of s to š (e.g., aws- → awš- [оухо : оушесе]). Both are assimilations with respect to the features *anterior* and *high*; both occur before vowels. If we assume that the progressive palatalization is early — prior to the first — we may formulate it as a constraint on the distribution of noncontinuant and continuant high consonants in certain environments. At the time when s', k, and g were the only high obstruents, the form of the progressive palatalization shows that a noncontinuant high consonant could only be anterior and strident (2.1) under circumstances similar to those of the change of s to š.

The specific conditioning factors of the progressive palatalization are high front vowels (i: and i) before the high noncontinuants k and g, and nonhigh back vowels (a: and a) after them. Additionally, the assimilatory effect of i apparently was not blocked by the presence of a sonorant consonant between i and the velar. Thus, in sum, k and g became anterior and strident after a high front vowel (i: or i) and before nonhigh back vowels (a: or a), with the optional intrusion of a sonorant consonant between i and the velar. The change may be formalized as:

$$(1) \begin{bmatrix} +\text{high} \\ -\text{cont} \end{bmatrix} \rightarrow \begin{bmatrix} +\text{ant} \\ +\text{strd} \end{bmatrix} \ // \ \begin{bmatrix} +\text{voc} \\ +\text{high} \\ -\text{back} \end{bmatrix} ([+\text{son}]) \text{———} \begin{bmatrix} +\text{voc} \\ -\text{high} \\ +\text{back} \end{bmatrix}$$

Thus, k becomes c and g — ʒ under the proper circumstances; for example:

/kuniNgas kuniNgu:n- atikas atike/

kuniNʒas atıcas

OB кънлѕь кънагъіни отьць отьчє

Attempts to specify the chronology of the progressive palatalization are complicated by historical data which argue against its early occurrence. For the most part these are late borrowings from Germanic which show the change (e.g., пѣнѧꙃь), and Slavic toponyms in Greece which do not (e.g., Γαρδίκι : градьць; Mirčev 1958:48-49). One may attempt to explain such forms by assuming that the progressive palatalization occurred late in absolute terms, while the relevant rules were reordered and forms reinterpreted; for example, отькъ : отьсæ → отьсь : отьсæ → ОВ отьць : отьци. In this way the progressive palatalization came to precede the fronting of back vowels in the grammar (Illič-Svityč 1967:78 and Wukasch 1976). However, this explanation is contradicted by examples such as иго (< *jugo) in which the progressive palatalization did not take place after the root vowel became front.

In any event, the progressive palatalization occurred very early in the relative chronology suggested by the grammar of Proto-Slavic. This is indicated by the phonetic mechanism of the rule itself. Forms such as пѣнѧзь may have resulted from the application of existing patterns to borrowings of certain types. For forms such as Γαρδίκι and Russian *brusnika*, I would note Avanesov's view (1968) that there existed in early Slavic dialects an unevenly distributed tendency to generalize the suffix k for c.

The consonants which underwent the progressive palatalization were high; those that were the result of the change would have been nonback. As mentioned in the introduction, consonants that are high and nonback are always soft. Thus, the softness of c and ҙ which were produced by the progressive palatalization is a concomitant of the change.

The mechanism of the progressive palatalization tells us nothing about the feature *coronal*. We may suppose that c and ҙ were phonetically, but not phonologically, marked for this feature. Their general feature specifications would be something like:

[c] : [−sonorant, +high, −back, +anterior, +coronal (?), −labial, −voiced, −continuant, +strident]

[ҙ] : [−sonorant, +high, −back, +anterior, +coronal (?), −labial, +voiced, −continuant, +strident]

II. The First Regressive Palatalization of Velars

3.2. Although the first palatalization is a relatively straightforward process, the new chronological position which we attribute to it requires additional comment. There have been four recent attempts to provide a precise formulation for the change:

Chomsky and Halle 1968:421-24, Halle and Lightner (see Channon 1972:35), Lunt 1974:197, and Scatton 1975:52.

Lunt and Scatton approach the problem from a synchronic point of view, the former for Old Bulgarian, the latter for New Bulgarian. Both consider the alternation of g with ž, not ǯ. This forces them to complicate the rule with the condition that a velar undergoing the change becomes continuant if it is voiced.[5]

The theoretical position reflected in Chomsky and Halle's treatment of the regressive palatalizations of Proto-Slavic (1968:419-30) is particularly interesting. They propose that the first palatalization took place in two successive stages: (1) k → k', g → g', x → x' and (2) k' → č, g' → ǯ, x' → š. They formalize the first as:

$$[-\text{ant}] \rightarrow [-\text{back}] \;//\; \underline{\hspace{1em}} \begin{bmatrix} -\text{cons} \\ -\text{back} \end{bmatrix}$$

(Nonanterior consonants are nonback before nonback vowels or j.)

The second is an instance of the persistent rule (C) (2.2):

$$\begin{bmatrix} +\text{high} \\ -\text{back} \end{bmatrix} \rightarrow [+\text{strident}]$$

(Soft consonants become strident.)

Above we adopted Machek's view (1958) that the progressive palatalization applied only to k and g. Additionally, we assumed the early change of s → š, not s → x.[6] This leads us to propose that x did not yet exist when the first palatalization applied. Thus, the change affected only k and g; for example:

	/atike/	/gena:/
(2)	atik'e	g'ena:
(C)	atiče	ǯena:
OB	отьче	жена

Večerka 1972:54-55, who justifiably questions the existence of any phonetic change of s to x whatsoever, explains the appearance of x as movement towards system symmetry. The appearance of the new alternation s ~ x is represented schematically by Večerka in the following way:

$$\begin{array}{c} \check{c}+i \; : \; \check{z}+i \; : \; \check{s}+i\,[7] \\ |\quad|\quad\;|\quad|\quad\;|\quad| \\ k+u \; : \; g+u \; : \; \check{s}+u \end{array}$$

$$\begin{array}{c} \check{c} \; : \; \check{z} \; : \; \check{s} \\ |\quad\;|\quad\;| \\ k \; : \; g \; : \; \emptyset \end{array}$$

Later:

$$\begin{array}{c} \check{c}+i \; : \; \check{z}+i \; : \; \check{s}+i \\ |\quad|\quad\;|\quad|\quad\;|\quad| \\ k+u \; : \; g+u \; : \; x+u \end{array}$$

$$\begin{array}{c} \check{c} \; : \; \check{z} \; : \; \check{s} \\ |\quad\;|\quad\;| \\ k \; : \; g \; : \; x \end{array}$$

It follows then that s did not become x, only later to return to š before front vowels and j; rather š (from s) was replaced by x before back vowels and w. Consequently we reformulate the first stage of the first palatalization as:

$$\begin{bmatrix} -\text{son} \\ -\text{ant} \end{bmatrix} \rightarrow [\alpha\text{back}] \;//\; \underline{} \begin{bmatrix} -\text{cons} \\ \alpha\text{back} \end{bmatrix}$$

(Nonsonorant nonanterior segments — at this stage š, g, and k — become [+back] or [−back] depending on the following nonconsonantal segment: nonanterior consonants are nonback before front vowels and j, but back before back vowels and w.)

This rule may be combined with rule (C) as:

$$(2) \begin{bmatrix} -\text{son} \\ -\text{ant} \end{bmatrix} \rightarrow \begin{bmatrix} \alpha\text{back} \\ -\alpha\text{strd} \end{bmatrix} \;//\; \underline{} \begin{bmatrix} -\text{cons} \\ \alpha\text{back} \end{bmatrix}$$

Because the new nonback consonants are high, they are also strident. Clearly, at this early time there are no soft consonants, i.e., [+high, −back], which are not strident as well. Consonants introduced by rule (2) probably had the following feature specifications:

[č] : [−sonorant, +high, −back, − anterior, +coronal (?), −labial, −voiced, −continuant, +strident]

[ǯ] : [−sonorant, +high, −back, −anterior, +coronal (?), −labial, +voiced, −continuant, +strident]

[x] : [−sonorant, +high, +back, −anterior, −coronal, −labial, −voiced, +continuant, −strident]

The feature *coronal* poses problems for the phonetic characterization of these three consonants. By origin, the noncontinuants č and ǯ were noncoronal. š, on the other hand, was probably coronal; however, in new alternations it was opposed to noncoronal x. Rule (2) gives us no reason to suppose any changes with respect to *coronal*, but the results of the change permit us to assume certain conflicts which later may have caused additional changes and eventually led to differences in the way č, ǯ, and š developed in the various Slavic languages. Early fluctuation with respect to *coronal* could in fact have been fluctuation between alveopalatal and palatal dorsal consonants.

The following examples illustrate the application of the progressive and first regressive palatalizations:

/awša- awšese staːrike staːrikas duzgjas geːba:/

(1) staːricas
(2) awxa- staːriče duzǯjas ǯeːba:

OB оухо оушесе старьчє старьць дъждь жаба

III. −as Becomes −us

3.3. Before considering the remaining changes related to the general tendency of consonants to become nonback contiguous to other nonback segments, we need to specify when -as (-os) became -us before a morpheme boundary. Word-final yers in the nominative singular of o-stem nouns (and perhaps also in the dative plural of nouns and first person plural of verbs) are believed to be reflexes of -os (-as), -jos (-jas). The formant of the comparative adjective is also related to -jas/-jos (Meillet 1964:229-30).

The change -as → -us has been explained in various ways (Mareš 1963, Georgiev 1969, Gâlâbov 1973). Whatever the explanation, one thing is certain: the change was very early — not prior to the progressive palatalization of velars, but no later than the fronting of back vowels after soft consonants and j (below). The loss of the final consonant in -us took place before word-final s changed (4.8). For example:

/staːrikas saldjas+jas#jas/

(1) progressive
    palatalization   staːricas
(2) first regressive
    palatalization
(3) -as → -us   staːricus saldjus+jus#jus

    OB   старьць   слаждьшь+и

IV. Vocalic Fronting

3.4. The general tendency for assimilation with respect to *front* applied to vowels as well. As a result of a well-known early Proto-Slavic change, back vowels became front after soft consonants and j:

(4) $[+\text{vocalic}] \rightarrow [-\text{back}] \; // \; \begin{bmatrix} +\text{high} \\ -\text{back} \end{bmatrix}$ ——

As a consequence of rule (A) (2.2), high vowels did not occur here — before another vowel.

In all probability (4) applied to all back vowels. Examples such as OB доуши, земли (ja:j → je:j → ji:) contradict the claim that it did not apply to a:.[8] Further, it must be emphasized that all changes which affected vowels and following nasal consonants took place *after* fronting. This fact contradicts Stieber's contention (1969:28) that -jǫ and -jǫt in first singular and third plural present tense verbal forms, resp., constitute evidence that the change of ä to ě followed the introduction of nasal vowels.

We believe that vowel fronting and nasalization were rather far apart chronologically. Nasalization was one of the changes which applied to sequences of *vowel + sonorant consonant* and was close in time to liquid metathesis; it was relatively late, and there are signs that it was still taking place in Old Bulgarian. On the other hand, vowel fronting occurred early — before the second regressive palatalization and the elimination of diphthongs.

Thus, all vowels became front by assimilating to preceding soft consonants and j. The soft consonants which invoked the change were c and ʒ from the progressive palatalization, s' (e.g., the pronoun сь), and č(j), ǯ(j), and š(j).[9] The front vowels found after č, ǯ, and š are original. Fronting is very common, chiefly due to the great frequency of j in Proto-Slavic. The following are examples of the change:

```
        /kanjas  gena:  sta:ricas  juga-  zemja:j  staja:N/

(1)                     sta:ricas
(2)              žena:
(3)     kanjus          sta:ricus
(4)     kanjis          sta:ricis  jiga-  zemje:j  staje:N

OB      кон'ь   жена   старьць    иго    земли    стонж
                                         земи
```

Obviously, fronting took place after the progressive palatalization, after the change of -as → -us, and before the loss of diphthongs. Our analysis does not specify the relative chronology of fronting with respect to the first regressive palatalization.

V. aj and a:j Become e:

3.5. The mechanism of the change of **aj** and **a:j** to **e:** differs from that of the loss of other diphthongs (rule 10a): while the second involves raising, the first involves regressive assimilation with respect to the frontness of **j** and lengthening. Additionally, the elimination of other diphthongs shares a number of features with other later changes, while the elimination of **aj** and **a:j** is closely related to the fronting of other vowels.[10]

aj and a:j become e: after the fronting changes described in the preceding section and, as we have long known, before the second regressive palatalization of velars. The change takes place before consonants and at the end of words. Before vowels the diphthong is unaffected; cf. OB мои, достоинъ, таинъ. Thus:

$$(5) \quad a(:)j \rightarrow e: \ // \ \underline{\quad} \left\{ \begin{matrix} C \\ \# \end{matrix} \right\}$$

Or more precisely:

$$\overset{1}{\begin{bmatrix} +voc \\ +back \end{bmatrix}} \overset{2}{\begin{bmatrix} -cons \\ -voc \\ -back \end{bmatrix}} \rightarrow \overset{1}{\begin{bmatrix} -back \\ +tns \end{bmatrix}} \ // \ \underline{\quad} (CX)\#$$

(Back vowel and front glide become tense [long] front vowel before a consonant or word boundary.)

Note that the original underlying back vowel is not marked for *tense*. Thus:

```
     /berajs  berajte  žena:j  drawgaj  kanjaj/
(4)                                     kanjej
(5)  bere:s   bere:te  žene:   drawge:
OB   бери    берѣте   женѣ    дроусѣ   кон'и
```

The fronting of back vowels and the change of **aj** and **a:j** to **e:** significantly increased the frequency of front vowels. At a certain point, this led to the opposite change — the backing of front vowels.

VI. The Second Regressive Palatalization of Velars

1. k, g, x

3.6. The appearance of the front vowel e: from aj and a:j reintroduced the conditions for velar palatalization. This time, however, there were three velars to be affected: x, as well as g and k. Under the influence of a following front vowel, back consonants became nonback, anterior, and, as a consequence of rule (C), strident: k → c, g → ʒ, x → s.[11] For example:

	/raNka:j	drawgaj	magajte	kajla:/
a(:)j→e: second regressive palatalization	raNke:	drawge:	mage:te	ke:la:
	raNce:	drawʒe:	maʒe:te	ce:la:
OB	рѫць	доусѣ	мосѣте	цѣла

This change can be formalized as:

$$(6) \begin{bmatrix} -son \\ +back \end{bmatrix} \rightarrow \begin{bmatrix} +ant \\ +strd \end{bmatrix} \bigg/\bigg/ \underline{} \begin{bmatrix} +voc \\ -back \end{bmatrix}$$

The second regressive palatalization is also essentially an assimilation to a contiguous front segment. However, it is difficult to explain why the resulting nonback consonants became c, ʒ, and s instead of č, ǯ, and š. Here, one must keep in mind the overall development of Proto-Slavic. c and ʒ from the progressive palatalization occurred mainly in nominal formants before grammatical endings; e.g., -ьць, -ьце, -ица, -ʒа. The new consonants resulting from the second regressive palatalization also occurred most frequently before nominal endings: in the singular, plural, and dual of the o- and a-declensions; e.g., рѫць, рѫцѣхъ, доуси, бозѣ. It is possible that morphological factors and morpheme structure influenced the change of the velars to c, ʒ, s.[12]

2. w

The second regressive palatalization was the first change to give different results in different Slavic dialects. Particularly interesting is the contrast of kv and gv in West Slavic vs. cv and ʒv (zv) elsewhere. A number of explanations have been proposed for this difference (e.g., Lekov 1960:70); we propose another here.

All of the consonantal changes described up to this point represent stages in the reorganization of the Proto-Slavic phonological system. We have seen the system acquire high strident nonback consonants at the expense of back high nonstrident consonants. Assimilatory tendencies are particularly strong, for they even affect vowels. The single back segment which remains to undergo this process (though perhaps it might have been subject to some earlier changes) is the high back glide w. As a result of the second regressive palatalization, w would have become anterior and strident, while remaining labial, sonorant, high, continuant, voiced, and noncoronal. Taken together, these features specify v'. The feature *high* is not permanent for this segment (see rule E in 2.2), and it later behaved like v.

Thus, we have reason to believe that the change of w to v began in those instances where w was followed by a front vowel. This can be accounted for by generalizing rule (6) to:

$$(6') \quad [+\text{back}] \rightarrow \begin{bmatrix} +\text{ant} \\ +\text{strd} \end{bmatrix} // \underline{\quad} \begin{bmatrix} +\text{voc} \\ -\text{back} \end{bmatrix}$$

(6') applies not only to forms such as ke:la: → ce:la:, but also to those such as kwe:t- → kv'e:t- and gwe:zda: → gv'e:zda:.[13]

In South and East Slavic we suppose that the palatalization was passed back, to the left: kw → cv' and gw → ʒv' (Lekov 1968:45). Because palatalization is not observed in forms such as ogni (where g did not become ʒ — *ozni — before anterior n), we must suppose that w, not v', stood between the velar and the front vowel. In other words, kw changed directly to cv', with both consonants simultaneously assimilating to the front vowel — not only k → c , w → v', but kw → cv'. Of these two back segments, the second is sonorant.

FRONTING

In order to account for kw → cv' and gw → ʒv', rule (6') must be reformulated as:

(6″) ($\begin{bmatrix} -\text{son} \\ +\text{back} \end{bmatrix}$) [+back] → ($\begin{bmatrix} +\text{ant} \\ +\text{strd} \end{bmatrix}$) $\begin{bmatrix} +\text{ant} \\ +\text{strd} \end{bmatrix}$ // ―― [−back]

(k → c, g → ʒ, x → s, w → v', kw → cv', gw → ʒv', xw → sv' before front vowels.)

The change of w to v did not apply in all positions at the same time. The next relevant change made w consonantal before a vowel; for the results of this change see the discussion of rule (10a). The general change of w to v before vowels represented the extension of (6″). The rule's domain may be formalized as:

(7) $\begin{bmatrix} -\text{voc} \\ +\text{lab} \end{bmatrix}$ → [+cons] // ―― [+voc]

(w becomes v before vowels.)

Up to this point we have considered changes united by the general tendency to assimilate with respect to *front* (or nonback): the velar palatalizations, a(ː) → eː, and the fronting of back vowels. Applied to consonants and perhaps the back glide w, these changes are accompanied by the repeated application of the persistent Proto-Slavic change (C), which makes every soft (i.e., nonback high) segment strident. These changes *did not* apply to dental or labial consonants before front vowels.

Notes

1. In fact the various chronologies represent different explanations for the change. Avanesov 1947 and Bernštejn 1961:40-41 relate the so-called *syllabeme* to the softening of consonants before front vowels for a short period at the time of the disintegration of Proto-Slavic. The recently published correspondence between Jakobson and Trubetzkoy (Jakobson 1975:138) shows that they believed in the late appearance of softening of this sort in Russian, for example. Žuravlev 1961, 1965, and 1966 attributes what he calls "group synharmony" to a very early period — before the elimination of diphthongs. Jakobson 1971:27 believes that we are not in a position to establish with certainty the relative chronology of the palatalization of consonants before front vowels. In the last analysis, Jakobson takes "syllabic synharmony," "syllabic synchronic monism," and "syllabic uniformity" to mean the general tendency towards progressive and regressive assimilations (1971:25).
2. There is no particular reason to connect this process with "syllabic synharmony" for (1) the assimilation may take place across syllable boundaries (cf. the progressive palatalization, where consonants are influenced by the following vowels), and (2) there is no reason not to assume that phonologically hard consonants were followed by front vowels at this particular point in time.
3. See Ježova 1968 and Channon 1972. The latter provides a detailed survey of virtually all of the work on the subject.
4. See Avanesov 1968 and Channon 1972:31-32 concerning the alternation k ~ c in suffixes.
5. Compare Lunt:

$$\begin{bmatrix} -\text{son} \\ +\text{back} \\ <+\text{vcd}> \end{bmatrix} \rightarrow \begin{bmatrix} +\text{cor} \\ -\text{ant} \\ <+\text{cont}> \end{bmatrix} // \underline{\quad} \begin{bmatrix} -\text{cons} \\ -\text{back} \end{bmatrix}$$

and Scatton:

$$\begin{bmatrix} +\text{cons} \\ -\text{ant} \\ <+\text{vcd}> \end{bmatrix} \rightarrow \begin{bmatrix} +\text{cor} \\ +\text{strd} \\ <+\text{cont}> \end{bmatrix} // \#X \underline{\quad} \begin{bmatrix} +\text{syll} \\ -\text{back} \end{bmatrix} Y\#$$

6. In his letters to Jakobson, Trubetzkoy speaks of the change as s → š → x (Jakobson 1975:7).
7. It is more likely that ž was ǯ at this time.
8. See, for example, van Wijk 1949-50, who does not assume a change of ia: → ja: → je: in the prehistoric period, and, disagreeing with Jakobson, writes: "Obviously [Jakobson] attributes far too much significance to Old Bulgarian, where every a → ê (æ) after soft consonants." However, there were already dialect differences in Old Bulgarian with respect not to the change of a: → e:, but to the later change of e: (ě) → a:.
9. The chronology of the loss of j after ǯ, č, š from the first regressive palatalization is not clear (4.11).
10. In the history of the Germanic languages, the change aj → e before the seventh century is related to changes known as i-Umlaut or "front mutation" (Scargill 1951:24).
11. See Večerka 1972 for discussion of the alternation x/š in West Slavic.
12. There have been similar attempts to explain the relationship between the progressive and second regressive palatalizations (Illič-Svityč 1967:78).
13. Lekov 1968:45, while examining the second regressive palatalization, also speaks of a change giving kv' and gv'.

CHAPTER THREE

The Elimination of Closed Syllables

4.0. The title of this chapter refers to a number of developments which entailed changes in consonant clusters and the loss of consonants at the end of words. The general process, extending over a substantial period of time, includes the following Proto-Slavic and Old Bulgarian developments:

1. changes in groups containing anterior consonants;
2. changes in groups containing w and j; regressive assimilations for the feature *high*: elimination of diphthongs; dental palatalizations;
3. changes in word-final position;
4. changes in consonant clusters with initial back segments;
5. changes in delayed release consonants: t:, t':, d':, č, ǯ, c, ʒ;
6. changes in groups containing strident consonants: sts, štš, ždž (stv, skv, vdv);
7. changes in groups with initial sonorant consonants.

Taken together, these changes led to differences among the Slavic languages and to the first divergent processes in Bulgarian dialects.

I. Clusters Containing Anterior Consonants

4.1. Leskien (1919, §32) records the following consonant clusters in Old Bulgarian:

bl	br	gv	kv	gl	gn	gr	dv	zv	zg
zd	sk	st	zdr	str	zl	sl	zn	kl	kn
kr	pl	pr	sv	sk	sl	sm	sn	sp	skl
skr	stv	tv	tr	xv	xl	xr	mr	nr	ml
vr	vl	svr	skl	skvr	zr	xvr	šl	žl	žr
čr	čl								

Leskien noted that b, p, t, d were deleted before s, t, n, m. Seliščev 1951 provides convincing examples for the change of pt → t, bd → d, tn → n, dn → n, bn → n, pn → n, dm → m, ts → s, ps → s; for example: teptej → tetej (OB тети), da:dmi → da:mi (OB дамь), wapsa: → wasa: (OB оса), supnus → sunus (OB съпъ), zna:jeNts → zna:jeNs (OB зналъ). In all of these cases anterior noncontinuant obstruents are lost before all anterior consonants except v and l. The existence of the clusters tv, dv, cv, zv in Old Bulgarian is extremely important, for it demonstrates that clusters of anterior consonants changed (1) before w became v after consonants, (2) before w was lost after labial consonants (e.g., bw → b; OB облакъ), and (3) before kw became cv before front vowels (i.e., before the second regressive palatalization of velars). The existence of dl, tl in West Slavic and their absence in South and East Slavic (except for new cases resulting from the metathesis of liquids) indicate an early differentiation; cf. Polish modlitva, mydło and Russian *molitva, mylo*. It is likely that the East and South Slavic forms result from the generalization and expansion of the earlier rule. However, a conclusive explanation for the difference would require a detailed study of the history of the liquid consonants in the Slavic languages. The phonetic characteristics of liquids are very unclear, and their evolution needs special study.

Clusters with initial nonanterior consonants were relatively more stable. This is suggested by the dental palatalizations, which — because they applied to the cluster kt — took place before the loss of back consonants before nonsonorants (4.14).

Thus, at a very early stage, anterior noncontinuant obstruents (b, p, d, t) dropped before all nonliquid anterior consonants. This rule may be formalized as:

$$(8) \begin{bmatrix} -\text{son} \\ +\text{ant} \\ -\text{cont} \end{bmatrix} \rightarrow \emptyset \; // \; \underline{\hspace{1cm}} \; \begin{bmatrix} -\text{voc} \\ +\text{ant} \end{bmatrix}$$

Leskien explains exceptions to this rule, such as топнѫти and погыбнѫти, as late changes involving morphological generalizations; cf. канѫти (pn → n), осльнѫти (pn → n), оувѧнѫти (dn → n).

II. Early Changes of l and N

4.2. No one has asked why clusters with initial anterior sonorants (nasals and l) did not change when clusters with other anterior consonants did, but only *later* — with the process of nasalization and the change of r before consonants. Perhaps it was the case that sonorants simply developed independently. Perhaps the fact that l is also a continuant was relevant. On the other hand, perhaps l and the nasals were preserved because they had already undergone some other change which had removed them from the domain of (8). This would have been the case if they had become nonanterior and, eventually, back, i.e., l → ʎ or ɫ, n → ŋ.[1] This hypothesis is supported by a number of later developments.

In general, there is greater evidence for the change of n to ŋ than for l to ʎ or ɫ. Serbo-Croatian dialects perhaps preserve the old state of affairs with l and ɫ. After the metathesis of liquids, the back lateral could have come to occur before vowels as well (cf. Bulgarian, Russian, Polish). Modern Bulgarian dialects attest different types of l with various distributions; the explanation of these facts requires detailed experimental studies. Generally, in the dialects we observe the fluctuation of l, ʎ, l' before vowels and ʎ, ɫ, w before consonants or word-finally (Seliščev 1929, Stojkov 1956, 1962, 1968, Kotova 1963 and 1974, Stankov 1974). We leave aside clearly later changes, such as l' → j and softening before soft consonants; e.g., *búlka* : *búl'k'i*.

We can only hypothesize that "Central European" l was an early feature of the Slavic languages, that at some early stage of development it became ʎ or ɫ before consonants, and that these later came to occur before vowels as a result of liquid metathesis and changes affecting ъʎ, ьʎ, ʎ (and ɫ). The phonetic specification of ʎ would be:

[+consonantal, +vocalic, +sonorant, −high, +anterior, +back, +coronal, −labial, +voiced, −strident, +continuant];

ɫ is:

[+consonantal, +vocalic, +sonorant, +high, −anterior, +back, −coronal, −labial, +voiced, −strident, +continuant].

4.3. What is the evidence for the early change of n to ŋ? On the basis of their study of a variety of languages, Chen and Wang 1975:267 describe phonological processes related to the opening of closed syllables terminating in nasal consonants. It appears that nasal consonants pass through several stages before merging with preceding vowels: (1) m → n, (2) n → ŋ. Chen and Wang propose the following general stages of development:

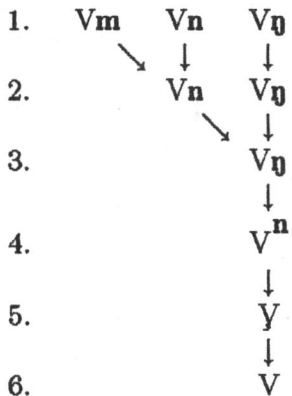

Nasalization is discussed in detail below (9.0–9.7). In order to better understand the details of nasalization, we must specify as precisely as possible the features of the nasal consonant which causes the nasalization of the preceding vowel.

We know that in the oldest glagolitic alphabet the characters which represent the nasal vowels consist of the letters for oral vowels followed by a separate raised letter for nasality: ⰔⰅ, ⰔⰅ, ⰔⰅ (Dobrev 1969). Trubetzkoy claims that the separate mark of nasality denotes a nasal consonant. There have been many objections to this view. Most recently Mošin 1973:44 argues that Ⰵ could not represent a nasal consonant because the existence of a separate glagolitic letter for n makes it superfluous. However, when Trubetzkoy used the symbol N for a nonspecific nasal consonant, he had in mind ŋ, not n — a view which he expressed in a letter to Jakobson in 1929 (Jakobson 1975:128). The assumption that the original vocalization of glagolitic Ⰵ was ŋ solves a number of problems raised by abecedariums and clarifies several aspects of the development of glagolitic. Additional evidence that Ⰵ originally designated ŋ is provided by spellings such as аⰅгел- in SPs: 40b, 25, 42a, 17, 42b, 1, 177a, 21, 127a, 5. Von Arnim 1930:62 considers these spellings "pre-Pannonian."

CHAPTER THREE

In the glagolitic of Zo, Euch, Cloz, and elsewhere, ⱔ stands for the non-iotated front nasal. We can explain this development on the basis of what was probably its original name: *en*. After the nasalization of vowels in several Old Bulgarian dialects ⱔ, called *en*, became the symbol for ę.

Indirect evidence that the change of n to ŋ is a process related to the loss of open syllables is provided by the distribution of n and ŋ in modern Russian: here ŋ occurs before a velar followed by an obstruent, while n occurs before a velar followed by a sonorant (Avanesov 1971:82-84).

Sequences of V+ŋ developed differently in different Slavic languages. In most Bulgarian dialects ŋ was lost after the nasalization of the preceding vowel. In Salonika dialects ŋ assimilated to the following consonant: *dъmp, pent, krъnk*. A similar development is observed in dialects of Kashubian, some of which have forms with aŋp, aŋt, aŋk, aŋs, while others show assimilation: amp, ant, aŋk, aŋs (Tolstaja 1966:136).

For Proto-Slavic, then, it is important to recognize that nasal consonants were backed before consonants and, probably, word-boundaries:

(9) [+nasal] → [+back] // —— (CX)#

This rule introduced VŋC and Vŋ#. The feature specifications of ŋ are:

[+consonantal, −vocalic, +sonorant, +high, +back, −anterior, −coronal, +nasal, −labial, +voiced, −strident, −continuant].[2]

III. Regressive Assimilation for Height

4.4. This assimilation includes changes of vowels and consonants before high segments — Vj, Vw, VŋC, Vŋ#, Cw, Cj, CC' — and a number of closely related developments. The changes of vowels before high segments are usually referred to as the monothongization of diphthongs, and those of consonants as the dental palatalizations. The present treatment of these changes is new in the following respects:

1. It relates both developments to a single general tendency.
2. It systematically examines two aspects of each change:
   a. the raising of the consonant or vowel before the high segment;
   b. the loss of the second, high segment.

This analysis allows us to propose a new explanation for the development of nasal vowels in the individual Slavic languages and Bulgarian dialects.

IV. Regressive Assimilation for Height: Vowels

1. Changes before j and w; elimination of diphthongs

4.5. The diphthongs which change at this stage are ej, ew, and aw. (For the development of aj see 3.5.) Most scholars believe that the vowels in original Proto-Slavic diphthongs were short (e.g., Stieber 1969:17). The elimination of diphthongs created long high vowels: front nonlabial i:, front labial ü:, and back labial û:.[3]

Until now little attention has been paid to one very important fact: ej became ij or i before consonants and glides as well as before vowels; consider OB трьѥ, триѥ (←treje) and зима (←zejma:). However, aw did not change before vowels; compare коупоуѭ, коуповати: aw → û before nonsyllabic segments, but aw → ov before vowels. This fact suggests the following pair of ordered rules:

1. w → v before vowel;
2. e and a are raised before j and w (prior to the loss of diphthongs per se).

E.g., **zejma:** → **zijma:**, OB зима; **rewtej** → **riwtij**, OB рюти; **awxa-** → **uwxa-**, OB оухо; **treje** → **trije**, OB трыѥ, триѥ.

The raising of vowels under the influence of following glides is an assimilation with respect to the feature *high*. The formalization of the rule shows the regressive influence of **j** and **w** on the preceding vowel:

(10a) $[+voc] \rightarrow [+high] \; // \; \underline{\quad} \; \begin{bmatrix} -cons \\ +high \end{bmatrix}$

(a → u and e → i before w or j.)

The diphthong **aj** did not undergo this rule because it had already become **e:** before consonants or word-boundaries by the application of rule (5). It is necessary, however, to stipulate that (10a) does not apply to **aj** followed by a vowel.

The raising of vowels before glides is typologically very common. The changes of **ej** to **ij** and **ew** to **iw**, for example, have often been described in historical studies of the Germanic languages (e.g., Scargill 1951:15 and 16, Lehmann 1955:355, Guxman 1962:74, 94, 106, Vennemann 1971:114).

Old Bulgarian forms such as кон'и (loc sg) and тиха vs. костьи illustrate another detail of this development: before a consonant or word-boundary the vowel in the diphthong is lengthened, whereas before a vowel it remains unchanged. Additionally, the glide **w** causes the preceding vowel to become labial. Altogether we propose the following development:

	tijxa:	**kanjij**	**riwtij**	**kastiji**
	ti:jxa:	**kanji:j**	**rü:wti:j**	
OB	тиха	кон'и	рюти	костьи
				костеи

Thus, **ij** → **i:j**, **iw** → **ü:w**, **uw** → **ů:w**. This intermediate change can be expressed by the following rule:

(10b) $[+voc] \rightarrow \begin{bmatrix} +tns \\ \alpha lab \end{bmatrix} \; // \; \underline{\quad} \; \begin{bmatrix} -cons \\ \alpha lab \end{bmatrix} (CX)\#$

Obviously, a later rule is needed to delete **j** and **w** after the new long vowels: **iːj → iː, üːw → üː, ůːw → ůː**. Thus, (10b) is immediately followed by:

(10c) $\begin{bmatrix} -\text{cons} \\ +\text{high} \end{bmatrix} \rightarrow \emptyset \; // \begin{bmatrix} +\text{voc} \\ +\text{high} \\ +\text{tns} \end{bmatrix} \underline{\quad\quad}$

(Nonconsonantal high **j** and **w** are deleted after the long high vowels **iː, üː,** and **ůː**.)

Recall that rule (A) prohibits the occurrence of high vowels before other vowels.

Rule (10c) requires further consideration. The change of **iːj → iː, üːw → üː,** and **ůːw → ůː** reveals an important feature: **w** is lost after labial vowels, while **j** is lost after nonlabial vowels; in other words, the high labial glide is deleted after high labial vowels, and the high nonback nonlabial glide is deleted after high nonback nonlabial vowels. Compare rule D (2.2), as well as the loss of **w** after labial consonants and **j** after nonlabial soft consonants, which are also high and nonback (4.11).

Thus the loss of **ej, ew,** and **aw** is a process involving three separate changes: (1) raising vowels before **j** and **w**, (2) lengthening vowels before **j** and **w** followed by a nonsyllabic segment or word-boundary with the concomitant labialization of the long vowel before **w**, (3) loss of **j** and **w** after long high vowels. For changes of **i** and **u** before vowels see 8.2-8.12.

The changes described here occur after the change of **aj** to **eː** and the change **w** to **v** before vowels, which in turn take place after vowel fronting. For example:

	/wajawjet-	wajawaːtej	awšese	treje	kanjaj	zejmaːj/
(4)	wajewjet-	wajewaːtej			kanjej	
(5)						zejmeː
(7)	vajewjet-	vajevaːtej				
(10a)	vajiwjet-	vajevaːtij	uwšese	trije	kanjij	zijmeː
(10b)	vajüːwjet-	vajevaːtiːj	ůːwšese		kanjiːj	ziːjmeː
(10c)	vajüːjet-	vajevaːtiː	ůːšese		kanjiː	ziːmeː
OB	воюѥтъ	воѥвати	оушесе	трьѥ	кон'и	зимѣ
					(loc sg)	(loc sg)

The appearance of the labial vowels ü: and û: as a result of the elimination of diphthongs introduces two new vowels into the phonological system and creates the possibility of new oppositions (Žuravlev 1968:40). This represents the beginning of the complex process leading to the reorganization of the vocalic system, a process which varied throughout the Slavic languages and their dialects, but which did exhibit a number of elements common to all of them. Before describing this process, however, we need to consider other changes related to regressive assimilation for the feature *high* and the simplification of other consonant-glide sequences.

2. Vowel changes before ŋ

4.6. If vowels were raised before the high sonorants j and w, one might reasonably expect them to be raised before the high sonorant nasal ŋ as well. The raising of short vowels before n might be assumed on the basis of the general tendency which I have called regressive assimilation for height. This assumption is made even more appealing by the fact that it sheds light on a number of aspects of the development of the Slavic languages which otherwise are inadequately explained.[4] See, for example, the discussion of the reorganization of the vocalic system (chap. 4). Examples of the proposed change are:

/raŋka: beraŋt pladaŋs kanjeŋs/

ruŋka: beruŋt pladuŋs kanjiŋs

OB рѫка берѫ плодъı кон'ѧ
         (aor) (acc pl) (acc pl)

There is insufficient evidence for the claim that this change also applied to long vowels at this early stage; consider forms such as ženaːŋs (женъı), ženaːŋ (женѧ). Later developments present problems which need to be investigated in the light of additional data drawn from the historical dialectologies of the other Slavic languages.

As a working hypothesis, we propose the following rule: short vowels are raised before ŋ. At this time, as a consequence of the application of rule (9), ŋ occurred only before consonants or word-boundaries. Thus the raising rule may be formalized as:

(11) $\begin{bmatrix} +\text{voc} \\ -\text{tns} \end{bmatrix} \rightarrow [+\text{high}] \;\; // \;\; \underline{} \begin{bmatrix} +\text{nas} \\ +\text{high} \end{bmatrix}$

(e → i and a → u before ŋ.[5])

We need to keep in mind that prior to the loss of diphthongs u is a high back vowel unmarked for *labial*, while after the loss of diphthongs it functions as nonlabial.

The raising of vowels before nasals is not restricted to the Slavic languages. For example, the changes em → im, en → in, and eŋ → iŋ have been proposed for Proto-Germanic (Guxman 1962:93-94). In Baltic dialects and elsewhere, in, im, un, um are believed to have developed from en, em, an, am, resp. (Zinkjavičjus 1972:6).

One may object to rule (11) on the grounds that there is no evidence that it applies in roots — that is, for example, there is no evidence for an early Bulgarian form such as **muŋka:** (мѫка). However, the rule is motivated by the following considerations:

1. In a great number of Bulgarian dialects the nasal vowels and the yers developed in the same way.

2. Prothetic w appeared before high back vowels which are not labial; cf., въноукъ, въімѧ, съвѧзъ, New Bulgarian *vъdica*, *vъglen*, but оучити, оудъ, отъ, оправьдати.

3. Borrowings into other Balkan languages replace the back nasal vowel with a high back vowel followed by n. In Rumanian, borrowings with un are considered older than borrowings with î, e.g., **dumbravă**, OB дѫбрава, **dungă**, OB дѫга, **scump**, OB скѫпъ; cf. **trîmbă**, OB трѫба. The front nasal is similarly replaced. In examples such as **colindă**, OB колѧда, **grindă**, OB грѧда, **oglindă**, OB оглѧдало, we cannot explain i as the result of a Rumanian sound change (Mirčev 1958:74).

4. The assumption that the back nasal vowel was vocalized as uŋ explains Slavic and Old Bulgarian fluctuations of oy and ѫ. Consider the reflexes of the back nasal in East Slavic, Serbo-Croatian, Czech, and Slovak, as well as OB doublets such as ноужда ~ нѫжда, гноусъ ~ гнѫсъ, моудити ~ мѫдити, скѫдьнъ ~ скоудьнъ, гроубъ ~ грѫбъ. It appears that here we are dealing with old changes of uŋ to uw and uw to uŋ: the

"deconsonantalization" of ŋ and the "consonantalization" of w. These changes were abetted by features shared by w and n, [+sonorant, +high, +back]. Mirčev 1958:107 provides support for this proposal: "The confusion of the two vowels [oy and ж, B.V.] dates from a rather early period, when they were very close to one another in both acoustic and articulatory terms."

3. Changes of ж and oy
(ŋ → w; w → ŋ)

The deconsonantalization of ŋ (uŋ → uw) has considerable importance for Common Slavic. Essentially an assimilation, the change may be formalized as:

(12) $\begin{bmatrix} +\text{son} \\ +\text{high} \\ +\text{back} \end{bmatrix} \rightarrow [-\text{cons}] \; // \; \begin{bmatrix} -\text{cons} \\ +\text{high} \\ +\text{back} \end{bmatrix}$ ──

(High back sonorant consonant ŋ becomes nonconsonantal w after the high back vowel u.)

As a result of the loss of diphthongs by (10b) and (10c), the new diphthong uw would be replaced by a high back labial vowel.[6] Consider Russian forms such as *muka* and *zubi*.

Rule (12) explains the lack of parallelism in the developments of the nasal vowels in those Slavic languages in which the back nasal became u. While the Bulgarian and Polish reflexes of the nasals are identical with respect to height — ǫ and ę, ъ and e, a and æ (→ e), Serbo-Croatian has u (high) and e (nonhigh), and Russian u (high) and a (low). This asymmetry is due to the fact that in the early stages of Russian and Serbo-Croatian there was only *one* nasal vowel, the front nasal: in place of the original back nasal we find the result of the old change of uŋ to uw.

The individual stages in the development of uN to u and iN to ę are attested by Old Russian borrowings in Finnish (Mikkola 1894 and V. Kiparsky 1958), as well as by eleventh-century Old Russian texts (carefully analyzed by Kolesov 1971).

Sławski 1947 describes and examines in detail Slavic roots in which ѫ and оу alternate. He concludes that examples in which denasalization appears to have taken place make up only about 25 percent of the data. On the basis of Old Bulgarian examples and data from modern Bulgarian and Polish dialects, he identifies 56 cases of secondary "nasal infix" and 13 cases of denasalization. His data suggest that uw became uŋ primarily after nasal consonants, while uŋ became uw in the environment of labials. In the environment of the sonorants r and l and the velars k and g, uŋ and uw were apparently unstable. With r and l, uw tended to become uŋ, and vice versa with k and g. For example: ноужд- ~ нѫ(ж)д-; моуд- ~ мѫд-; гноус- ~ гнѫс-; скѫдьнъ ~ скоудьнъ; кѫтъ, кѫшта ~ *skut-*; гроубъ ~ грѫбъ; троудъ ~ трѫдъ; гѫд- ~ гоуд- (*gъdulka* and *gusla*); *ručej* ~ *rъčej*; (*x*)*ruštel* ~ (*x*)*rъštel*; perhaps *bъbrek* ~ *bubrek*, *pъp* ~ *pup*. For complete data see Sławski 1947 and Mirčev 1958:107.

Thus, we come to the general conclusion that uŋ and uw readily replaced one another in the Slavic languages. The change of uŋ to uw gave one of the earliest Slavic isoglosses. In Bulgarian dialects the general tendency was for uŋ to replace uw, which reflected an earlier state with unchanged sequences of *back vowel + nasal consonant*. Instances with ѫ for оу, predominantly after nasal consonants, represent old dialect variations within the territory of Bulgarian.

Glagolitic texts have нѫ(ж)д-, while cyrillic texts have нѫ(ж)д- and ноу(ж)д-. In Sav, for example, the form occurs once with ѫ and twice with оу. In En ноуждѧ occurs on 24a, 4. Supr regularly has ноу(ж)д-. The verb моудити ~ мѫдити occurs with оу in glagolitic manuscripts. Zo has both оу and ѫ. SPs clearly prefers forms with ѫ: не замѫди 53b, 19-20, 85b, 20, нѫждаахъ сѧ 50a, 9; въз(г)нѫша сѧ 141b, 24.

At present we cannot give even a tentative general rule for the change of uw to uŋ in Bulgarian dialects due to the lack of clear etymologies for all examples. We can only offer a single, particular rule for the change of uw to uŋ after nonlabial n (nuw → nuŋ):

(13) $\begin{bmatrix} +\text{son} \\ +\text{high} \\ +\text{back} \end{bmatrix} \rightarrow \begin{bmatrix} +\text{cons} \\ +\text{nas} \\ -\text{lab} \end{bmatrix} \;//\; \begin{bmatrix} +\text{cons} \\ +\text{nas} \\ -\text{lab} \end{bmatrix} \begin{bmatrix} -\text{cons} \\ +\text{high} \\ +\text{back} \end{bmatrix} \underline{}$

This formalization clearly shows the assimilatory nature of the change.

The following examples illustrate the order of rules (10a), (10b), (10c), (11), (12), and (13), which produce variants with ѫ and oy in Old Bulgarian:

	/nawd-	nawd-	skaŋd-	skaŋd-/
(10a)	nuwd-	nuwd-		
(11)			skuŋd-	skuŋd-
(12)				skuwd-
(13)		nuŋd-		
(10b)	nů:wd-			sků:wd-
(10c)	nů:d-			sků:d-
OB	ноудити	нѫдити	(о)скѫдьнъ	скоудьнъ
	ноужда	нѫжда		

4. Changes before r and l

4.7. If vowels changed before the sonorants j and w and, under certain circumstances, before ŋ, it is natural to ask whether they changed before the sonorants r and l — even if their phonetic properties in Proto-Slavic are not entirely clear. We have seen that vowels before j and w ([+sonorant, -vocalic, -consonantal]) changed when j and w were followed by a consonant, another glide, or word-boundary. Diphthongs with ŋ ([+sonorant, -vocalic, +consonantal]) changed before a consonant or word-boundary. We might anticipate even more limited conditions for the change of vowels before r and l, which are [+sonorant, +vocalic, +consonantal].

Short vowels before r or l followed by a consonant, j, or w did not change. Are there cases where er → ir, ar → ur, el → il, al → ul before word-boundary? One uncertain case is the vocative form of r-stem nouns, e.g., ma:ter, dukter. Assuming that e is raised to i before r#, we would expect the development of ma:tir and duktir, which would later become ma:ti, dukti (*matь, dъštь*) with the loss of word-final r.[7] The Russian nominative forms *mat'*, *doč'* have, in fact, not been satisfactorily explained, although the reduction of i: to i has been suggested (*mati → matь*).

Other forms which may involve raising before r# are the third person verbal endings -tъ and -Ntъ, which may derive from the Indo-European medial endings *-tor, *-ŋtor. This explanation is proposed by Gâlâbov 1973, who also assumes the "narrowing" of vowels before word-final r. A compelling argument for the putative relationship between the Indo-European medial endings and the Slavic third person verbal endings would provide support for the existence of the Proto-Slavic changes er → ir and or → ur before word-boundary.

V. Word–Final Changes

4.8. Additional instances of changes before nasal consonants are observed at the ends of words. They are of two types: consonant deletions and vowel mutations.

First, word-final consonants preceded by short vowels are lost:

	/maːteres	pladuŋ	tat/
	maːtere	pladu	ta
OB	матєрє	плодъ	то

This rule can be formalized as:

$$(14) \quad C \rightarrow \emptyset \ // \ \begin{bmatrix} +\text{voc} \\ -\text{tns} \end{bmatrix} \underline{\quad} \#$$

Rule (14) takes place after vowels have been raised before high sonorants and, therefore, after back vowels have become front after soft consonants and j — a change which itself follows the change of as to us:

CHAPTER THREE

	/suːnus	kanjas	kastiN	berajs	kanjaNs/
(3) as→us		kanjus			
(4) fronting		kanjis			kanjeNs
(5) aj→eː				bereːs	
(9) N→ŋ			kastiŋ		kanjeŋs
(11) eŋ→iŋ					kanjiŋs
(14) C→∅	suːnu	kanji	kasti		
OB	сынъ	конь	кость	бєри	кон'ѧ
			(acc sg)		(acc pl)

After word-final consonants are lost after short vowels, only the following word-final sequences of consonants or vowels and consonants remain: VːC, V(ː)ŋs, V(ː)ŋt, V(ː)st, V(ː)ss, V(ː)rs, Vːŋ (see rules 8 and 14). If we accept prevailing views of the etymologies of Proto-Slavic endings (Meillet 1964 and 1934, Stang 1966, Georgiev 1969, Mareš 1963), we need to explain the following changes: beruŋs → бєрѫ, maliŋs → молѧ, pladuŋs → плодꙑ, kanjiŋs → кон'ѧ, kazaːŋs → козꙑ (acc pl), kazaːs → козꙑ (gen sg and nom pl), zemjeːŋs → земл'ѧ, maːteːr or maːteːrs (Mareš 1963:53) → мати, iduŋt → идѫ (pl aor), viːdeːss → видѣ, viːdeːst → видѣ, znaːjeːŋ → знаѭ, pladaːs[8] → плодꙑ (inst pl).

These changes can be accounted for by three ordered rules:

1. All vowels are high and long before word-final nonnasal continuant (r or s)[9]; a sonorant consonant may occur between the vowel and the final consonant without impeding the change:

aːs	→	uːs	u(ː)ŋs	→	uːŋs
eːs	→	iːs	i(ː)ŋs	→	iːŋs
(eːr	→	iːr)	eːŋs	→	iːŋs
(eːrs	→	iːrs)	aːŋs	→	uːŋs

Formally:

$$(15) \quad [+\text{voc}] \rightarrow \begin{bmatrix} +\text{high} \\ +\text{tns} \end{bmatrix} // \underline{\quad} ([+\text{son}]) \begin{bmatrix} +\text{cont} \\ -\text{nas} \end{bmatrix}$$

This rule applies after the loss of diphthongs, after the raising of vowels before ŋ, and after the loss of word-final consonants after short vowels:

	/berajs	maːteːr	pladaNs	kanjaNs	kazaːs/
(4)				kanjeNs	
(5)	bereːs				
(8)					
(9)			pladaŋs	kanjeŋs	
(11)			pladuŋs	kanjiŋs	
(14)					
(15)	beriːs	maːtiːr	pladuːŋs	kanjiːŋs	kazuːs
OB	бєри	мати	плодъı	кон'ѧ	козъı

	/zemjaːNs	beraNts	suːnus	znaːjaNts/
(4)	zemjeːNs			znaːjeNts
(5)				
(8)		beraNs		znaːjeNs
(9)	zemjeːŋs	beraŋs		znaːjeŋs
(11)		beruŋs		znaːjiŋs
(14)			suːnu	
(15)	zemjiːŋs	beruːŋs		znaːjiːŋs
OB	зємл'ѧ	бєръı	сынъ	знаѩ

2. It is certain that at this point nasal consonants were lost between uː and word-final s: uːŋs → uːs. Consider, e.g.: **pladuːŋs** → плодъı and **kazuːŋs** → козъı, but **kanjiːŋs** → кон'ѧ and **maliːŋs** → молѧ. Thus:

(16) $\begin{bmatrix} +\text{nas} \\ +\text{high} \\ +\text{back} \end{bmatrix} \rightarrow \emptyset \;//\; \begin{bmatrix} +\text{high} \\ +\text{back} \end{bmatrix} \underline{\quad\quad} [+\text{cont}] \;\#$

This change is an obvious dissimiliation: a high back nasal is lost after a high back vowel. The loss was probably abetted by the assimilatory influence of the following continuant, which encouraged the loss of closure in the nasal (Nikolov 1970:166). Considering the changes prior to (16), we must emphasize that the vowel before (ŋ)s could only be long. For example:

/pladu:ŋs   beru:ŋs   zemji:ŋs/

pladu:s   beru:s

OB плодъ   беръ   земл'ѧ

3. The last change is well known: word-final nonnasal consonants, regardless of their number, are deleted:[10]

(17) $\begin{bmatrix} +\text{cons} \\ -\text{nas} \end{bmatrix}_n \rightarrow \emptyset \ // \ \underline{\quad} \ \#$

For example:

/pladu:s kanji:ŋs ma:ti:r iduŋt vi:de:ss vi:de:st/

pladu: kanji:ŋ   ma:ti: iduŋ   vi:de: vi:de:

OB плодъ кон'ѧ   мати   идѫ   видь   видь
                              (aor)

The order in which the word-final rules apply is absolutely fixed; other orders produce incorrect forms.

Rule (15) deserves special attention: all vowels become high and tense in the environment: ———[+sonorant] s#. Thus, u → u:, i → i:, a: → u:, e: → i:. Rule (15) is crucial for understanding a number of problems. The fact that word-final s plays a special role in these processes is not itself a new claim.[11] What is new is the recognition of a series of related rules and the precise specification of their form and the order in which they apply.

To recapitulate then:

1. The changes discussed in this section took place within Proto-Slavic — after the fronting of vowels, the change of **aj** to **e:**, and the raising of vowels before nasals.

2. Changes in the quality of word-final vowels followed the loss of word-final consonants after short vowels. The change of **as** and **os** to **us** was early and had no relationship to rule (15).

3. The single reflex of the diphthong **aj** was **e:**, while the change of **e:** to **i:** before word-final **s** was general, applying regardless of the source of **e:**.

The contrasting reflexes e: and i: from aj (e.g., бери vs. берѣте) have been explained in different ways — most often on the basis of intonational or accentual differences. Bernštejn 1961:197 concludes from a critical survey of existing proposals that "at present we are justified in making the following claim: the diphthong o̭i became e_2 in Proto-Slavic; in certain cases — under conditions which remain unclear — word-final o̭i became i."

If we accept the Proto-Slavic changes proposed above, the explanation of the development of бери from bere:s is the same as that proposed by Bernštejn 1974:190 for камъı: the raising and lengthening of word-final vowels under certain conditions. The development of (ka)mon, (ka)man, or, more precisely, (ka)mans (with the generalized masculine ending of the o-, u-, and i-declensions; Stang 1966:219, Gâlâbov 1973:12) suggested by Bernštejn may be represented in our terms as:

/(ka)mans/

(9) kamaŋs
(11) kamuŋs
(15) kamu:ŋs
(16) kamu:s
(17) kamu:

OB камъı

The word-final changes of rules (14), (15), (16), and (17) explain a number of controversial cases, such as мати, камъı, the forms of singular masculine and neuter present active participles (e.g., берѫ and молѧ), word-final ъı in paradigms of o- and a-stem nouns, the second person singular imperative of first conjugation verbs, and others.

The ending -ъı for the genitive singular and nominative plural of a-stem nouns (e.g., женъı) can be explained as: a:s → u:s or (for the genitive) a:ŋs → u:ŋs → u:s. In the case of the instrumental plural of o-stem nouns, the proposed rules exclude the possibility of oj (aj) → ъı. Mažiulis's proposal (1973) for a Balto-Slavic instrumental-locative suffix -os (-as) is more likely.

On the basis of our analysis, it follows that a front nasal vowel in the nominative singular of n-stem nouns (e.g., имѧ, брѣмѧ) could develop only if another consonant, s or t, followed the nasal consonant (Stang 1966:219-20).

CHAPTER THREE

The nominative plural of o-stem masculine nouns, -i, can be explained as a generalization of the ending of jo-stems (Georgiev 1969:57), where -jaj → -jej → -ji. Alternatively, word-final s may have been extended here by analogy to other declensions (u-, a-, and i-stem nouns, and pronouns; Mareš 1962:20 and 1963:55). In the latter case the development would have been: -ajs → -eːs → -iːs → -iː.

The phonological treatment of the word-final vocalization of Old Bulgarian does not, of course, exclude the possibility that some endings must be explained morphologically. Nor can we rule out interactions among various inflectional paradigms or the replacement of one ending by another. These processes would have resulted in the generalization of one given ending for two or more morphological forms (see Georgiev 1969 for details). In this regard, the generalization of the accusative plural ending -ѧ to other cases of ja-stems, in opposition to -ъі of a-stems is typical. Compare:

genitive singular
 женъі овьцѧ[12] for *овьци
  from jaːs → jeːs → jiːs

nominative plural
 женъі овьцѧ for *овьци

accusative plural
 женъі овьцѧ

In dual nominative, accusative, and vocative forms, -ѣ is opposed to -и: женѣ vs. овьци. Our explanation for this contrast differs somewhat from Georgiev's 1969:97-99.

Rules (1), (2), (3), (4), (5), and (6) — changes united by what we refer to as the tendency to assimilate with respect to the feature nonback — are obligatorily ordered in a way that probably reflects their relative chronology. Likewise, the rules which represent changes related to the loss of closed syllables, regressive assimilation for *high*, and word-final changes — (8), (9), (10a), (11), (12), (13), (10b), (14), (15), (16), and (17) — are strictly ordered with respect to one another. It is difficult, however, to relate these two larger sets of rules one to the other. In fact, the question is: What relation does the second set of changes have to the second regressive palatalization of velars? One thing is certain: rule (8), the loss of anterior consonants in clusters (e.g., ts → s), precedes rule (6), the second regressive palatalization. We can also establish that (15), the raising and lengthening of vowels before final s, occurs after (5), the change of aj to e:.

Van Wijk 1949-50:294 assumes that the word-final changes were a long process, consisting of two stages: an early one, during which the phonetic principles of Indo-European word-final syllables were still valid, and a late one, during which final syllables opened. Our analysis suggests the need to re-examine van Wijk's contention — with a certain amount of skepticism.

Conventionally we will order the rules related to the second set of processes after those related to the first; either way, correct forms are produced:

	/gena:s	atikaN	gardaN	beraNt/
(1)		atic'aN		
(2)	žena:s			
(4)		atic'eN		
(8)				
(9)		atic'eŋ	gardaŋ	beraŋt
(5)				
(6)				
(11)		atic'iŋ	garduŋ	beruŋt
(14)		atic'i	gardu	
(15)	ženu:s			
(16)				
(17)	ženu:			beruŋ
OB	женъı	отьць	градъ	берѫ
	(nom pl)	(acc pl)	(acc sg)	(aor)

	/zemja:Ns	magajs	nesaNts/
(1)			
(2)			
(4)	zemje:Ns		
(8)			nesaNs
(9)	zemje:ŋs		nesaŋs
(5)		mage:s	
(6)		maʒ'e:s	
(11)			nesuŋs
(14)			
(15)	zemji:ŋs	maʒ'i:s	nesu:ŋs
(16)			nesu:s
(17)	zemji:ŋ	maʒ'i:	nesu:
OB	землʼѧ	моѕи (acc pl)	нєсъі

To conclude this survey, we summarize the situations in which we expect и, ъі, the nasal vowels, and the yers in Old Bulgarian endings:

и   i:
        i:s
        ajs → e:s → i:s
        jaj → jej → jij
        ej   → ij   → i
        (e:r → i:r → i:)

ъі   u:
        u:s
        a:s → u:s
        aNs → uNs → u:Ns → u:s
        a:Ns → u:Ns → u:s
        aNts → aNs → uNs → u:Ns → u:s
        a:Nts→ a:Ns → u:Ns → u:s
        u:ts → u:s

CLOSED SYLLABLES

Ѧ (ѥ)[13]   i:N
iNs → i:Ns → i:N
i:Ns → i:N
e:Ns → i:Ns → i:N
ja:Ns → je:Ns → ji:Ns → ji:N
eNs → iNs → i:Ns → i:N
eNt → iNt → iN
iNt → iN
i:Nt → i:N

Ѫ (ѧ)   a:N
aNt → uNt → uN
uNt → uN

Ѩ (ѩ)   ja:N → je:N

ь (ѣ)   i
iN → i
eN → iN → i
jas → jus → jis → ji
(er → ir → i)

ъ (ѣ)   u
uN → u
aN → uN → u
as → us → u

CHAPTER THREE

VI. Regressive Assimilation of Consonants for Height; Dental Palatalizations

1. Softening of consonants before j

4.9. Consonants tended to be raised under the influence of the segments which followed them. Before the simplification of clusters of Cj, dental consonants were subject to well-known changes referred to as the dental palatalizations. Typological studies of various languages show that the palatalization of consonants follows a definite hierarchy:

1. velars
2. dentals
3. labials

In Chen's opinion (1973:176-83) this order is so consistent that successive stages are predictable. If this is so, we must suppose that in the early stages of the softening of front consonants before j, labials were not affected. It is the absence, or the weakness, of softening in labials before j which Trubetzkoy 1930:395-96 relates to the appearance of "epenthetic l": here j is "consonantalized," becoming l'. (For unconvincing criticism of this position see Kalnyn 1961:7.)

The dental palatalizations are at once among the most interesting and most complex questions in the phonological development of Proto-Slavic. One particularly difficult problem is the behavior of tj and dj in dialects which later developed into Bulgarian and which are reflected in the written monuments of Old Bulgarian. It is well known that their Bulgarian reflexes are št and žd and that they are identical to the reflexes of *stj, *sk + front vowel, *kt + front vowel, and *zg + front vowel.

Rules for the dental palatalizations have been the subject of a number of recent studies. Chomsky and Halle 1968:429-30 examine the first stage of the development — the softening of consonants before j — in relation to the two regressive palatalizations of velars. Scatton 1975:108-109 describes the changes on the basis of facts of the modern language. Lunt 1974:199 provides a synchronic analysis of the Old Bulgarian (his Old Church Slavonic) data and proposes a set of ordered rules to account for them within its grammar. The following treatment offers an interpretation which, taken as a whole, is new. Let us then consider the changes which gave rise to alternations such as: носити ~ ношѫ, съмотрити ~ съмоштрѫ, мыслити ~ мышлѣаше, свѣтъ ~ свѣшта, троудъ ~ троуждѫ, могѫ ~ мошти, съблазнити ~ съблажнѭ.

4.10. We begin by assuming that every coronal consonant becomes nonanterior, nonback, and high (alveopalatal or palatal) before the nonanterior nonback high sonorant segment j: s → š, z → ž, t → t', d → d', n → n', l → l', r → r'. This change may be formalized as:

(18) $[+\text{cor}] \rightarrow \begin{bmatrix} +\text{high} \\ -\text{ant} \end{bmatrix} // \underline{} \begin{bmatrix} -\text{cons} \\ -\text{voc} \\ -\text{back} \end{bmatrix}$

2. The deletion and consonantalization of j and w

4.11. After the softening of coronal consonants, j is lost; e.g., t'j → t', šj → š. Recall persistent rule D (2.2), which limits the occurrence of contiguous nonback (soft) segments. The appearance of epenthetic l after labial consonants indicates that j was not lost in this environment because — as we have suggested — at this stage the labials were not soft before j. The rule deleting j would be:

$j \rightarrow \emptyset // \begin{bmatrix} +\text{cons} \\ +\text{high} \\ -\text{lab} \end{bmatrix} \underline{}$

Or:

$j \rightarrow \emptyset // \begin{bmatrix} +\text{cons} \\ +\text{high} \end{bmatrix} \underline{}$

(j is deleted after high nonlabial consonants *or* after all high consonants — given the assumption that at this time all high consonants in this position are nonback.)

It is necessary to note, however, that in addition to the loss of the nonback nonlabial glide j after certain consonants, the back glide w disappeared after nonhigh labial consonants: облакъ, обити, облѣшти, обѧзати, where bw → b; the rules which delete both glides may be combined. Lunt 1974:199 suggests the following formalization:

$$\begin{bmatrix} -\text{cons} \\ -\text{voc} \\ \alpha\,\text{lab} \end{bmatrix} \rightarrow \emptyset \;//\; \begin{bmatrix} -\text{syl} \\ -\alpha\,\text{high} \\ \alpha\,\text{lab} \end{bmatrix} \underline{}$$

(**j** is lost after soft nonlabial consonants; **w** is lost after hard labials.)

If we order this rule after the dental palatalizations (18), then it may be slightly simplified:

$$(19)\; \begin{bmatrix} -\text{cons} \\ -\text{voc} \\ \alpha\,\text{lab} \end{bmatrix} \rightarrow \emptyset \;//\; \begin{bmatrix} -\text{cons} \\ \alpha\,\text{lab} \end{bmatrix} \underline{}$$

(Labial glides are deleted after labial consonants; nonlabial glides are deleted after nonlabial consonants.)

Next, we propose a similarly parallel development to account for epenthetic **l**: the consonantalization of **j** to **l'**[14] after labial consonants and that of **w** to **v** after nonlabials; cf. земл҄ѣ, творити:

$$(20)\; \begin{bmatrix} -\text{voc} \\ \alpha\,\text{lab} \end{bmatrix} \rightarrow [+\text{cons}] \;//\; \begin{bmatrix} +\text{cons} \\ -\alpha\,\text{lab} \end{bmatrix} \underline{}$$

It is difficult to specify the exact position of this rule with respect to other rules considered here.

It is well known that forms with and without epenthetic l vary greatly in Old Bulgarian written records (for details see Miletič 1886, von Arnim 1930:228-35). Not only do the environments in which l occurs vary within a single text, but there is variation among texts. It has been shown that epenthetic l is least likely to occur before и and ь (van Wijk 1957:106): e.g., земи, земь. Perhaps the explanation of this fact is related to rule D (2.2). In addition, the *absence* of epenthetic l shows a definite tendency to be generalized before grammatical endings. Miletič 1886:244 observes "a force opposed to labial *l*" in Old Bulgarian, principally in Zo and Supr. This "force" can be explained by the early softening of labials and the consequent absence of the consonantalization of j to l' in some dialects. In Slavic studies, however, it is generally believed that epenthetic l appeared everywhere and that later l' became j or was deleted altogether (van Wijk 1957:106-108).

The solution to this problem is tied to the explanation of forms with ь and ъ in Supr, Sav, SPs. Consider, for example, Supr възлюбьюнъіи 56, l. 16, осклабьюнь 47, l. 29-30, поставьѭши 47, l. 28-29 vs. поставл'ѣѫ 49, l. 25; SPs земъь 27b, 20, 39a, 18, земьѫ 109b, 7, земъѩ 27a, 6, избавъѭ сѩ 19b, 18. In all likelihood, forms with ъ in SPs are only an orthographic feature: they occur in those parts of the manuscript where ъ is written for ь (von Arnim 1930:10). We contend that the occurrence of ь in such examples is due to the phonetic sequence of *hard consonant* + j (that is, the absence of any change in groups of *labial* + j) or to the intrusion of a short high vowel, which would have inhibited the consonantalization of j. In the first case two lines of development were possible: CjV → Cl'V or CjV → C'V; in the second there was only one: CjV → CijV → CiV → CjV. (Recall the above hypothesis regarding the relatively later palatalization of labial consonants.)

Once softened, labial consonants exclude the appearance of epenthetic l. Forms such as оумръщвено Euch 73b, 9 and оумръщвенъіхъ SPs 131a, 7, show clearly that tv became t'v' — that labials softened preceding dentals.

3. Changes before soft consonants

4.12. The softening of consonants before other soft consonants suggests a generalization of (18) at some particular time; consider examples such as: съмоштрѭ, изоштренъ, съблажнѭ, оумръщвенъ. E.g.:

/bla:znj-/

$$Cj \to C'j \quad \text{bla:zn'j-}$$
$$j \to \emptyset \quad \text{bla:zn'-}$$
$$CC' \to C'C' \quad \text{bla:žn'-}$$

The last change is the result of a rule which makes consonants high and nonanterior before other high nonanterior consonants. This represents a generalization and simplification of rule (18):

$$(18') \quad [+\text{cons}] \rightarrow \begin{bmatrix} +\text{high} \\ -\text{ant} \end{bmatrix} // \underline{\quad} \begin{bmatrix} -\text{syl} \\ +\text{high} \\ -\text{back} \end{bmatrix}$$

(Consonants are alveopalatal or palatal before nonsyllabic high nonback segments, i.e., before j or soft consonants.)

It is essential to note that this change does *not* apply before front vowels. This agrees with Paul Kiparsky's observation (personal communication) that the segments which invoke palatalization are ordered as follows:

1. j
2. other soft consonants
3. high front vowel (i)
4. nonhigh front vowels (e, ä)

This hierarchy represents the increasing generalization of a rule raising the vocalization of consonants before high nonback segments:

1. $C \rightarrow C' // \underline{\quad} \begin{bmatrix} -\text{cons} \\ -\text{voc} \\ +\text{high} \\ -\text{back} \end{bmatrix}$

2. $C \rightarrow C' // \underline{\quad} \begin{bmatrix} -\text{voc} \\ +\text{high} \\ -\text{back} \end{bmatrix}$

3. $C \rightarrow C' // \underline{\quad} \begin{bmatrix} +\text{high} \\ -\text{back} \end{bmatrix}$

4. $C \rightarrow C' // \underline{\quad} [-\text{back}]$

The discrete stages of this process are important for understanding the evolution of Bulgarian dialects. Individual dialects have passed through various sets of stages in the hierarchy, while at different historical points the range of environments in which softening took place led to different results.

For example, it is impossible to explain the vocalic development of Rhodope dialects without assuming that at some early time consonants were softened before the high front lax vowels ь and ѧ (ĭ and ĭŋ). Regarding the original vocalization of nasal vowels see 4.6.

4. Velars and front vowels

4.13. The dental palatalizations of Proto-Slavic are essentially assimilations for *high* and *nonanterior*: the articulation of consonants shifts rearward; e.g., s → š, z → ž. Conditions for the same changes are shown by combinations of velars (high and back) and front vowels. Consider:

$$/\text{agni} \quad \text{makti:}/$$
$$\text{agn'i} \quad \text{makt'i:}$$
$$\text{OB} \quad \text{огн'ь} \quad \text{мошти}$$

This change applies only to noncontinuant coronal consonants t and n. (d does not occur here.) We may formulate the rule as:

$$(20) \begin{bmatrix} +\text{cor} \\ -\text{cont} \end{bmatrix} \rightarrow \begin{bmatrix} +\text{high} \\ -\text{ant} \end{bmatrix} \mathbin{/\!/} \begin{bmatrix} +\text{cons} \\ +\text{high} \\ +\text{back} \end{bmatrix} \text{------} [-\text{back}]$$

Note the relevance of [+high], [−anterior], and [−back] for both (20) and (18′); we may combine them as follows:

$$(18'') \begin{bmatrix} +\text{cor} \\ <-\text{cont}> \end{bmatrix} \rightarrow \begin{bmatrix} +\text{high} \\ -\text{ant} \end{bmatrix} \mathbin{/\!/} \left\{ \begin{array}{l} \text{------} \begin{bmatrix} -\text{syl} \\ +\text{high} \\ -\text{back} \end{bmatrix} \\ < \begin{bmatrix} +\text{cons} \\ +\text{high} \\ +\text{back} \end{bmatrix} \text{------} [-\text{back}] > \end{array} \right\}$$

(A coronal consonant is soft before j or other soft consonant; if the coronal consonant is noncontinuant, it is softened also between a velar consonant and a front vowel.)

5. The deletion of velars

4.14. We know that when closed syllables were eliminated in Proto-Slavic, velars were deleted before nonsonorants:

	/re:kx-	re:kste	pakt-/
	re:x-	re:ste	pat-
OB	рьхъ	рьстє	потъ

The same change probably applied to forms with soft coronal consonants:

	/rekt'i:	dukt'er-	nakt'i/
	ret'i:	dut'er-	nat'i
OB	решти	дъштєр-	ноштъ

The rule is:

(21) $\begin{bmatrix} +\text{cons} \\ +\text{back} \end{bmatrix} \rightarrow \emptyset \ // \ \underline{} \ [-\text{sonorant}]$

6. t', d' become šč, žǯ

a. t' → t':, d' → d':

4.15. Next, how do t' and d' become št and žd? Let us begin by recalling the claim that Proto-Slavic soft consonants were "long." For example, Bernštejn 1961:168 asserts that "soft plosives were pronounced more energetically than corresponding fricatives" and that "long consonants other than *t'* and *d'* lost their length very early." Following this tradition, we too assume that soft t' and d' were long; however, we will represent this length with the feature *delayed release* (Chomsky and Halle 1968:318ff.). Thus:

(22) $\begin{bmatrix} -\text{son} \\ +\text{high} \\ +\text{cor} \\ -\text{cont} \end{bmatrix} \rightarrow [+\text{delayed release}]$

(t' → t':, d' → d':.)

CLOSED SYLLABLES

b. t'ː → št', d'ː → žd'

4.16. This change can be related to the well-known change of tt to st: paːdtiː → paːttiː → paːstiː (пасти), mettiː → mestiː (мести). Morphophonemic tt, dt were probably [tː]; thus, the change was tː → st rather than tt → st. It follows then that when anterior nonhigh delayed release tː became st, its nonanterior high counterpart t'ː became št'.[15] The general rule for these changes is:

(23) $\begin{bmatrix} -\text{strd} \\ +\text{del} \end{bmatrix} \rightarrow \begin{bmatrix} +\text{cont} \\ +\text{strd} \\ -\text{del} \end{bmatrix} \begin{bmatrix} -\text{cont} \\ -\text{strd} \\ -\text{del} \end{bmatrix}$

(Nonstrident delayed release consonant splits into two nondelayed release consonants, the first of which is strident and continuant.)

For example: metːiː → mestiː, med'ːaː → mežd'aː, dut'ːiː → duštiː.

c. t' → č, d' → ǯ

4.17. According to persistent rule C (2.2), soft consonants become strident; e.g., k' → č or c, g' → ǯ or ʒ, x' → š or s:

(C) $\begin{bmatrix} +\text{high} \\ -\text{back} \end{bmatrix} \rightarrow [+\text{strident}]$

Thus, št' and žd' became šč and žǯ, merging with the results of the first regressive palatalization — sk' → šč, zg' → žǯ. Typical Bulgarian examples develop in the following way:

	/medj-	isket-	agni	dukter-	pakt-	metti:/
						(met:i:)
(2)		isčet-				
(18)	med'j-	iščet-	agn'i	dukt'er-		
(19)	med'-					
(21)				dut'er-	pat-	
(22)	med':-			dut':er-		
(23)	mežd'-			dušt'er-		mesti:[16]
(C)	mežǯ-			duščer-		
OB	мєжда	иштєтъ	огн'ь	дъштєрь	потъ	мєсти

Subsequent changes in Bulgarian dialects applied to šč and žǯ.

The difference between Bulgarian and the other Slavic languages may be due either to the contrasting nature of the soft consonants — Bulgarian t': vs. t' elsewhere — or to different relative orderings of rules (23) and (C).

This description of the changes producing tt → st, tj → šč, and kt → šč differs substantially from that proposed by Lunt 1974:158-59, who posits the following rules:

1. tj → tč; dj → dǯ
   t → č after k, g

2. t, k, s, x → s before t and d
   t, k, s, x → š before č and ǯ

   d, g, z → z before t and d
   d, g, z → ž before č and ǯ

Accordingly tj and kt, for example, develop as:

	tj	kt
1:	tč	kč
2:	šč	šč

This treatment is distinguished by its generality and simplicity, but it leaves several issues unexplained. (1) The presumed change of pakt- to pat- (потъ) indicates the loss of the velar rather than its mutation before t. (2) The change of t to št before soft consonants (e.g., оумръштвєнъ, изоштрєнъ) remains unexplained. (3) If j becomes č and ǯ in tj and dj, if tč and dǯ become šč and žǯ, and if kt → kč → šč, it is not clear why kj does not become kč and eventually šč. The fact that the changes occur at different times and reflect different processes suggests that there are two different assimilatory tendencies, each of which needs to be clearly formulated.

Nevertheless, it is noteworthy that Lunt too relates the change of tj to šč to the change of tt to st — though in a different way. He proposes (1974:220) a general Old Bulgarian rule for st, šč, žǯ:

$$[-\text{son}] \rightarrow \begin{bmatrix} +\text{cont} \\ +\text{cor} \\ \alpha\text{ant} \end{bmatrix} // \underline{\hspace{1cm}} \begin{bmatrix} -\text{son} \\ -\text{cont} \\ +\text{cor} \\ \alpha\text{ant} \end{bmatrix}$$

(All obstruents — except labials — are continuant and coronal before noncontinuant coronal obstruents; before anterior consonants these new consonants are anterior, and vice versa: t, d, s, z, k, x → s before t, d, but š, ž before č, ǯ.)

However, we must keep in mind that Lunt's goal is to give the simplest and most general synchronic account for the Old Bulgarian facts; he is not concerned with reconstructing Proto-Slavic sound changes.

A significant difference between our treatment and Lunt's is our view of tt as tː. In this respect our treatment also differs from Chomsky and Halle's (1968:430).

VII. Delayed Release Consonants and Clusters with Strident Consonants

1. šč → št, žǯ → žd,
   sc → st;
   stv → st, skv → sk

4.18. As a result of the changes considered above, the number of strident segments and their frequency of occurrence increased substantially. To the old sibilants s, s', z, and š, the various palatalizations and other related changes added ǯ, č, š, ʒ', s', c', and v, which occurred alone or in combinations such as šč, sc, and žǯ. The relative frequency of strident consonants also increased due to the change of tt to st and the loss of consonants before s. At this point, one might expect some reduction in the number of strident consonants or, at least, in their frequency of occurrence. This, indeed, took place, affecting for the most part č, ǯ, c, and ʒ. The reason that this particular group of consonants was affected may be found in the nature of affricates. (1) They are [+delayed release]: delayed release consonants tend, as we have seen, to split into two consonants at this time. (2) In principle, an affricate consists of a noncontinuous element followed by a continuous element; the extent to which the two components are connected may vary (Richter 1940:1-38). Thus, we are justified in assuming that ždž, štš, and sts served as intermediate stages in the development of žǯ, šč, and sc to žd, št, and st. (See also Leskien 1919, §412.)

The dissolution of affricates has parallels in the dissolution of other noncontinuant delayed release consonants, d':, t':, and t:. In both cases, a noncontinuant delayed release consonant splits into two segments, a strident continuant followed by a nonstrident noncontinuant. Apparently, there exits a phonetic constraint, which we may express as:

$$\sim \begin{bmatrix} +\text{delayed release} \\ -\text{continuant} \end{bmatrix}$$

After a strident continuant, that is, in žǯ, šč, and sc, voiced *and* voiceless affricates (ǯ, č, and c) split; elsewhere only voiced affricates (ǯ and ʒ) are effected.[17] The dissolution of šč, žǯ, and sc is accomplished by the following rule:

(24) $\begin{bmatrix} -\text{cont} \\ +\text{strd} \end{bmatrix} \rightarrow \begin{bmatrix} -\text{cont} \\ -\text{strd} \end{bmatrix} \begin{bmatrix} +\text{cont} \\ +\text{strd} \end{bmatrix} // \begin{bmatrix} +\text{cont} \\ +\text{strd} \end{bmatrix}$ ──

(Preceded by a strident continuant, a strident noncontinuant, which is delayed release by convention, splits into a nonstrident noncontinuant followed by a strident continuant.)

Notice the similarity between rules (24) and (23).

The resulting clusters are then simplified by the loss of the last segment: štš → št', ždž → žd', and sts → st:

(25) $\begin{bmatrix} +\text{cont} \\ +\text{strd} \end{bmatrix} \rightarrow \emptyset // \begin{bmatrix} +\text{cont} \\ +\text{strd} \end{bmatrix} \begin{bmatrix} -\text{cont} \\ -\text{strd} \end{bmatrix}$ ──

(A strident continuant is deleted after a strident continuant followed by a nonstrident noncontinuant.)

Thus:

	/iščezn-	dužǯi	duščer-	marisce:ji/
(24)	ištšezn-	duždži	duštšer-	maristse:ji
(25)	ištezn-	duždi	dušter-	mariste:ji
(OB)	иштєзн-	дъждь	дъштєр-	морьстьи

Rule (25) is clearly dissimilative. It is motivated not only by the behavior of sibilants, but also by that of the strident continuant v. Consider the following alternations observed in old written records: сквозѣ and скозѣ, листвиє and листиє, and in newer forms such as: (v)digna ← vdvigna (въдвинѫти), storja ← stvorja (сътворити). Likewise in several examples from SPs: църъсто 27a, 3, засъвѣдѣтєльстоунѫ 109b, 1-2, оскрънишѩ 139b, 7-8. Rule (25) accounts for all of these changes.

CHAPTER THREE

2. Old Bulgarian ⱋ/ⱎⱅ, щ/шт, сц/ст

4.19. Old Bulgarian manuscripts show dialect differences based on the absence or presence of rules (24) and (25). These differences appear in variations between ⱋ vs. ⱎⱅ (щ vs. шт) and ⱌⰲ vs. ⱌⱅ (сц vs. ст); for example, свѣща ~ свѣшта; морьсцѣи ~ морьстѣи.

For glagolitic we may suppose that at least originally ⱋ and ⱎⱅ denoted different things. We assume that in cyrillic щ was — or could have been interpreted as — a ligature for ш and т; we cannot make the same assumption for glagolitic. The letter ⱋ is clearly related to ⱎ and ⱋ, not to ш and т. The confusion of ⱋ and ⱎⱅ in glagolitic roughly reflects the fluctuation of šč and št. Of course, the manuscripts do not directly display the dialects of the scribes who copied them; rather, differences are due to the variant orthographic norms of Old Bulgarian.

We find ⱋ in manuscripts connected to the older glagolitic tradition: the oldest portions of SPs, Euch, and Ril, most of Ass and OchrFol, and part of the later hand of Zo. In Ass ⱋ is more frequent in the second part of the text (written in a single column). щ is characteristic of Sav, Und, and En. ⱎⱅ is the norm for Zo and Cloz. In Mar ⱎⱅ predominates: in our samples the frequency of ⱋ to ⱎⱅ is 121 : 261. In general, ⱎⱅ is found in glagolitic texts which are considered the "jungere Überlieferungschicht" (von Arnim 1930:66) — together with the new nasal ⱔ and ⰸ for ⰷ.

The distribution of sc and st coincides only partially with the distribution of ⱋ and ⱎⱅ. In Mar, Zo, and Cloz — besides ⱎⱅ — we find sc almost exclusively. In Ass st alternates with sc: 32 vs. 7. According to von Arnim 1930:206, we find sc together with ⱋ in the older portions of SPs, but st and ⱎⱅ in its "more cyrillic" sections; sc and ⱋ are characteristic for Euch and the later hand of Zo. Among the cyrillic manuscripts, щ and сц are typical for Sav, while шт and ст are typical for Supr and MacFol. According to Kul'bakin 1929:187 сц is customary for the earliest translated works.

The texts indicate that the dissolution of šč and sc ceased during the Old Bulgarian period and that the geographic distribution of the change was uneven. On the other hand, they show that the dissolution of žǯ (→ ždž → žd) was carried out. While the reflex of tj has its own letter, the reflex of dj does not.

For the latter we find ⰆⰄ or жд (with the exception of a single occurrence of ⰆⰄⰆ in Mar; Lunt 1959). On the basis of this evidence most investigators have assumed that in the oldest glagolitic records Ⱋ represented k', which was paired with the letter Ⰼ used for g' in Greek borrowings in surviving copies. According to this hypothesis, which originated with Durnovo, Ⱋ and Ⰼ were the reflexes of tj and dj, resp., in the oldest glagolitic. Velčeva 1973:105-24 discusses and criticizes this hypothesis and several of its recent variants on the basis of paleographic and philological data.

We must reiterate that voiced affricates are less stable than voiceless affricates. Consider ȝ and ӡ, which became ž and z, resp., everywhere — not only after strident continuants. č and c did not change in this way. As Perkell 1969 points out, the asymmetrical behavior of voiced and voiceless affricates is probably related to the fact that voiced consonants are nontense (lax), while voiceless consonants are tense (see also Chomsky and Halle 1968:325-26). These facts lead us to assume that glagolitic Ⱋ for šč and ⰆⰄ for žd may represent the actual state of affairs in ninth-century Old Bulgarian. It is possible that this was the dialect of Salonika, where šč later became št. There are traces of šč and žd in contemporary southern Bulgarian dialects (in the areas of Razlog and Strandja), while šč and žȝ are found in south-western dialects (in the areas of Kastoria and Korçë; e.g., *lešča, šěrka, košča, bašča, vežȝa, mežȝa*).

Thus, we may reconstruct three early Old Bulgarian dialects with a considerable degree of certainty:

1. Dialects with šč and žȝ, which Mirčev 1958:171 claims "have not been preserved in Old Bulgarian linguistic monuments because they were unknown to the Salonika dialect of Cyril and Methodius, [but] which today are fairly common in the dialects of Macedonia and South-west Bulgaria"; here rule (24) has not applied.

2. Dialects with šč and žd, preserved in the original glagolitic with Ⱋ (ш + Ⱍ)[18] and ⰆⰄ, and representing a stage in the development of the Salonika dialect and other dialects with šč and žd; here rule (24) applied only to voiced affricates:

$$(24') \begin{bmatrix} -\text{cont} \\ +\text{strd} \\ +\text{vcd} \end{bmatrix} \rightarrow \begin{bmatrix} -\text{cont} \\ -\text{strd} \end{bmatrix} \begin{bmatrix} +\text{cont} \\ +\text{strd} \end{bmatrix} \mathbin{/\!/} \begin{bmatrix} +\text{cont} \\ +\text{strd} \end{bmatrix} \underline{\qquad}$$

3. Dialects with št and žd, shown most clearly in manuscripts such as Supr and MacFol; here (24) has applied.

Thus, for example:

dialect type:	1		2		3	
	šč	žǯ	šč	žǯ	šč	žǯ
(24′)				ždž		
(24)					štš	ždž
(25)				žd	št	žd
OB			ш	жд	шт	жд

Finally, we must mention one extremely significant detail: Old Bulgarian vowels alternate after щ (шт) and жд in the same ways that they do after ш, ч, and ж. Moreover, the substitution of ѫ for ѧ in Middle Bulgarian texts occurs after щ and жд in the same way as it does after ш, ч, and ж. This fact is crucial for the chronology of the confusion of nasal vowels, for it shows that the confusion appeared in some Bulgarian dialects — not in Bulgarian as a whole — before the changes of šč and žǯ to št and žd, resp.

3. ǯ → ž and ʒ → z

4.20. The instability of voiced affricates led to the change of ǯ to ž and ʒ to z in all environments. This process passed through two phases.

1. The connection between the two components of the affricates weakened: ǯ → dž and ʒ → dz by a rule similar to (23) and (24):

$$(26) \begin{bmatrix} -\text{cont} \\ +\text{strd} \\ +\text{vcd} \end{bmatrix} \rightarrow \begin{bmatrix} -\text{cont} \\ -\text{strd} \end{bmatrix} \begin{bmatrix} +\text{cont} \\ +\text{strd} \end{bmatrix}$$

(Voiced, that is lax, strident noncontinuant splits into a nonstrident noncontinuant followed by a strident continuant.)

2. At this point — after the application of rules (8) and (21) — no clusters of *nonsonorant* + *continuant consonant* remained; this fact can be formalized as the phonetic constraint:

$$\sim [-\text{sonorant}] \begin{bmatrix} -\text{sonorant} \\ +\text{continuant} \end{bmatrix}$$

Consider specific examples of the application of rules (8) and (20): ts → s, ps → s, kš → š, ks → s, kx → x, e.g. These can be expressed as a single rule:

(27) $[-\text{son}] \rightarrow \emptyset \; // \; \underline{\quad} \begin{bmatrix} -\text{son} \\ +\text{cont} \end{bmatrix}$

(Obstruents are deleted before continuant obstruents.)

Consequently, dž becomes ž and dz — z.

The dissolution of voiced affricates is an old phenomenon. To judge by the fact that glagolitic and cyrillic each have a single letter for ž from the dental palatalizations and ʒ́ from the first velar palatalization, but separate letters for ʒ and z, we may suppose that ʒ́ changed earlier than ʒ. Nevertheless the shape of the letter ⰅⰉ, which contains an element of ⰄⰀ 'd' (Ilčev 1972:24), suggests that the creator of glagolitic may have known the variant ʒ́.

4. ʒ in Old Bulgarian orthography

4.21. Old Bulgarian records clearly confuse ʒ and з. ʒ predominates in Ass (126:5), Ril (7:1), and Mar (188:45). The older situation with ʒ is preserved also in SPs, the second part of Zo, En, and part of Hil. з predominates in Zo (122:39) and Cloz (12:1); it is also typical for Euch, Supr, OstE, and Sav. We lack data for the epigraphic monuments. There is an exceptional example in the seal of George the Syncel (*Georgi Sinkel*), which dates from the ninth to tenth centuries: гй помози робоу геѡргїѹ чрьньцю и сункелѹ блъгарьс(кѹмѹ) (Ivanova 1955:84-86 and 133). In the MacFol, which shares, to some extent, the graphic characteristics of the epigraphy of Preslav and Dobrudja (Δ, ж, only ь, ю, ьр, шт), ᵹ and з fluctuate (2:2).

It is difficult to establish, of course, the distribution of ᵹ and з in Old Bulgarian dialects. But it is beyond doubt that з replaces ᵹ principally in manuscripts in which we find initial a in words such as авити, акъı, агнѧ (5.2). This feature is essentially north-eastern. Today ᵹ occurs widely throughout Bulgarian, mainly in western and southern dialects. However, it is generally a secondary development in words such as *naᵹat* and *bъrᵹo*. Old examples have been replaced outright or ᵹ has been replaced by g by analogy; e.g., *drugi*, *nogi*, *pomogni*. Forms such as *ᵹvezda* and *noᵹe* are believed to contain secondary ᵹ and are not very helpful.

We have even less evidence for the change of ǯ to ž. It is interesting that in many Rupa dialects ž replaces ǯ not only in Slavic but also in Turkish words (old hypercorrections?). More recently ǯ in fact replaces ž in literary words (new hypercorrections). Given supporting data on ǯ and ž, we might be able to explain anomalies in Thracian and Rhodope dialects as results of the late loss of ǯ and its uneven replacement by ž, and to regard Rhodope forms such as ǯæba as archaic.

In any case, we find evidence for the affricate origin of ž not only in Old Bulgarian texts but in those of Old Russian and Middle Bulgarian as well. So, for example in the *Izbornik of 1076*, we find the very interesting example бежделѣза (← bež želěza ← bez želěza). Also, it is characteristic that vowels after ž sometimes behave as they do after č, but not as they do after š (5.3, 7.2, 7.5).

VIII. Dental Epenthesis and Its Relation to Liquid Metathesis

4.22. It is possible that the increased number of continuants in Proto-Slavic may explain another process, the appearance of t/d between anterior and nonanterior continuants: sr → str, zd → zdr (e.g., OB остръ, пьстръ, струѩ, издрешти, въздрѣмати, въздрасть). This change is not ordinarily considered to be related to the loss of closed syllables, but is assumed to be older. To the extent that the loss of closed syllables comprises a series of processes which affect the number and frequency of various consonants and glides and their co-occurrence, dental epenthesis has something in common with it.

Dental epenthesis is a dissimilative process: a coronal noncontinuant appears between two coronal continuants; the intrusive consonant takes on the voicing feature of the preceding consonant, but differs from it with respect to *strident*. The rule can be formalized as:

$$(28) \quad \emptyset \rightarrow \begin{bmatrix} +\text{ant} \\ +\text{cor} \\ -\text{cont} \\ \alpha\text{vcd} \end{bmatrix} \bigg/\bigg/ \begin{bmatrix} +\text{ant} \\ +\text{cor} \\ +\text{cont} \\ \alpha\text{vcd} \end{bmatrix} \underline{} \begin{bmatrix} -\text{ant} \\ +\text{cor} \\ +\text{cont} \end{bmatrix}$$

At this point — after clusters containing s/š and z/ž have changed — the rule may apply only to sr and zr.

4.23. Clusters of two continuant consonants, the first a sonorant and the second an obstruent, are also eliminated. Every sequence of *liquid + consonant* undergoes two well-known changes: liquid metathesis (Georgiev 1964 and 1968) and the development of so-called syllabic ṛ and ḷ (Velčeva 1973a). These changes are not dealt with here.

After the metathesis of liquids, which took place in late Proto-Slavic or, more precisely, in preliterary Old Bulgarian, the rule of dental epenthesis continued to apply in certain dialects, where it affected new groups of sr, zr, and even žr. Mirčev 1958:145 distinguishes two types of Bulgarian dialects:

1. dialects in which dental epenthesis did not apply to the results of liquid metathesis (e.g., *ostъr* and *pъstra*, but *sreda* and *srebro*, *sreštа*, and *žrebe*);

2. dialects — mostly western — in which epenthesis also applied in cases resulting from metathesis (e.g., *streda*, *strebro*, *nastrešten*, *ždrelo*, *žrebe*; see BDA, vol. 1, map 72 for examples in far south-eastern dialects) and even from the loss of weak yers or changes affecting ŗ (e.g., *strodjavam se*). Several forms of this origin (e.g., *zdrač* and *stъršel*, have made their way into the literary language.

In dialects of the first type, liquid metathesis took place *after* the completion of dental epenthesis. Examples such as малдичиє, балтины, and палтъ from the tenth century (Mirčev 1958:139), found in John the Exarch and explained as north-eastern Old Bulgarian archaisms, may support this claim. The late epenthesis of t and d is least typical of north-eastern dialects.

It is rather arbitrary to divide dialects into two types on the basis of dental epenthesis. In fact, their variety is much greater. On the basis of material contained in the commentaries to the first volume of the BDA, we may conclude generally that on the borders of dialects of the second type there appear hypercorrective tendencies to generalize sr and zr in examples such as *sesra* and *zrave* (cf. *sestra*, *zdrave*). In and around these dialects, the commentaries record locations where young speakers use the opposite hypercorrections, generalizing str and zdr to produce forms such as *strokove* and *straženie* (*srokove*, *sraženie*).

Notes

1. Bernštejn 1961:165 proposes an early change of m to n before consonants or word-boundary.
2. Chomsky and Halle 1968:177 consider ŋ to be noncontinuant; according to Voyles 1967:653 it is continuant.
3. û denotes a high back labial vowel — OB oy.
4. Trubetzkoy mentions a similar notion in a letter to Jakobson in 1921: "At the time of complete unity, the groups *ent* and *ont* became *ęnt*, *ǫnt* with closed *ę*, *ǫ*" (Jakobson 1975:16).

5. The neuter accusative singular ending was not subject to this change (OB село, поле). Presumably the pronominal ending -at was generalized to this case at some earlier time.
6. A similar deconsonantalization of high back consonants and the appearance of new diphthongs of *high vowel + glide* is also observed in the history of the Turkic languages.
7. This assumption does not agree with Vladimir Georgiev's explanation (1961 and 1969:130-31) of the vocative of r-stems. He reconstructs the development: ma:ter → ma:te, dukter → dukte, bra:ter → bra:te, with the subsequent extension of this ending to o-stems.
8. This form follows the etymology of Mažiulis 1973.
9. According to Gâlâbov 1973:17, in this change both r and s behave like continuants, "as opposed to plosives."
10. The greater stability of nasal consonants in word-final position has parallels in other languages; for example, Japanese, where the only consonant that occurs in this position is nasal.
11. See Meillet 1934, §166, Bernštejn 1961:145, Mareš 1963:53-54, Gâlâbov 1973, Lunt 1974:198-99. To explain word-final changes, Mareš proposes a theory based on the so-called *mora* (unit of length), while Gâlâbov suggests a tendency for vowels to narrow in certain positions. Vladimir Georgiev entirely rejects the possibility of special phonological changes in word-final position and seeks solutions in morphology and syntax.
12. Old Czech and Old Russian forms with ѣ (доушѣ, землѣ for доушѧ, землѧ) are probably the result of early nasalization and lowering. See 9.0 regarding conditions for nasalization.
13. The glagolitic designations reflect the distribution of ⰵ, ⱔ, and ⱗ in early glagolitic (without the letter ⰵ for ѧ).
14. Forms such as *zemn'a* and *Damn'an* in Bulgarian dialects show that the consonantalization of j could give n' as well as l'.
15. For a similar explanation see Lightner 1966: tj → ttj → stj → st'j → št'j → št' → št. Scatton 1978 is preferable: tj → t' → t't' → št' → št.
16. The two changes tt → st and t' → št', though expressed in a single rule, may have occurred at different times.
17. Voiceless affricates show greater stability. In this regard, see Avanesov 1974:173-74, Zinder 1963, Bulygina 1971:90-91.
18. On ⱛ as an original glagolitic letter, see Velčeva 1973.

Chapter 4

Reorganization of the Vocalic System

5.0. The elimination of diphthongs and the introduction of two new high vowels, ů: and ü:, triggered a complete reorganization of the vocalic system of Proto-Slavic (Žuravlev 1968:40). The appearance of the two vowels had the following consequences:

1. The number of high vowels increased, which entailed utilization of the other "vertical" contrast *high*, in addition to *low*. Vowels were then redistributed, and a new series of mid vowels ([-high, -low]) — e, ᴧ (ъ), and o — appeared.

2. The feature *labial* became distinctive.

3. The feature *tense* became redundant: at a given point in the development of Bulgarian dialects the distribution of tense vs. nontense became conditioned by stressed vs. nonstressed.

4. In the course of changes affecting the features *high* and *labial*, vowels became unstable with respect to *back*.

Jakobson et al. 1928 note an important regularity in the development of linguistic systems: "The disappearance or appearance of a correlation often leads necessarily to a radical restructuring of the system." In other words, a series of innovations may take place in order to reintroduce stability into a system.

In all Proto-Slavic dialects, vocalic innovations apply — to one degree or the other — to high as well as low vowels. Here we consider only those changes characteristic for Bulgarian.

The most complex changes in the vocalic system applied to high vowels. The number of high vowels, as we have seen, was significantly increased after the elimination of diphthongs — by the appearance of ů: (оу) and ü: (ю) and by the increased frequency of u (ъ) and i (ь) before nasal consonants. At this stage of development, oppositions among the high vowels were very complex, involving the features *back*, *labial*, and *tense*. At this point, these vowels became critical links in the vocalic system and underwent substantial changes, involving the appearance of prothetic glides and affecting ü:, u: (ы), the yers, and the nasal vowels.

I. Prothetic j and w

1. Prothetic glides before the high vowels i(:) and u(:)

5.1. The appearance of j and w (later v) before initial vowels has been described many times (e.g., Meillet 1906, 1934: §§93-101, Trávníček 1928, Lang 1910, Fortunatov 1919:236-38, Vaillant 1950:185ff., Bernštejn 1961:185-87). In general two points are in dispute: (1) Do all instances of the changes in question have the same chronology and the same explanation? (2) Were the changes primarily the result of some effort to eliminate hiatus arising from the loss of word-final consonants, or were they part of the general development of the Proto-Slavic vocalic system?

In recent years a number of special studies of prothetic glides in Proto-Slavic have appeared: Šylo 1949, Nieminen 1956, Shevelov 1963, Žuravlev 1965. Both Shevelov and Žuravlev relate the appearance of prothetic glides to the development of the Proto-Slavic vocalic system in general. Shevelov places the changes between the first and fifth centuries and explains them as the systematic "transformation of vowels into phonetic units with rising sonority; just as $e \rightarrow {}_e a$ and o and a merge in ${}_o a$, i and u presumably become ${}_i i$ and ${}_u u$, resp." (Shevelov 1963:260). In this respect, Shevelov is not far from Meillet's view (1934: §§94-95) of early prothesis before i(:) and u(:). Shevelov claims that the prothetic vowels were introduced in three stages and applied to all vowels.

Žuravlev also considers the changes to be very old — older than the first palatalization of velars. He tries to find their explanation in early delabialization and palatalization. In his terms, the vowel features *flat* and *sharp* passed to preceding consonants or otherwise appeared before the vowels as prothetic glides.

Several clarifications are necessary:

1. It would be overly ambitious to propose an absolute chronology for the changes in question before establishing their relative chronology. In any case, Bulgarian hydronyms, such as въıть from Thracian *utus* (Georgiev 1960:34), show that the change was still in effect after the Slavs arrived on the Balkan Peninsula.

2. Prothetic **w** did not occur before round vowels in Proto-Slavic; this fact casts doubt on Shevelov's claim that the original prothesis took place before every high back vowel.[1]

3. There is no convincing evidence for the old prothesis of **j** or **w** before **o** (ă). The exception вон'ѣ, вонѩ is apparently related to *wѫxati (Diels 1932:76), modern Bulgarian dial. *vĭxam*, *vĭxav* (Conev 1919:87).

4. The appearance of prothetic glides before initial nasal vowels (ѩ, вѫ, гѫ) is evidence that the process was still in effect after the changes eŋ → iŋ and aŋ → uŋ.[2] That is, the appearance of prothetic glides before high vowels took place after the raising of vowels which accompanied the elimination of diphthongs.

5. Žuravlev's explanation is related to his theory of "group-phonemes" (Žuravlev 1961, 1965, 1966), which in turn is based on the assumption that in early Proto-Slavic all consonants were softened before front vowels. Our interpretation excludes the early development of palatalization because of the existence of a rule which makes all soft consonants strident. Consequently, Old Bulgarian forms such as дьтѧ and тебе contradict the theory of early Proto-Slavic "synharmony."

Two facts must be explained: (1) the regular prothesis of **w** and **j** before initial high vowels and the irregular prothesis of **j** before оу, є, ѣ, and а; (2) the absence of any prothetic element whatsoever before о. Of course, here we have in mind an early period in the development of the Slavic languages and, in particular, Bulgarian dialects.

In the system which we attribute to Old Bulgarian, the prothesis of **w** and **j** before u(:) and i(:) is explained primarily by the necessity to increase the contrastive resources of high vowels, a necessity which emerged after the loss of diphthongs or, more precisely, after regressive assimilation of vowels for *high* before j, w, and ŋ. As a consequence, initial i(:) → ji(:), iŋ → jiŋ, u(:) → wu(:), uŋ → wuŋ. For example, ima:ŋ → jima:ŋ (OB имѧ), iŋti: → jiŋti: (ѩти), i:ti: → ji:ti: (ити), iŋzu:ku → jiŋzu:ku (ѩзыкъ), utara: → wutara: (вътора), u:saku → wu:saku (въісокъ), su + uŋzu → su + wuŋzu (съвѫзъ)[3]; cf. New Bulgarian *vĭdica*, *vĭsénica/gĭsénica*, *vĭglen*, *vĭtъk*, *vĭtre*, *vĭbel*, *vĭže*, *vĭtъl*, *vъgъréc*, *vĭzel*.

THE VOCALIC SYSTEM

Keeping in mind that etymological **j** occurred before initial ü:, we describe the distribution of **j** and **w** as: **j** occurs before high front vowels, and **w** before high back nonround vowels. **w** could neither appear nor remain before round vowels as a consequence of phonetic constraint D (2.2):

$$\sim [w] \ // \ [+\text{labial}]$$

(w is unstable in the environment of labial consonant or glide.)

Thus, for example, оухо, оучити, оумрѣти. Likewise in languages where uŋ → ů: (uŋ → uw): Russian *údica*, *úgol'*.[4] In Slavic languages in which uŋ did not become ů:, prothetic **w** did not disappear but became consonantal. Besides the Bulgarian examples given above, we may cite Polish *węgieł*, *więgiel*, *węzeł*, and Polabian *vęgil*.[5]

The Proto-Slavic rules for the introduction of prothetic **j** and **w** before high vowels are:

$$\emptyset \to j \ // \ \# \text{——} i(:)$$
$$\emptyset \to w \ // \ \# \text{——} u(:)$$

They may be generally formalized as:

(29) $\quad \emptyset \to \begin{bmatrix} -\text{voc} \\ -\text{cons} \\ \alpha\text{back} \end{bmatrix} \ // \ \# \text{——} \begin{bmatrix} +\text{voc} \\ +\text{high} \\ \alpha\text{back} \end{bmatrix}$

This rule is constrained or followed by (D), which itself can be formalized as:

(D) $\quad \begin{bmatrix} -\text{voc} \\ -\text{cons} \\ +\text{lab} \end{bmatrix} \to \emptyset \ // \ [+\text{labial}]$

Thus, the following distribution arises in initial position:

$$\text{ji}(:) \qquad \text{wu}(:)$$
$$\text{ů:} \qquad \text{jü:}$$

In this way the oppositions of front vs. back vowels (including ü: and ů:) and back labial vs. back nonlabial vowels are reinforced.

On the other hand, the oppositions of i: vs. i and u: vs. u are reduced.

Glides did not survive in these positions. In OB ji(:) became i:, and w — v. For ji(:) → i: and ij → i(:), see 8.2 and 8.3. At this point, it should be noted that initial ji(:) became i: in all Bulgarian dialects before the loss of the yers; e.g., *ime, imam, igla, igraja*. (Compare the loss or vocalization of i (ь) in Czech: (j)*meno,* (j)*mam, jehla,* where the development of the yers in initial position apparently took place later.)

Initial w became consonantal. For this change either the features *high* and *back* or the feature *labial* could have greater phonological importance. In the first case w became velar g, in the second — labial v. In this regard, consider the variation *gŭsénica* vs. *vŭsénica* in modern Bulgarian dialects. The change of w to v is accomplished by the following rule, discussed earlier:

(7) $\begin{bmatrix} -\text{voc} \\ +\text{lab} \end{bmatrix} \rightarrow [+\text{cons}] \; // \; \underline{\hspace{1em}} \; [+\text{voc}]$

In the change of w to g, the high back glide became consonantal, preserving its velar features [+high, +back] and losing sonority and labiality. The change took place before the high back vowels u(:) followed by the high back nonlabial consonant ŋ; i.e., initial w → g before ѫ:

(30) $\begin{bmatrix} -\text{voc} \\ +\text{high} \\ +\text{back} \end{bmatrix} \rightarrow \begin{bmatrix} +\text{cons} \\ -\text{son} \\ -\text{lab} \end{bmatrix} \; // \; \# \; \underline{\hspace{1em}} \; \begin{bmatrix} +\text{voc} \\ +\text{high} \\ +\text{back} \end{bmatrix} \begin{bmatrix} +\text{cons} \\ +\text{high} \\ +\text{back} \\ +\text{son} \\ -\text{lab} \end{bmatrix}$

This change took place in several separate instances; e.g., New Bulgarian *gŭsénica, gŭžva*. The earliest example is found in SPs 137a, 3-4: гѫсьницѩ.

Prothetic g is preserved before labial vowels. This may explain forms such as Russian *gusenica*, Serbian *guž*, and numerous examples with g and ɣ in Ukrainian dialects (Žuravlev 1965, Čalâkov 1968).

THE VOCALIC SYSTEM   Page 93

It is noteworthy that w → g in Bulgarian dialects only before the back nasal vowel, not before ъ or ы. Is it possible that the velar consonant ŋ impeded the change of w to v? Is it possible that the glide was preserved longer before the nasal uŋ?

If we assume that Cyril did not always indicate j before vowels, then perhaps he did not always indicate the glide w. This is one of the possible explanations for Old Bulgarian forms such as ѫдоль, ѫгль, ѫже, ѫзъкъ, ѫродъ, ѫтроба, ѫсѣница, and ѫтрь (here ѫ represents glagolitic Ⰴ) alongside гѫсѣница, съвѫзь, въ-, вы-. Fixed norms, perhaps codified in Moravian and Pannonian literary centers, also played a definite role in scribal practice. In any event, Salonika dialects have forms with initial prothetic v: *vŭnʒ́i, vŭnʒ́il*, and *vŭtak* in the villages of Suxo, Visoka, and Ajvatovo (Gołǫmb 1960-63:213, 231, 234).

In the context of the changes examined at this stage, the change of w to v indicates the nonlabiality of following back vowels: **wupi:ti:** → **vupi:ti:** (OB въпити), **wu:soka:** → **vu:soka:** (OB высока). In general, the change of w to v in this position took place neither simultaneously nor uniformly throughout the dialects of Old Bulgarian. We observe clear variations in the reflex of Proto-Slavic initial wu-: *vnúk* (*ʃnúk*) and *unúk*, *vnétre* (*ʃnétre*) and *unétre*, *vnátre* (*ʃnátre*) and *unátre*, *vzémem* and *úzmem*, *v* (*ʃ*) and *u* (in dialects with *u-* from *vu-*, the old locative preposition въ and the ablative oy merge).

In western dialects, forms with u- from vu- are probably old. u instead of v is often encountered even in modern eastern dialects, but they are to be taken as later developments. Mirčev 1958:143 cites forms from the seventeenth century: оурѣме, оуратъ for врѣме, вратъ.

The old contrast between v- and u- is evidence that the same two rules, (1) the change of w to v and (2) the development of the yers, applied in different relative orders (1.1). In dialects with u-, the weak yers were lost before the change of prothetic w to u: wuC- → wC- → uC-. In dialects with v, w became v before the loss of the weak yers: wuC- → vuC- → vC-.

Apparently the development of wC- differed from that of vC-. Before consonants, w was vocalized (recall the changes that eliminated diphthongs in which w followed by a consonant caused lengthening of the preceding vowel (rule 10b). This change may be considered a variant of rule (7) (3.6):

(7′) $\begin{bmatrix} -\text{cons} \\ +\text{lab} \end{bmatrix} \rightarrow [+\text{vocalic}] \; // \; \underline{\quad} \; C$

(w → ŭ before consonants.[6])

Thus, we assume general underlying forms for all Bulgarian dialects with prothetic w before high back nonlabial vowels: wu-, wuː-, wuŋ-. Dialect differences, then, were due to subsequent changes which applied to w and to the yers.

Forms such as *jáže, jáglen,* and *játok,* found in several western dialects, pose an interesting problem: Do they show later prothetic developments or the change of w to j? In my opinion, neither answer is correct. Rather, here we see the results of very interesting interdialectal processes which generalize particular patterns. In all likelihood, prothetic j began to appear in forms of this sort in dialects in which the back nasal vowel had a labial reflex, o or ô (e.g., *pót, jóže* in the dialect of Debar). Prothetic w would not have been preserved before a labial vowel. The appearance of j may be explained as the interaction of forms with initial o from ѫ and forms with initial ѩ (cf. the change of ѩ to ѭ). Reiter 1964, Ugrinova 1951, and Vidoevski 1962 show that particular patterns are also generalized where a- and u-dialects meet. Thus, forms such as *júže, júzel, jútok* in the dialect of Skopje occur together with or close to forms such as *játrva, jádro, jázik* (with old ѩ → ѭ; Ugrinova 1951:12) and *jágrca* (from *вѫгрьць; Vidoevski 1962:50). Reiter 1964:58 cites forms such as *jadica, jažica, jaglen* alongside *janʒa, jatrva, jačmen.*

In dialects where ѩ → je, initial je was generalized. Vidoevski 1962:50 cites *ezik* [sic], *jetrva, jegrk*; Gianelli and Vaillant 1958 cite *eglenje* and *ečimen.* The coexistence of an old form with w alongside a newer one with j is recorded by Mazon 1936:28 in an archaic Bulgarian dialect in Southern Albania: *jangárec* vs. *wangórec.*

Despite all of the changes and fluctuations in the forms, it is clear that late Proto-Slavic exhibits the following general initial syllables containing high vowels and prothetic glides: ji(ː), wu(ː), and ŭː. With the exception of o (ă), which shows no prothesis, the other vowels are subject to considerable etymologically conditioned variation: e vs. je, a vs. ja. After the change of jüː to ŭː, we also encounter examples with initial jŭː as well as ŭː.

2. The iotation of nonhigh vowels

5.2. The merger of initial vowels with or without j is a tendency already identified — though rather unclearly — by Fortunatov 1919:243 as the reason for new instances of prothetic j. The earliest examples probably involved eː (ѣ). After the fronting of vowels and the change of jaː to jeː, the distinction between jeː and eː was eliminated in initial and intervocalic positions: eːd → jeːd- (OB ѩдъ), eːsin → jeːsin- (ѩсьнъ), as jeːma (OB ѩмо-же) and jeːrasti (ѩрость). After the late Proto-Slavic change of jæ (←jeː) to ja, conditions arose for the elimination of the contrast ja vs. aː: агнѧ → ѩгнѧ, агода → ѩгода. Perhaps it was only with regard to a and æ that the notion of avoiding hiatus had any significance (cf. the difference in the iotations of aː and a (←o)).

Today, forms without j before a are characteristic of north-eastern dialects and of those south-eastern dialects which descend in a wedge southward from the Balkan Mountain and sub-Balkan areas. Most of the population of western Moesia is not original or native to this area. Consequently it is difficult to say whether forms with initial a are a generally old northern feature or a specifically north-eastern one. In the future, historical dialectology should shed greater light on the nature of the old division between northern and southern dialects. It should not be forgotten that the Balkan Mountain naturally separated the early tribes, their habitations, and movements into northern and southern. Even today there are great similarities among the dialects of southern Macedonia, Thrace, and Strandja — despite complex forces favoring their historical differentiation. This supposition is supported by another old, surviving isogloss, the adverbial morpheme -y; compare: the old forms акъі, тогъі the new north-western forms *kogí, segí, togíva*, north-eastern *kogí, segí, togíz(i)* as opposed to Balkan and southern forms *segá, kogá, togáva, togá(zi), togáj* and the general new form *áko* (old ѣко and акъі).

Old Bulgarian glagolitic manuscripts also have forms with initial a and ѣ: ѣвити/авити, ѣгнѧ/агнѧ, ѣко/акъі, агода, ѣще/аще, ѣбие/абие. Cloz shows the most consistent use of initial ѣ. The greatest frequency of a occurs in Euch: авити (regularly in 38 cases), акъі 47a, 22, агньци 3b, 10-11, агньче 15a, 4, агнець 16b, 4, 5. In Ass ѣвити and авити occur as 32 : 21; also ако (twice), и ако (once), акъи (twice). In Маr ѣвити exceeds авити

38 : 33. Examples with авити predominate in Zo. ѣ is most frequent in John — that part of the manuscript which is considered linguistically the oldest. Von Arnim 1930:184 makes several interesting observations regarding the use of ѣ in initial and word-internal positions after vowels in Zo: from Matt. 6:4 to Luke 10:12 авити vs. ѣвити is 28 : 2; from Luke 17:30 to John 21:14 the relation is 2 : 18; in examples of the type добраѣ vs. добраа the corresponding proportions are 29 : 8 and 6 : 12. We find a similar distribution in SPs, where the scribe in part A behaved like the scribe of the second half of Zo, and vice versa. The form акъі is found in Zo (Matt., Mark, Luke), Euch, Ass, Supr, and John the Exarch.

We observe a clear tendency to generalize j before ů; cf. jü → ju — ů → ju. The spread of j is apparent in a number of manuscripts. For example, in Mar оуже occurs 10 times vs. 35 for юже. In Sav оуже occurs 6 times, юже 12. In Zo, Mar, Sav, Euch, SPs, and Supr оутр- outnumbers ютр- (оутро, оутрьнъ, заоутрьнъ) by 102 to 25. The greatest percentage of examples with ю- is found in Mar and SPs (Nieminen 1956:26). Modern forms such as *jútro*, *júžina* are found in western dialects in the vicinity of Kjustendil, Sofia, and elsewhere. The use of iotated u, and even iotated o, is particularly common in folk songs: *jútro*, *júmre*, *jóšte*, *jóči*, *jóti*, for example.

The iotation of e is not treated here because glagolitic did not have a separate letter for je. There is, however, a very interesting question which deserves special consideration: why was iotated e not generalized in Bulgarian dialects, when the following circumstances favored it:

1. the great percentage of etymological **je** (Fortunatov 1919:243) and the great frequency with which certain forms containing je occurred (e.g., the anaphoric pronoun ѥго, ѥмоу,...);

2. the increased occurrence of forms with initial je due to the change of jiŋ → ję; e.g., jiŋzu:ku → języ:ku (Shevelov 1963:250).

Apparently some factor, or factors, opposed the expansion of je — which is clearly suggested by changes such as добраѥго → добраего → добрааго, доброуѥмоу → доброуемоу → доброуоумоу.[7] To judge by the present state of affairs, we may conclude that this tendency was strongest in western and southern dialects.

Most often the appearance of initial j and w in Proto-Slavic is explained by rules of external sandhi: either the tendency to avoid hiatus or the "law of rising syllabic sonority" ("steigende Sonoritätswelle"; van Wijk 1931:39-40, 46-47). Theoretically these proposals are appealing, but practically they leave many questions unanswered. There are vowels, like o, which are not iotated. With other vowels iotation occurs sporadically or is even avoided. Later developments may lead to the elimination of j. The very term "rising sonority" is imprecise. What rising sonority is to be found in new consonant clusters such as str, zdr, and skvr? The very fact that Proto-Slavic words and morphemes could begin with vowels casts doubt on the theory of rising sonority.

Nevertheless there were intra-word factors which favored the appearance of prothetic glides. There is evidence of this in frequent examples of the iotation of a and ů after i (Nieminen 1956:25). For example, in the alternation of оутр-/ютр- in Old Bulgarian manuscripts, it turns out that 28% of all examples with ю occur after i, while less than 1% with oy are in this position. Thus, the preceding vowel provides the basis for the generalization of a given pattern with the prothetic glide. The choice of the particular word-initial pattern to be generalized is conditioned by the character of the initial vowel itself and by existing types of contrastive oppositions.

In 2.2 we introduced persistent rule A, which accounts for the change of high vowels to glides under certain circumstances. Thus, in Proto-Slavic i(:) → j and u(:) → w in the environment of the nonhigh vowels a(:) and e(:); for example, ia(:)→ ja(:), a(:)i → a(:)j.

The occurrence of high vowels contiguous to other high vowels was avoided in order to preserve vocalic oppositions and to preclude changes such as:

$$u(:) + u \rightarrow u: (ъі)$$
$$i(:) + i \rightarrow i: (и)$$
$$i(:) + u \rightarrow ju$$
later $$u + i(:) \rightarrow ъі$$

It is significant that the prothesis of w and j preserves initial vowels, sometimes even strengthening their invariant contrast. But it does not always preserve the preceding vowel. Consider frequent examples such as въ истинѫ → въістинѫ, въ инѫ → въі инѫ

(New Bulgarian *vínagi*), сътворитъ и → сътворитꙑ и, прѣдамь и → прѣдамє и, съмѣритъ и → съмѣрито и.

Essentially the same phenomenon is observed in the development of certain forms with the definite article, for example, zʌtь + ътъ → zʌtjъtъ (*zét'ə(t)*, *zék'ə*, *zék'o*), pѫtь + ътъ → pѫtjъtъ (*pŭt'ə(t)*, *pŭk'ə*, *pŭk'o*, *pák'o*) — with the regular change of i (ь) to j in the environment of vowels (Mirčev 1958:186).

Usually alternations like *zét* : *zét'o* are taken as proof of the lost Proto-Slavic palatalization of consonants before the front vowel ь (5.1). Allegedly, the palatalization was preserved in definite forms (Ščepkin 1906:103, Popova 1962:9).

In western Bulgarian dialects (as well as in some eastern dialects in Strandja (Bojadžiev 1973)), the change of t to k' and d to g' occurs only before j which comes to follow consonants as a result of the loss of weak yers: grozdьje → grozdje → grozg'e, gostьje → gostje → gosk'e, ladьja → ladja → lag'a. A form such as *pák'a* in the dialect of Botevgrad can not be from pѫt'+ъt, regardless of how we explain the eventual word-final soft consonant; it must come from pѫtь+ътъ → pѫtjъt(ъ). Examples with k' and g' clearly show the nature of the change: tьъ → tjъ → t', not tь→ t'.

II. The Evolution of ü:

5.3. The labial vowel ü: did not remain front. As in other Indo-European languages (e.g., English), in Slavic the feature [+labial] did not long remain compatible with [−back].[8] ü: could develop in two directions: it could become [+back] while remaining [+labial]; it could remain [−back] while becoming [−labial]. The study of Old Bulgarian texts shows that these changes did not occur uniformly in all positions or in all dialects.

The original glagolitic alphabet represented ü: with the letter Ⱓ, the components of which are similar to the letters for i: — Ⱇ, Ⰹ, and Ⱔ. This is additional evidence that Ⱓ originally represented a high front vowel.[9] Old cyrillic manuscripts, such as MacFol, lacked the letter ю. In MacFol we find glagolitic Ⱓ. This suggests that the creators of cyrillic were representing a dialect in which the change of ü: to (j)û: had already taken place. In Hil we find the oldest form of cyrillic ю: |-о, which suggests a connection with glagolitic Ⱓ.

оі, the second "cyrillic variant" of ю, occurs first in En: въѕлоібенс 36b, 6-7. Another early monument in which we find examples of оі is one of the hands of the addenda to Ass (e.g., 112b left, 117a bottom, 121b, 125a, 130a, 131b, 132b, 133b, 134b, 136a, 150b). This hand is very similar to that of the second glagolitic scribe. The use of оі (150b) and ѫ, Ѧ, and ъ connect the addenda of Ass to En. оі is found in many Middle Bulgarian manuscripts, e.g., SlepA, Bol, and SlepT. In the second, archaic hand of manuscript 1/12 in the library of Rila Monastery (a gospel from the thirteenth to fourteenth centuries), оі occurs with °у for оу, which reminds one of оі. The letter оі was probably introduced in a provincial scribal school as a cyrillic letter different from ю.[10]

The elimination of ü: took place in the following circumstances:

1. *After labial consonants.* Examples such as блюдѫ, плюти from *bewd-, *pew- indicate an old change of ü: to jû: after labial consonants. In this position j became l'. The change is old and is found in all dialects of Slavic.

2. *After soft consonants and* j. In general we can conventionally distinguish two different patterns in the use of ю in Old Bulgarian manuscripts, one "glagolitic," the other "cyrillic." In the vast majority of glagolitic manuscripts the occurrence of ю is etymologically correct, regardless of environment; for example, шю, чю, жю, цю, лю, and so on. The glagolitic manuscripts Euch, Zo, Cloz, Ril, SPs, and OchrFol, and cyrillic Sav are most consistent in this regard. In these manuscripts examples of оу for ю are rare; e.g., вражъдоуѭща Euch 34a, 12, ашоутъ SPs 42b, 2 and 43b, 12. Mar, Ass, the later hand of Zo, and BojP very frequently violate this norm.

	цю : цоу	шю : шоу	жю : жоу	чю : чоу	щю : щоу	ждю : ждоу
Mar:	22 : 9	47 : 19	3 : 0	21 : 1	67 : 28	11 : 0
Ass:	19 : 2	22 : 33	2 : 0	17 : 0	22 : 42	54 : 4

This variation shows one clear pattern: examples of оу after ш are greater than after ж and ч. The same pattern is observed in the use of a for ѣ. (For ъ/ь see below.) The similar patterning of ж and ч reflects the original pronunciation of ž as ǯ. The variation after щ/жд is also significant: it connects these clusters with other hushing consonants. To judge from the data, Mar shows more traces of the affricated articulations šč and žǯ than Ass. (Cf. also the changes ѣ → a (7.1) and ь → ъ (8.14) after hushing consonants.)

The norm in Supr and OstE[11] is шоу, жоу, чоу, штоу (щоу), ждоу. One example is found in the Vladislav inscription: исходѦщоу. The norm is most often violated after ч. In many Middle Bulgarian manuscripts (e.g., Pir, KE) the norm is шоу, жоу, ждоу, щоу, but чю (with fluctuations after ж). En is an early representative of this norm: here шоу occurs twice, щоу five times, жоу and чюдеса (37b, 9) once each.

In both cyrillic and glagolitic manuscripts we find ю (ⱙ) at the beginning of words, after vowels, and after the letters for sonorant consonants. Some exceptions occur after p (Ščepkin 1899:290). ию and иоу alternate in foreign nouns, e.g., июда (see Diels 1932:13, 43 for explanation).

Despite the impossibility of clearly distinguishing OB ю = ü/jü from ю = jů, there is evidence of the beginning of the change of ü to (j)ů, which appears inconsistently in the texts.

3. *After hard consonants.* In the course of the loss of ü, there are some fluctuations among ů, jů, and i after hard consonants. For the most part these involve l; one case occurs after t — tüždь (← *teud-). In Old and early Middle Bulgarian texts we find great variation in the latter example: тоуждь, цюуждь, штюждь, стоуждь, штоуждь, чюждь, чоуждь. Forms with щ (шт) are the result of tj → šč → št. In тоуждь we see the change of ü to ů. These forms indicate fluctuation between ü: → jů: and ü: → ů:, perhaps facilitated by the reinterpretation of тоуждь as related to the adverb тоу 'there'.

The alternation тоуждь/штоуждь is clearly reflected in Old Bulgarian texts. тоуждь is essentially typical of glagolitic, штоуждь and штюждь of cyrillic. Divergences from this norm are rare in glagolitic texts (von Arnim 1930:212). In this respect Zo shows some variation, e.g., по тоуждемь же не їджтъ. нъ бѣжжтъ отъ н'єго ѣко не знажтъ штюждєго гласа (John 10:5).

Von Arnim 1930:212 connects штоуждь/штюждь with northern or north-eastern Bulgarian dialects reflected in the texts. Mirčev 1958:141 explains the later forms чоуждь/чюждь as dissimilation in штоуждь/штюждь.

Today the forms *túg* and *túgi* (from earlier тоуждь) are characteristic of many south-western dialects. *čužd- (čuzd-)* covers the largest part of Bulgarian linguistic territory, replacing the descendants of штоуждь completely and those of тоужд- partially. In modern Salonika dialects we find *čúst, čúzda*. Mazon 1936:132 records an old form *čuždži* in a gospel dating from 1847 found in Korçë.

The confusion of оу and ю after л appears relatively late in the manuscripts. The first examples are from En: лю for лоу and vice versa. Mirčev and Kodov 1965:208 refer to these as "*l*-anomalies." Examples are very common in SlepA and many thirteenth-century texts, e.g., лоубити ~ любити, полоучити ~ полючити, лоуна ~ люна. Examples such as *lúbam, klúcet* beside *mliáko, hliábo* are recorded for south-western dialects in the sixteenth century (Giannelli and Vaillant 1958). The connection of this change to the phonetic properties and the historical development of l needs to be studied on the basis of full descriptions of individual dialects.

In general then we can can say that ü is replaced by û or jû in Bulgarian dialects. This change can be formalized as:

(31) $\begin{bmatrix} +\text{vocalic} \\ +\text{labial} \end{bmatrix} \rightarrow$ (j) [+back]

(Labial vowels are back; j appears irregularly.)

In some dialects and in some positions (mainly after l) ü survived longer than in others. In these instances it could become i, remaining front while losing its labiality; e.g., lübe → libe. Forms such as *klíč*, *zaklíčam*, *líl'ak* are widely attested in the modern dialects. In the Čerged prayers from the sixteenth century, there are examples such as *blidi* (блюди), *listo* (людьство), *ligem* (людьємъ). In the Trojan tale of the fourteenth century we find the example ипитеръ (Mirčev 1958:130). In these cases the change is:

(32) $\begin{bmatrix} +\text{vocalic} \\ -\text{back} \end{bmatrix} \rightarrow$ [−labial]

(Front vowels are nonlabial.)

The general basis for these two changes is a constraint against front labial vowels:

∼ [+vocalic, −back, +labial]

In order to conform to this constraint a front labial vowel becomes either [+back] or [−labial].

III. ЪI and the Evolution of the Vocalic System

5.4. With respect to ю we tentatively distinguished two major dialectal or chronological systems: one with two labial vowels ü: and û: (reflected in original glagolitic), the other with the beginnings of the change of ü: to û: (reflected in certain cyrillic texts). In the second system we see the tendency for only back vowels to be labial. In turn, this system shows that one of the first changes among the oppositions of high vowels was the reduction of four long, high vowels to three:

THE VOCALIC SYSTEM

	back	labial
оу	+	+
ы	+	−
ю	−	+
и	−	−

→

	back	labial
оу	+	+
ы	+	−
и	−	−

We know that in most Bulgarian dialects another change affecting the high vowels — y → i — commenced after the twelfth century (Mirčev 1958:118). Thus, as the nonlabial high back vowel became front, the tendency for high round vowels to be back came to an end. After this change the system of long high vowels was even simpler:

	back	labial
оу	+	+
и	−	−

This constraint can be formalized as:

$$\begin{bmatrix} +\text{vocalic} \\ +\text{high} \\ +\text{back} \\ +\text{labial} \end{bmatrix} \text{ or } \begin{bmatrix} +\text{vocalic} \\ +\text{high} \\ -\text{back} \\ -\text{labial} \end{bmatrix}$$

which can be generalized to:

$$\begin{bmatrix} +\text{vocalic} \\ +\text{high} \\ \alpha \text{ back} \\ \alpha \text{ labial} \end{bmatrix}$$

The rule for the change of y to i is:

(33) $\begin{bmatrix} +\text{vocalic} \\ +\text{high} \\ -\text{labial} \end{bmatrix} \rightarrow [-\text{back}]$

(High nonlabial vowels are front.)

CHAPTER FOUR

This change took place in Bulgarian dialects *after* the loss of the yers. Otherwise, not only y, but also ъ, would have become nonback, leading to e as the reflex of both yers.

Rule (33) also occurred before the softening of consonants before front vowels. We find no trace of any contrasts before y and i, or before old ъ and ь.[12] See also 5.1 for word-final palatalization in cases such as *pъt'* and *zet'* (Popova 1962 and Kočev 1968 explain them differently).

Our analysis contradicts the widely-held opinion that Proto-Slavic consonants were generally palatalized before front vowels and that the vocalizations of the yers and nasals were identical in Middle Bulgarian: nonpalatalized consonants before the reflexes of the back nasal and back yer, palatalized consonants before those of the front nasal and front yer; i.e., Съ vs. С'ъ (Mirčev 1958:115).

Glagolitic did not have a separate symbol for *yeri*, the old long back nonlabial vowel. On the basis of his analysis of glagolitic texts, statistical data, and comparison with dialects of Salonika, Gâlâbov 1952 and 1974 attempts to prove that y and ъ early merged in the dialect reflected in the original glagolitic. He supports this claim with previously overlooked examples of the confusion of y and ъ in glagolitic texts (Gâlâbov 1974:520). Such examples are found in Mar, SPs, Euch, and Cloz — but mostly in the verb слъіш(ати)/слъш(ати). Gâlâbov concludes (1974:519) that "the creator of the original glagolitic alphabet based his work on a dialect in which Proto-Slavic y did not have its own reflex, different from the vowels otherwise represented by glagolitic letters; or, in other words, Proto-Slavic y merged with one of the other vowels in the dialect."

Indeed, the data on ъ from ъі in Salonika dialects, for example the dialect of the village Visoka, are unambiguous: *sъn, sanót* (сынъ), *kъtka, kъsalo, bъl, sъt, mъška, pъtam, plъtka, vъm'a, grindъt'a* (грѧдъі-)(Gołomb 1960-63:183). However, in order to confirm Gâlâbov's hypothesis, one serious question must be answered. If the merger of y and ъ is an early occurrence in the dialect of Visoka, why do we find secondary nasalization after ъ but not after y; cf. *bъnčva, lъnžá, bъnc, bъnzó*?

IV. The Development of Nonhigh Lax Vowels:

a → o

6.1. The increased number of high vowels led to changes not only in their contrasts with respect to one another but in the vocalic system as a whole. A new vertical opposition appeared: vowels now contrasted not only as [±high] but also [±low]. A third row appeared, consisting of mid vowels, [-high, -low] (Jakobson 1963:13). Already existing nonhigh vowels became mid lax ε and ʌ and low tense æ and a. Conventionally, we may represent these changes as: e → ε, a → ʌ, e: → æ, a: → a. The rule which carried out these changes, so critical to the development of the Bulgarian vocalic system, can be formalized as:

$$(34) \begin{bmatrix} +\text{vocalic} \\ -\text{tense} \end{bmatrix} \rightarrow [-\text{low}]$$

(Lax vowels are nonlow.)[13]

This is a persistent rule in Bulgarian dialects. Its application is observed in the development of unstressed ѣ; e.g., *ml'áku* or *mlǽku* but *mlεkár*. It appears in the so-called reduction of unstressed a, e.g., *glʌvá*, where the unstressed vowel, being lax, becomes nonhigh.

The nonhigh nonlow vowels ε and ʌ were likely to take on the tenseness (length) of the other nonhigh vowels. This process was connected with the appearance of labialization in the back mid vowel.[14] It is difficult to fix the time of this change. Greek toponyms of Slavic origin were borrowed with a, e.g., γαρίτσα, καρούτα, μαγούλα (Mirčev 1958:45). Georgiev 1964:6-7 places labialization in the ninth century (also Mirčev 1958:50).

The glagolitic letter ꙙ has parallels in ꙗ 'ѫ', ъ 'ъ', ь 'ь', э 'є', and ꙗ 'ѧ'. It is obvious that the element ɔ is common to the shapes of all lax vowels; however, glagolitic offer no evidence of the labiality of the vowel represented by ꙙ. In cyrillic, Greek o replaces ꙙ.

Evidence of the interaction of the features *tense* and *labial* is also observed after stress became dynamic. The old distinctive opposition with respect to length (*tense*) was replaced by one conditioned by stress: stressed vowels became tense, unstressed vowels — lax. Scatton 1975:14 formalizes this rule in the following way for New Bulgarian:

$$(35) \begin{bmatrix} +\text{vocalic} \\ \alpha\text{stress} \end{bmatrix} \rightarrow [\alpha\text{tense}]$$

This rule began to apply after the loss of weak yers and the loss of old quantitative correlations (Jakobson 1963).

It is reasonable to assume that *akane* as an old development was possible in Rhodope dialects of Bulgarian, in which the mid vowel from old ă remained nonlabial everywhere until some late time, and that the introduction of rule (35) had something to do with labialization. Thus, the development of o in all positions took place according to the rule:

$$(36) \begin{bmatrix} +\text{vocalic} \\ -\text{high} \\ -\text{low} \\ +\text{back} \\ +\text{tense} \end{bmatrix} \rightarrow [+\text{labial}]$$

(Back nonhigh nonlow tense ʌː is labialized; see also 8.1.)

V. Low Tense Vowels

1. æ → a

7.1. Here we consider one of the early instances of the instability of late Proto-Slavic vowels which were opposed with respect to the feature *back* and which occurred in the environment after soft consonants and j. Front low tense vowel æ becomes back a; e.g., žæba → žaba (жаба), jæm- → jam- (ιaмь).

Reasons for this change are found in the development of the phonological system itself. From the processes we have already considered, it is clear that the early shift of vowels was part of a general tendency in the system towards a more forward vocalization — a tendency which appeared in a number of assimilations: the palatalizations of consonants and the fronting of vowels. These changes increased the frequency of front vowels in the system.

The dental palatalizations of late Proto-Slavic represent another tendency: the raising of vowels and consonants before high, predominantly sonorant segments. This tendency not only increased the number of high vowels, but also the number of nonanterior nonback consonants, at the expense of anterior consonants. The increase in the number of soft dorsal consonants ([-anterior, -back, +high]) essentially reflected a tendency for vocalization to shift rearward; this tendency affected vowels as well.

Consequently there are several reasons for the shift of æ to a:

1. the instability of the vocalic system containing a number of new oppositions;

2. the high frequency of front vowels;

3. a tendency to shift vocalization rearward;

4. morphological factors: a tendency to merge the endings of hard and soft stems (cf. мѫжа, наша as отрока, бѣла).

This change was a progressive assimilation: the earliest examples occurred after nonanterior consonants and j, most frequently after the continuants š, ž, j; less frequently after c, č, ǯ; least frequently after sonorants. The change is indicated by fluctuations of the following sorts in Old Bulgarian texts: шь/ша, жь/жа, чь/ча, ль/лıа, нь/нıа, рь/ра/рıа.[15] For example, чьсъ vs. часъ, воль vs. волıа. The change of æ to a took place after the elimination of diphthongs and after the dental palatalizations.

Unfortunately, existing descriptions of modern Bulgarian dialects do not allow us to relate the systems found in Old and Middle Bulgarian records to those of the modern dialects. These developments ought to be one of the central concerns of Bulgarian historical dialectology for several reasons:

1. Old and Middle Bulgarian texts are clearly differentiated with respect to the distribution of the letters designating the low vowels in various environments.

2. The results of the change varied throughout Bulgarian dialects.

3. The change was closely tied to the so-called *jat-shift*.

4. These problems are controversial not only for paleoslavistics (van Wijk 1949-50:299-300), but also for historical dialectology.

7.2. Old and Middle Bulgarian texts show great variation with respect to the distribution of ь, а, and ꙗ (glagolitic Ⰰ and ⱔ) in various environments. We may tentatively distinguish the following characteristic types of Old Bulgarian orthographic systems:

1. An archaic system with no change: жь, шь, чь, ць, ждь, нь, ль, рь, ь. This system is found occasionally in Mar and SPs and in isolated examples in other glagolitic texts. As for cyrillic, it occurs in DE and BojE. жь, чь, шь are the norm only in KF, where ь occurs fifteen times and а twice. In SPs ь occurs after hushing consonants mainly in what von Arnim calls part A — the part containing most of the presumably original glagolitic features. Examples of ь are not numerous, but they are interesting as violations of the norm: ша : шь :: 171 : 0, жа : жь :: 77 : 5, ча : чь :: 66 : 6, ца (шта) : ць (шть) :: 113 : 4, жда : ждь :: 16 : 1. The use of Ⰰ after hushing consonants in glagolitic coincides approximately with the absence — or traces of the absence — of ⱔ from the orthographic system, the hanging arrangement of letters on the line, and the use of ⱏ and ⱐ. This is substantiated by one of the cyrillic manuscripts, DE, which generally preserves the norms of original glagolitic. In this text the use of ь after hushers co-occurs with the presence (as a norm) of three nasals, ѫ, ѧ, and ѩ, vestiges of hanging writing, and ь for ꙗ.

Philological analysis of glagolitic manuscripts has established that in the original glagolitic graphic system Ⰰ was written after letters for soft ([+high, -back]) consonants and j. Moreover, forms such as ьгнѧ and ьвити indicate that the early Proto-Slavic fronting of vowels after [+high, -back] segments remained in effect even after the iotation of initial a; cf., *jægne*, *jæbʊlka*, and *jæk* in modern southern Bulgarian dialects. Rhodope dialects preserve the greatest number of forms of this sort.

With a certain degree of approximation, we may suppose that the original glagolitic alphabet reflected a system with æ after soft consonants and j. This view is justified by philological analysis, the classification of texts on the basis of paleographic characteristics, and comparison of the contemporary Rupa (Rhodope and Thracian) and southern Macedonian dialects. The alternation of žǽbi (žébi) : žába beside bǽli (béli) : b'ál may indicate the later change of žæ → ža.

2. ша, жа, чѣ, цѣ, ждѣ, нѣ, лѣ, рѣ. This system reflects an old dialect in which æ is preserved after the soft noncontinuants č and ǯ. The data given above for SPs hint at this system. In Ass examples with ѣ are: плаштѣницѧ 11d, 7, чл҃чѣ 49d, 25, 123b, 28, 91c, 15, чѣетъ 85b, 25, плацѣницеѥ 111a, 3, запечѣтьлѣвъше 111b, 27, чл҃ѣ 127b, 15, чѣса 39a, 10, ицѣте 35a, 23, 69b, 26-27. These examples may be vestiges of an archaic type of glagolitic. Another vestige of this sort in Ass is ѩ for ѥ in 196 cases.

Isolated examples of ѣ after hushing consonants in Mar, Zo, the late hand of Zo, and Und occur after ч (ч), ж (ж) (for ǯ and ž see above). There is a single example in the Vladislav inscription: коньчѣ же сѧ.

We find ша, жа, чѣ, ца, жда, нѣ, рѣ, лѣ, ꙗ (or ѣ) as an established norm in Middle Bulgarian texts such as SlepA, GP, Stam, KE, and others from the thirteenth and fourteenth centuries. This was apparently a prominent orthographic norm, which left lasting traces in the Middle Bulgarian literary tradition.

Uncovering evidence of this system in the modern dialects would require very careful investigation. Traces have been effaced by later changes, such as morphological levelings and the shift of ѣ to a and e. For example, in the dialect of Pirdop, we find forms such as šápka, šápki, žápka, and žaléa, but čáša, čéši, játka, érica. These forms allow us to reconstruct with some degree of probability an Old Bulgarian dialect with ша, жа, чѣ, цѣ, and intervocalic ѣ. The change of чѣ to ча and jѣ to ja may have taken place later, at the same time as changes of ѣ, that is, simultaneously with changes such as snǽk → sn'ák. In these cases the hardening of š and ž is a consequence, not a cause, of the old change of жѣ to жа and шѣ to ша.

The orthographic system with ша, жа, чѣ has two major variants in the old texts: ша, жа, чѣ, нѣ, лѣ, рѣ, ѣ vs. ша, жа, чѣ, нѣ, рѣ, лѣ, ꙗ. We find the first in Und, SlepA, and GP. The second is infrequent in Old Bulgarian (cf. коньчѣ and ꙗже in the Vladislav inscription), but very common in Middle Bulgarian, occurring in KE, Stam, Pir, and many other manuscripts. Both types appear in Old Bulgarian more often as isolated intrusions of the dialects of the scribes than as fixed, accepted norms.

CHAPTER FOUR

Old and Middle Bulgarian data suggest the existence of late Proto-Slavic dialects in which the change æ → a was conditioned not only by the softness of the preceding segment but by two additional factors as well: its continuousness and sonority.

The change with the most limited range of application is жѣ → жа and шѣ → ша (vs. preserved чѣ, (j)ѣ, нѣ, лѣ, рѣ, eventually цѣ).[16] This change is probably early; its limited application is reflected in the complexity of the rule which produces it:

(37) $[+\text{low}] \rightarrow [+\text{back}]$ // $\begin{bmatrix} +\text{high} \\ -\text{back} \\ +\text{cont} \\ -\text{son} \end{bmatrix}$ ——

(æ becomes a after soft nonsonorant continuants — š and ž, sometimes s', z', štš, ždž.)

The second variant cannot be captured by a single general rule: j and the continuants do not constitute a natural class, sharing features which distinguish them from the sonorant consonants. There are three possible explanations for this system: (1) it is purely literary in origin; (2) it reflects a dialect with nonsoftened n, l, and r; (3) the feature *coronal* was relevant for the change, that is, ž, š, and j were palatal while č, n', l', and r' were alveopalatal. Unfortunately the data do not allow us to reconstruct specifications for the feature *coronal*.

3. ша, жа, ча, нѣ, рѣ, лѣ, ѣ. This system is a common norm in glagolitic manuscripts — Zo, Mar, Cloz, Euch, Ass. As for cyrillic manuscripts it occurs in MacFol and En. For example, En землѣ 26b, 7, 32a, 14, искоуша[етъ] 15a, 18, ѣстъ 5b, 11, дръжава 28b, 9, достоьниѣ 32a, 6, [раз]дѣльетъ сѧ 22b, 6, разарьитє 4a, 9, чашѧ 15a, 7, 15a, 12, ѣростъ 32a, 1, волѣ 20b, 9, н(ъı)нѣ 26a, 19, and many others. This orthographic system reflects dialects in which the range of the change was wider than in those already considered; the rule which produces it it is more general:

(37′) $[+\text{low}] \rightarrow [+\text{back}]$ // $\begin{bmatrix} +\text{high} \\ -\text{back} \\ -\text{son} \end{bmatrix}$ ——

(æ → a after soft nonsonorant consonants.)[17]

We find traces of a system of this sort in contemporary dialects with forms such as: *bǽl* (*bél*), *šápka*, *šápki*, *žába*, *žábi*, *čás*, *dъšterǽ* (*dъšteré*), *zemǽ* (*zemé*), *glavnǽ*; or: *b'ál*, *bǽli* (*béli*), *šápka*, *šápki*, *čás*, *zem'á*, *dъšter'á*, *glavn'á*, (*j*)*ábъlka*, *pol'ána*, *polǽni* (*poléni*), *játka*, *jǽtki*, (*jétki*). Dialects of the second type show the additional change of æ to a after soft consonants or j and before a hard consonant. This change is preceded by the softening of consonants before æ. The appearance of *jakane* in these dialects represents the generalization of the change of æ to a at a later time, when stressed vowels were tense and when new soft consonants had appeared before æ. Given the present state of our knowledge of Bulgarian dialects and their histories, we can relate the Old Bulgarian system with ша, жа, ча, нѣ, рѣ, лѣ, and ѣ to modern dialects of both types. There are traces of such dialects today in north-eastern areas, where, for example, we find: *šápka*, *šápki*, *čáši*, *čás*, but *pul'ána*, *pul'ǽni*, *jám*, *jǽri*, *dъšter'á*, *glavn'á* — with no alternation of a after š, ž, and č, but with alternation after j, r, n, and l (BDA, vol. 2).[18]

4. жа, ша, ча, нга, лѣ, ра, га. This orthographic system is found in Sav. The distribution of ѣ and a (га) appears at first glance strange and even improbable. In fact, it represents a transition from the previous type to one which we consider next, in 5. Here the change occurs everywhere except after l; it is more general than (37′), which applies only to nonsonorants. Examples from Sav include: своѭ 29, 1[19], нынѣ 5, 19, въпрашаетъ 5, 17, отъвѣща 5, 19, слышасте 9, 15, ближънѣаго 9, 16, прохождаше 12, 1, съконьча 12, 21, покланѣаше 12, 27, оставлѣѭ 92, 21, гакоже 93, 6, печальни 97, 21, отъвѣщаша 101, 26, грѣхѫ сѧ 103, 3, съвѣдѣтель 104, 14, земли 55, 15, but земьѣ 114, 8, аврамль 131, 23, црѣ, кесара 108, 26, разараѭ 121, 18, 113, 9-10.

5. ша, жа, ча, нѣ, лѣ, ра (рѣ), ѣ. This orthographic type is found in Supr, ZogrFol, and Old Serbian and Old Russian manuscripts. In this system the change has applied in all environments:

$$(37'') \quad [+\text{low}] \rightarrow [+\text{back}] \ // \ \begin{bmatrix} +\text{high} \\ -\text{back} \end{bmatrix} \underline{}$$

(æ → a after soft consonants and j.)

Examples from Supr include: поклан'ꙗнѥмъ сѧ 59, 22-23, молꙗахѫ 398, 10, родителꙗ зависти 389, 27, цѣсарь, цѣсарꙗ, and цѣсара. In Supr there are 206 instances of ѣ after *lj, *rj, and *nj versus 600 with ꙗ (Meyer 1928). ꙗ is very rare after p: 16 examples, as opposed to 77 with ѣ and 96 with a. Forms with pa probably indicate the secondary hardening of r'. Cf. forms such as сꙗмо in an inscription from the village of Basarab in northern Dobrudja (Mixailè 1964:155) and само in Supr.

The significant number of forms with ѣ after soft sonorant consonants in Supr suggest that two Old Bulgarian orthographic norms crossed here: one with ꙗ after vowels and ѣ after soft sonorant consonants, the other with ꙗ in both environments. Both norms are found in cyrillic. The following examples after sonorants are found in the short ZogrFol: оуꙗшнꙗти and съставлꙗти.

Today we find this system principally in Balkan and western Bulgarian dialects: šápka, čáša, žába, jám, zemjá, von'á, vól'a, búr'a (búra). It is the norm in the Bulgarian literary language. Because of the numerous examples of ꙗ, лꙗ, and нꙗ in Supr and OstE, these spellings are considered "classical" and are used as citation forms in all Old Bulgarian (Old Church Slavonic) dictionaries. This type became the norm neither in Old Bulgarian nor Middle Bulgarian. It is found as a violation of the norm in Middle Bulgarian.

The great variation in the distribution of Old Bulgarian ѣ and a (ꙗ) suggests early dialectal differentiations. We must emphasize that, on the basis of the formalizations proposed here, Old Bulgarian dialectal differences were due to greater or lesser degrees of generality of a single phenomenon. Doubtless, dialectal differentiations in this process were, and are, real. However, it is not excluded that the various stages in the change of æ to a represent a chronologically continuous process of increasing generalization. This is suggested not so much by the different degrees of generality (simplicity) in the changes reflected in Old Bulgarian records, as by the later variant of the change, the so-called *jat-shift*, which gradually spread over a large part of Bulgarian dialects. Clearly, the general tendency remained valid for a substantial period of time. The replacement of ǽ by á is a process which can still be observed today in south-eastern, particularly Thracian, dialects.

7.3. Finally, we must treat separately one particular instance of the change of æ to a — after strident anterior consonants, c, ʒ, s, z, as reflected in the alternations цѣ/ца, ʒѣ/ʒa, сѣ/са. Mirčev and Kodov 1965:208 cite the example цасароу in Supr as well as rather numerous examples from En, e.g., облѣцамъ же сѧ 5a, 17, прр̂цахъ 8a, 2, рѣцамъ 21b, 18, цалова[нї] 31b, 2, ѧзыцахъ 4b, 11-12, 18b, 8, цаножꙗ 3a, 4, ʒалѡ 26b, 4, трѣʒахъ 39b, 17. In Sav we find сѣ → ca (e.g., вьсакъ), but always цѣ.

In modern Bulgarian dialects, especially those of the west and south, this change is very wide-spread, e.g., *cána*, *calúvam*, *cádim*, *sákam*. This development took place at different times in different dialects. But one thing is common to all of them: æ became a at the time when the preceding consonant was soft. The change was *not* due to the hardening of the consonant, as is commonly believed. The forms *cál* and *c'ál* are the results of two similar changes applying at different times. The change in question must be explained as the old change of æ to a after soft consonants, e.g., шѣ → ша, чѣ → ча, and цѣ → ца. (See Scatton 1976 for a similar explanation.) This old change was not carried out in two cases: (1) if the anterior consonants had already hardened; (2) if the change would have applied in a dialect where it would have affected only soft continuants (type 2 above). Where anterior consonants had hardened (and therefore did not undergo the early change), they could subsequently resoften before æ, and then participate in the later *jat-shift*: thus, cǽl → c'ǽl → c'ál, as bǽl → b'ǽl → b'ál. In all cases the shift of æ to a was due to the softness of the preceding consonant; the change of c'a to ca and s'a to sa was secondary.

In Old Bulgarian, forms with ца are found in texts which otherwise follow an orthographic norm with ча. Of course, we are excluding early examples such as дѣвица and отьца, which are morphologically motivated.[20] On the other hand, not all Old and New Bulgarian dialects with ча show traces of цѣ → ца as well.

We will attempt to explain this last fact by looking first at a clear presentation of the relevant changes:

1. æ → a after š, ž, č, c', ʒ', s', j
2. the *hardening* of anterior c', ʒ', s' (cf. E, 2.2)
3. the *softening* of consonants before front vowels
4. the *jat-shift*
5. æ → e

CHAPTER FOUR

Differences are probably due to the absence of *softening* in western dialects and different orderings of the first two rules with respect to one another. (Changes in the length of vowels are disregarded in the following discussion.)

1. Dialects with *cála, cáli, čás, béla, béli*

	/c'ǽla	c'ǽli	čǽs-	bǽla	bǽli/
æ → a	c'ála	c'áli	čás-		
hardening	cála	cáli			
softening			does not apply		
jat-shift			does not apply		
æ → e				béla	béli
modern	cála	cáli	čás	béla	béli

2. Dialects with *céla, céli, čás, béla, béli*

	/c'ǽla	c'ǽli	čǽs-	bǽla	bǽli/
hardening	cǽla	cǽli			
æ → a			čás-		
softening			does not apply		
jat-shift			does not apply		
æ → e	céla	céli		béla	béli
modern	céla	céli	čás	béla	béli

3. Dialects with *c'ála, céli, čás, b'ála, béli*

	/c'ǽla	c'ǽli	čǽs-	bǽla	bǽli/
hardening	cǽla	cǽli			
æ → a			čás-		
softening	c'ǽla	c'ǽl'i		b'ǽla	b'ǽl'i
jat-shift	c'ála			b'ála	
æ → e		c'él'i			b'él'i
modern	c'ála	c'él'i	čás	b'ála	b'éli

2. æŋ → aŋ; ⱔ and ⱙ

7.4. One of the most controversial questions of Slavic paleography concerns the vocalization of the glagolitic letter representing the "third" nasal vowel ⱔ, transliterated with cyrillic ⱙ. Several substantial studies have recently treated this question from a variety of perspectives: Mareš 1963, Birnbaum 1963, Kolesov 1973, Mošin 1973. There are actually two problems: (1) Did the glagolitic letter represent a front vowel or j + *back vowel*? (2) Did the glagolitic letter represent a nasal vowel or a sequence of V + *nasal consonant*?

The second question is valid for *all* letters representing "nasal" vowels; it has already been discussed in 4.2. Here we must re-emphasize that this particular question cannot be answered generally, but only for particular, individual periods in the development of the Slavic languages and dialects. The nasalization of vowels before N[21] evidently did not occur at the same time in all Old Bulgarian dialects, nor did it occur at the same time in all environments in any given dialect. Glagolitic records offer evidence of two stages, Vŋ and y̨; cyrillic records show only y̨ (9.10).

Whether or not the letter for the third nasal represented a front vowel or a iotated back vowel has been widely debated. The prevalent opinion is that ⱔ was not jǫ or joN but a separate front vowel. This view, which originated with Fortunatov (Birnbaum 1963) and Ščepkin 1906[22], is most effectively set forth by Trubetzkoy 1954. On the basis of his analysis of glagolitic, Trubetzkoy (1954:64ff.) concludes that in the system upon which the first Slavic alphabet was based, the front vowels i, ь, ü, æ (ě), e(N), and öN occurred after j and soft consonants.

Some who have studied the phonological development of Proto-Slavic have tried to account for the appearance of the front vowel ö (öN). However, this particular vocalization for the third nasal can not be explained satisfactorily (Mareš 1963); Birnbaum's criticism (1963) is compelling in this respect.

Trubetzkoy's interpretation requires the assumption that æN became oN, which later was fronted to öN, not eN. Such early changes of æ to o and o to ö are not supported by the general development of the vocalic system. The changes of u(:) to i(:) and a(:) to e(:) are old; they preceded all phases of the loss of diphthongs containing j and w. The evolution of these diphthongs, for their part, shares features of the development of groups of V + nasal. Moreover, we find no other changes suggesting any tendency supporting the eventual change of e:N or a:N to öN. Thus, for the present there is no convincing evidence for the appearance of ö or öN.

Recently Mošin 1973:42-54 has proposed a new interpretation for the early glagolitic nasal letters: originally Ѧ represented ǫ and Ѥ — ę. This view is based on data from abecedariums and the *Skazanie o pis'menax* of the monk Xrabr. However, because these data can be explained in other ways, they are inconclusive.

The Munich abecedarium is particularly important for Mošin's hypothesis. In the glagolitic portion of the manuscript, we find Ѧ, Ѥ, and ѨѤ, in the cyrillic portion — three unique symbols. It must be noted, however that the behavior of these symbols is similar to that of certain features of late glagolitic texts (e.g., the distribution of Ѥ and ѨѤ in the glagolitic of the first hand of OchrE)[23]; for this reason these data are not compelling.

From what we have reconstructed up to this point, it follows that the third nasal was more likely to have been vocalized as æN than öN. The distribution of glagolitic ѨѤ corresponds to that of early Old Bulgarian æN. This is basically the case for Euch and, partially, for manuscripts of the oldest glagolitic type with three nasals, ѨѤ, ѨѤ, and ѨѤ. In the latter — KF, SPs, OchrF, and to some extent Ass — we find ѨѤ after *j and sonorant consonants. After ш, щ, ж, жд, ч, and ц, ѨѤ is replaced (though not always) by ѨѤ. It is precisely in SPs, KF, and Ass that traces of the vocalization æN for the third nasal coincide with traces of an old orthographic system with чь, шь, and жь. Cyrillic DE provides similar data.

The reading of ѨѤ as a front vowel coincides, of course, with the absence of the letter ꙗ in glagolitic and the use of ᴀ for every Proto-Slavic æ (from *e:, *ja:, and *aj). Additional support for the interpretation of ѨѤ as æN is the name of the letter in Abcd: *hie*; compare *hiet* for ь. In the Banduri abecedarium we find γέα and γέατ, resp., as the names of the two letters (see table in Vrana 1963). The oldest form of the letter ѨѤ can be reconstructed on the basis of the way it is written in Abcd, KF, and SPs: with a separate second element.

In our explanation of the nasal vowels, Ѥ of the oldest glagolitic is read as ŋ — a back high nasal consonant (4.3). This explains, additionally, the spellings ⰀѤⰃⰎ- (аѥгел-) in SPs.

Thus the change of ш☉є to шӡє (шѫ; e.g., OB нашѫ), ч☉є to чӡє (чѫ; e.g., OB плачѫ) must be explained as the change of æŋ to aŋ (compare the change of æ to a above).

Still to be explained is when and how aŋ and uŋ merged into a single nasal vowel. Did aŋ → uŋ or aŋ → ʌŋ? Did uŋ and a:ŋ become ɑ, or did they become ʌ? Probably this question must be answered concretely not only for the Slavic languages but for Bulgarian dialects as well.

In the history of Bulgarian, we cannot exclude the possibility of other paths of development in individual dialects: the absence of the change of æŋ to aŋ or the absence of the merger of uŋ and aŋ. Dialects of the first type would be the most archaic. We would expect to find in them forms such as *znáje*, *znájet*, *sp'ǽ*, but *berá*, *berát*. Dialects of this type are found in south-eastern Bulgarian.

Reconstruction is complicated by the following factors:

1. morphological leveling;
2. the possibility of later *jat-shift: sp'ǽ* → sp'á;
3. the root stress found over the largest part of south-eastern and western dialects: *čéta*, *vъ́rv'ʌ*.

From the point of view of the historical development of the Slavic languages, forms with æ are very old and are congruent with the Salonika dialect of the ninth century reflected in the glagolitic alphabet.

As the descendant of the second type, we would expect a system with *znájʌ*, *znájʌt*, *sp'á*, *sp'át*, *berá*, *berát*. These may be found in Bulgarian dialects in Aegean Macedonia (Ivanov 1972, map 117), as well as in south-eastern Bulgarian dialects in the area of Sliven, Burgas, and elsewhere.

7.5. Two features of glagolitic monuments deserve additional attention:

1. the alternation of ☉є and ӡє after hushing consonants;

2. the orthographic reform which replaced ☉є with ӡє after the letters for sonorant consonants.

The fluctuation of glagolitic ☉є and ӡє shares a great deal with the fluctuation of ѣ and a (ʌ and +). The norm for Zo, Mar, Ass, Ril, and others requires ☉є and ʌ after sonorants and j, but ӡє and + after other high consonants. Only in Euch do we find ☉є and ʌ in the first case, and ☉є and + in the second.

Examples which violate this norm, and the use of ѫє and ѧ after hushers represent, according to our interpretation, a more archaic, perhaps dialectal, phonological system. Examples with ѧ were listed above, and it was pointed out that they are most frequent in SPs, KF, and Ass. Excluding Euch, where they are the norm after hushers, examples with ѫє are also most frequent in SPs and Ass; however, they do not occur in KF.

Variants in SPs are distributed in the following way:

шѩ : шѫє   жѩ : жѫє   чѩ : чѫє   цѩ : цѫє   ждѩ : ждѫє

60 : 5   16 : 1   13 : 8   30 : 3   31 : 1

Consider the data given earlier in this chapter for a vs. ѣ in similar environments. Thus, for example: дш҃ѫє 51b, 15, 55a, 12, 70a, 20; прѣпоѣшѫєтъ сѧ 78a, 20; на(ш)ѫє 58a, 8; сълъжѫєтъ 78b, 11; оумочѫє 5b, 9; притъчѫє 57b, 1-2, 62a, 1; обличѫє 63b, 1, 64a, 15; наоучѫє 65a, 20; лачѫєщє 141a, 12; лачѫєщѧѧ 143a, 8; възвѣщѫє 50b, 7; полєщѫє 68a, 4; поропъщѫєтъ 73a, 3-4; хождѫє 56a, 8.

In SPs the ratio of ѩ to ѫє after hushers is 134 : 18; the ratio of ѫ to ѧ is 413 : 16. In this manuscript there are numerous errors and corrections which suggest uncertainty in the use of the letters for the front or back vowels after high sibilants or high sonorant consonants. For etymological æŋ the scribe hesitates among ѫє, ѩ, ѭ, є, even ѫ; for ѩ — between ѩ and ѫє: плачѫ (ѩ corrected to ѫ) 43a, 12, πενθῶν; възлачє (1 pers sg) 63b, 10; съхранє (1 pers sg) 19a, 22; зорѩ (acc sg) 94a, 17, φαῦσιν; землѩ (acc sg) 78a, 5, 133b, 2; въдовицѩ 123a, 19; на стьзѩ правыѩ 27b, 1; до дш҃ѩ моєѩ 82a, 4; моєѩ (gen sg, ѫє corrected to ѩ) 32b, 19; своєѩ (ѫє corrected to ѩ) 172a, 7-8; лъжѩ (acc sg, ѩ corrected to ѩ 71a, 10; веселѩєштє сѩ (ѩ for ѫє) 149a, 13; нашѩ (acc sg, ѩ or ѫє corrected to ѩ) 58a, 8.

In Ass we find 19 examples with ѫє, which violate the norm requiring ѩ: въложѫє 7b, 20; прр҃чѫє 39d, 19; положѫє 130a, 6, 69b, 1, 92d, 15; притъчѫє 44b, 11, 61d, 15, 121a, 21, 68a, 24-25, 122b, 4, 69d, 5-6; притєжѫє 67b, 27-28; плачѫєщѩ 81a, 14, стражѫє 85a, 14; лобъжѫє 90c, 24; съкажѫє 99c, 13; плачѫєщи сє 156a, 7; мръжѫє 157a, 17; плачѫєщии сє 123b, 22.

Additional evidence for the front vocalization of ѫє is the fact that in Ass this letter does not occur after ш, but mainly after ч, ж, and ц (for šč and ȝ see above), where the letters for the front vowels are most frequent (cf. ъ and ь, оу and ю, and a and ѣ). The confusion of etymological ѧ and ѩ (є) occurs in the following examples: каплѭштѧ 90a, 17-18; твор\ѧєщѩѧ 94c, 26-27; приємлѧтъ 42c, 19; ѣстоѧєщѩѧ 2d, 24; плачѧщı сѧ 119b, 5; помажѧтъ 11d, 28; лъжѧштє 113d, 17; въсплачѧт' сѧ 84b, 1; плачѧштии 113c, 16.

Examples of ждѧ and жѧ are found in two places in Mar. One example, плачѧ̂т'сѧ, occurs in Ril (V_3, 26). It is important to bear in mind that Ril is very close to Euch. This example — which even has the diacritic above ѧ as in Euch (and also KF) — is entirely predictable.

Examples of the front nasal instead of old ѧ (according to orthographic norms, ѩ or ѧ) are usually considered examples of the confusion of the nasals in Old Bulgarian. However, the confusion of the nasals, in principle, represents the confusion of the symbols for the front and back nasal vowels (ѫ and ѧ). If we assume that ѧ indeed represented æŋ, then the confusion of ѧ and ѩ is a genuine Old Bulgarian confusion of nasals. Examples like гл҃а (Cloz, En), приємѫщє and бєсѣдоуѫщими (En) are expected and predictable in phonological, but not graphic terms. Consider, additionally, the material from Sav given by Ščepkin 1903. In tenth-century epigraphy there is also one interesting example: писано бо єстъ поражѫ пастъира и разидѫтъ сѧ оцѧ (Mixaile 1964:160-63).

In Middle Bulgarian the representation of the old ѧ by the front nasal after н, р, and л, and in some texts also after vowels, established itself as an orthographic rule. Thus, it does not indicate genuine confusion of the nasals. (Cf. ѧ after sonorants and j after vowels in glagolitic, as well as the distribution of ѣ.)

The shape of ѧ with an upper triangular component in Abcd and KF and with an upper trapezoidal component in Zo is similar to the shape of glagolitic ѣ — Ⱑ.

In terms of the explanation proposed here, the early development of æŋ in Bulgarian dialects is reduced to two changes:

1. æŋ → aŋ after soft consonants and j (cf. the changes of æ to a);

2. the merger of aŋ with other groups of back vowel and nasal consonant.

The final result is the appearance of the back nasal after soft consonants and j; cf. OB ѭ, пишѭ, плачѭ, виждѭ, ицѭ. So for example:

	Old Bulgarian	пишѭ	жаба	берѫ
1.	New Bulgarian	píšʌ	žábʌ	berь̆
		/pišæŋ	žæba	beraŋ/
	æ → a	pišaŋ	žaba	
	aŋ → ѫ	pišѫ		berѫ
	finally	pišѫ	žaba	berѫ
2.	New Bulgarian	píšʌ	žábʌ	berá
		/pišæŋ	žæba	beraŋ/
	æ → a	pišaŋ	žaba	
	finally	pišǫ	žaba	berǫ

These models are given in the most general terms. Each separate dialect requires thorough analysis in order to establish the precise formulation of the relevant rules and the order in which they applied.

It must be re-emphasized that the change of æŋ (ѩ) to aŋ (ѭ) is a special case of the development of the change of æ to a (ѣ to a). Accordingly, æŋ should not have become aŋ in dialects which lack the change of æ to a, that is, with old forms such as жѣба, чѣсъ, ѣсти, видѣниѣ, and the like — except for examples due to morphological analogy. In the contemporary Rhodope dialect of the village of Trigrad, we find an archaic vocalic system with no trace of æ(ŋ) → a(ŋ): žǽba, jǽk, šǽpka, čǽs, jǽ ('I'); unstressed: večére, dúše, mréže, glávne, zém'e, igrájet, znájet, je (← ѩ), pájek. Stojkov 1962:21 explains je for ѩ in this dialect as the result of a series of changes: ѩ → jъ → ja → je. This complicated process is not very plausible. We may assume the direct change of unstressed æ to e.

The changes of vowels before ŋ and the change of æ to a varied in early Old Bulgarian dialects. Records from the tenth and eleventh centuries indicate variation with respect to norms and

THE VOCALIC SYSTEM

various solutions for the graphic representation of the low vowels after high consonants. Fluctuations of ⰀⰐ and +, Ⱏ and a/ⱑ, ⱔ and ⱔⰵ, ⰶ and ⱑⰶ, ⱔⰵ and ⱔⰵ, and ⰶ and ⰀⰐ represent not only differences in written norms, but also in chronology and dialect. The following major systems can be identified:

1. шⰀ   чⰀ   нⰀ   лⰀ   рⰀ   Ⰰ
    шⱔⰵ   чⱔⰵ   нⱔⰵ   лⱔⰵ   рⱔⰵ   ⱔⰵ

This system appears as a divergence from what is otherwise the norm, mainly in SPs.

2. шⰀ   чⰀ   нⰀ   лⰀ   рⰀ   Ⰰ
    шⱔⰵ   —   нⱔⰵ   лⱔⰵ   рⱔⰵ   ⱔⰵ

This is the system of KF.

3. ш+   ч+   нⰀ   лⰀ   рⰀ   Ⰰ
    шⱔⰵ   чⱔⰵ   нⱔⰵ   лⱔⰵ   рⱔⰵ   ⱔⰵ

This is the norm in Euch.

4. ш+   чⰀ   нⰀ   лⰀ   рⰀ   Ⰰ
    шⱔⰵ   чⱔⰵ   нⱔⰵ   лⱔⰵ   рⱔⰵ   ⱔⰵ

This system is found as a divergence from what is otherwise the norm in Ass and Euch.

5. ш+   ч+   нⰀ   лⰀ   рⰀ   Ⰰ
    шⱑⰵ   чⱑⰵ   нⱔⰵ   лⱔⰵ   рⱔⰵ   ⱔⰵ

This is the norm for Zo, Mar, Ril, and Ass.

6. ш+   ч+   нⰀ   лⰀ   рⰀ   Ⰰ
    шⱑⰵ   чⱑⰵ   нⱑⰵ   лⱑⰵ   рⱑⰵ   ⱔⰵ

This is the norm for Cloz; it is found as divergence from the norm in Zo, Mar, and SPs.

As a norm, in all of these types the front nasals ⱑⰵ, ⰵ (ⰀⰐ, Ⰰ, and Ⰰ) are not confused with ⱔⰵ or ⱑⰵ (ⱑⰶ, ⰶ).

The gradual replacement of ⱔⰵ by ⱑⰵ in this series of types is particularly interesting. In our treatment, this may represent the shift of front to back vowel, as well as the reinterpretation of ⱔⰵ as the symbol for j + ѫ in some glagolitic literary centers. In cyrillic, ѭ essentially represents j + *back vowel*. The following examples are taken from two glagolitic manuscripts, Euch and Cloz, which are diametrically opposed to one another in the use of ⱔ:

Euch: пицѭ нашѭ 13a, 13; пиѭщиимъ 14b, 5; глѭще 16a, 10; вонѭ 15b, 13; бѫдѫ/цѭѭ 24a, 1; страждѭщиимь 25a, 8; стрѣ/чѭцѭѭ 29a, 1; непомрачѭщиимь сѧ 32b, 10; землѭ 33a, 3; хвалѭ 36a, 16; хоцѭ 37b, 3; прошѭ 41b, 9; вечерѭ 46b, 3; разорѭ 48a, 9; отънѭдоуже 54b, 15.

Cloz: глѭште 1a, 38; похвальѭшта 1b, 12; рачъшѭѭ 2b, 23; поставлѭ 3a, 20; страждѫштеı 3b, 10-11; нашѭ дшѭ 4a, 12; волеѭ 5a, 37; бестоудънѭѭ couplѭ 5b, 35-36; чашѭ 7b, 21; волѭ 8a, 2; вражъдѫ 8b, 33.

Data from Zo illustrate a system intermediate between these two orthographic schools:

after л:

л ⱔ : л' ⱔ : л' ⱗ : л ⱗ

2 : 70 : 24 : 4

after н:

н ⱔ : н' ⱔ : н' ⱗ : н ⱗ

3 : 30 : 2 : 2

after р:

р ⱔ : р' ⱔ : р' ⱗ : р ⱗ

1 : 24 : 2 : 12

VI. High Lax Vowels

8.0. Here we include changes that applied to the yers and nasal vowels — specifically the high nontense (short) vowels (transcribed traditionally as *ŭ* and *ĭ*) and the groups uN and iN (ѫ and ѧ). The presumed Old Bulgarian vocalizations of these vowels were: ə, ɪ, əŋ, and ɪŋ, resp. ɪ was written ь in OB, ə — ъ. The changes of the high nontense vowels gave rise to considerable variation throughout Bulgarian dialects; for this reason separate historical analyses of all basic dialect types would follow the general formulations set out below.

A. The yers

Five major changes applied to the yers: "vocalization," regressive assimilation for *back*, changes of ь and ъ before j, the change of ь to ъ after certain consonants, and deletion.

1. "Vocalization" of the yers

8.1. At the outset we must specify what is meant by the term "vocalization." Grammars of Old Bulgarian ordinarily use this term to refer to the changes of ь → e and ъ → o. In fact, in a number of Old Bulgarian texts the change of ь to e is apparent, whereas the change of ъ to o is atypical (Zo, Supr, Ril, e.g.). Furthermore, in modern Bulgarian dialects the reflex e for ь is far more common than o for ъ. Of course, this does not mean that the high back nontense vowel ъ did not change in some Old Bulgarian dialects, or that it did not become a mid vowel in dialects where ь became e. Because terms like "dark vowel," "clear vowel," and "vocalization" are impressionistic and imprecise, it is preferable to refer to the change as the "lowering" of the yers (a term used by American linguists in recent years).

The lowering of the yers is a regressive assimilation for height. It applied in so-called "strong" positions: before syllables which themselves contain high nontense vowels, i.e., before C_1ъ or C_1ь, where C_1 denotes one or more nonsyllabic segments (consonants or glides). This rule is approximately:

(38) $\begin{bmatrix} +\text{voc} \\ -\text{tns} \end{bmatrix} \rightarrow [-\text{high}] \;//\; \underline{\qquad} \; C_1 \begin{bmatrix} +\text{voc} \\ +\text{high} \\ -\text{tns} \end{bmatrix}$

In order to avoid complicating the formulation of (38), let us informally add the condition that when several yers occur in successive syllables in a single word (often the "phonetic" word, which includes neighboring clitics), every second yer, counting from the end of the word, is lowered. For example дьнь → дєнь, дьньсьньjь → дьнєсьнєи. In all probability throughout the development of Bulgarian writing, ъ signified the high back yer ə, as well as the mid vowels ʌ and, later, ʹ[24] — after the onset of rule (35) above. For this reason, when дєнь and сънъ occur in the same manuscript, the forms may be written phonetically as denь and sʌnъ.

The new mid vowel ʌ from ъ tended to lengthen and labialize (like ʌ from ǎ); this could be accomplished by rule (36) (6.1 above). This tendency was opposed by the tendency for the reflex of ъ to merge with that of ѫ. For its part, the back nasal tended to develop into a nonlabial mid or low vowel (see 9.12 for details). The merger of ъ and ѫ is observed mainly in root morphemes.[25] In suffixes, prefixes, and the definite article, ъ was more independent, and it is precisely here that o developed more frequently (e.g., in modern dialects in the areas of Sofia, Botevgrad, and Salonika, in Thrace, and in Moesia). For example, dʹʐš or dáš, but sóberi, sópna se, takóf, dánok, vetъró (for details see Stojkov 1968). In many contemporary south-western dialects o occurs in root morphemes, as well: dóš, bóčva, vón.

Dialects in the area of Trân and Belogradčik and in the Rhodope Mountains have their own particular developments. In the first two, both yers have a ъ-reflex. In the Rhodope dialects ъ and ь usually merge in root morphemes and, very significantly, the appearance of labialization in these dialects is related to stress, that is, to the distribution of [+tense].

It is generally accepted that the "vocalization" of the yers in a given text is a dialect feature which indicates western Bulgarian origin. "'Vocalization' of the yers, especially the back yer to o, was characteristic of western Old Bulgarian dialects; in eastern Old Bulgarian dialects, to judge from textual evidence, this feature — particularly the vocalization of the back yer — was significantly limited" (Mirčev 1958:52). Often texts such as Cloz, Euch, SPs, and Ass are described as western and attributed to the Oxrid School, while Sav, Supr, MacFol, En, and Ril are described as eastern and attributed to a north-eastern literary center. This distinction can help to simplify many complex problems of Bulgarian dialectology; however, at the outset we should not assume that only two Bulgarian dialects are reflected in old written records. Doubtless, the real situation was far more complicated, and communicaton among literary centers — a factor little studied heretofore — was very substantial. Joining Euch and Cloz in one group merely obscures problems of historical dialectology before they can be formulated. The confusion of given letters in a single text may yield clear linguistic data only as a result of the analysis and investigation of complete graphic and orthographic systems. This investigation must take into account glagolitic-cyrillic parallels as well. Correspondences and similarities in Sav and Cloz or in Supr and Zo are undervalued as a result of attempting to uncover old orthographic *systems* which, above all, are supposed to reflect dialect systems. In other words, attempts to identify and to localize a system must precede attempts to localize deviations from it. And in attempting to understand divergences, it is critical to take into account all of the characteristics of a given manuscript.

So, for example, in three paleographically and orthographically different glagolitic texts, Ass, Euch, and SPs, we find confusion of ⰏⰍ (ъ), Ⰹ (o), and Ⰶ (ѫ). The confusion of ⰏⰍ and Ⰹ is interpreted as the "vocalization" of ъ; Ⰶ written as Ⰹ and Ⰶ as Ⰺ are explained as incomplete letters[26] (see 9.3 for examples with Ⰹ and Ⰺ for Ⰶ and Ⰶ, and vice versa). Were these vowels similar or identical? What features did they share — *labial*, *lax*, or the fact that they were all *mid*? To what extent did graphic proximity, or the source of the copied manuscript play a role? If there were many Old Bulgarian dialects in which o, ъ, and ѫ had the same value for *labial*, how was this dialect type lost? (This feature is found today only in the areas of Debar and the lower Prespa, and under stress in Rhodope dialects.)

These questions have to be answered concretely for each manuscript. In general, it must be emphasized that early in the development of glagolitic, the letter Ⰹ hardly could have designated the round vowel o (6.1). Mirčev 1958:50 makes the very important point that "early in the development of Old Bulgarian (the ninth century) a number of features characteristic of pre-literary Bulgarian were still preserved....The vowel *o* continued to be open. Its raising took place, it seems, later, in the course of the tenth and eleventh centuries."

2. ъ and ь before jV

8.2. Before jV the yers underwent various changes. Depending on the order of application of a number of rules which we have already considered — the lowering of strong yers, the lengthening of high vowels before j (see the loss of diphthongs), changes in groups of jV, and several others — the results of these changes differed.

Mirčev 1958:116-18 offers another opinion. Like van Wijk 1957:169ff., Mirčev proposes the early changes: ъj → ы, ьj → и. In his opinion, the resulting vowels retained certain of the properties of the yers, and this fact explains their particular development: "The yers changed qualitatively, but the ы and и which replaced them were still reduced vowels, like the yers from which they developed" (1958:116). He describes initial syllables and stressed syllables as strong (e.g., *bíja, šíja*), as well as syllables before j from i (e.g., *bólij, góstij*). Otherwise, before jV they are by definition *weak*; here i tends to disappear. According to Mirčev 1958:117, the development was гостиѥ → гостьѥ, with both forms pronounced as гостѥ in late Old Bulgarian. The data are so diverse and problematical that van Wijk, who also assumed original forms with и and ы, is often forced to admit that some forms regularly arose from *jer* + jV (1957:176).

In considering the elimination of diphthongs, we saw that the loss of closed syllables was related to the lengthening of vowels before j and the loss of this glide. This change took place in so-called closed syllables — before consonant or word-boundary. Before a vowel, ej was subject only to lengthening, becoming ij; e.g., treje → trije, OB триѥ and трьѥ. In Old Bulgarian texts we observe either the process or the results of later changes applying to ъjV and ьjV.

a. jь → (j)i

8.3. This change is early; e.g., имѧ, игла. However there is clear reason to assume that the difference between jь and ji survived for some time in certain morphemes, especially the anaphoric pronoun (Mareš 1964:14-16, 1971:172, Gâlâbov 1974:517). Thus,

(38′) jь → (j)i

b. "Vocalization" before jь

8.4. Consider болеи, костеи, грѣшьнои from earlier baliji, kastiji, and græ:šinuji. Using the Old Bulgarian symbols for the yers, we see that here ъjь → оjь (and perhaps also ajь) and ьjь → ejь. Mirčev, assuming original forms in which the changes ьj → и, ъj → ы, and jь → и had already taken place, is forced to claim that the vocalization of "reduced и and ы" occurred not before jь, but before j: bolii, božii, gostii → bolij, božij, gostij → болеи, божеи, гостеи; likewise грѣшьнои from грѣшьнъіи, свѧтои from свѧтъіи. This problem is very important, because it not only is related to uncovering the exact nature of the change, but also to specifying the chronology of the possible stages in the process. First of all, do we find in modern Bulgarian dialects, or even in Old Bulgarian texts, examples in which not only ъjь and ьjь, but also etymological ъji and ьji have changed to ei and oi? While listing every possible position with "reduced ы, и" or "tense yers," van Wijk does not cite a single form which might have developed as ьji → ij → ej. Contrary to Bulgarian dialects, Russian shows "vocalization" of stressed yers before j; e.g., béj, šéj, mój from old ьji, ъji.[27]

The data show that forms such as свѧтои, бечестъноі, гостеи, and болеи may be derived regularly only from forms with ъjь and ьjь. The terms "reduced и and ы" and "tense yers" are entirely superfluous.

The proper nouns Radój and Dragój/Drági are interesting, for they show the clear relationship between the change of ъjь to оjь and stress, and the connection between the tenseness of the vowel and the change with respect to labial. The question arises, whether forms such as Rádi are the results of the changes ъjь → yi → ii or ъjь → aj → y → i. Compare the alternation of stressed and unstressed Russian endings: bol'nój, ploxój, takój vs. zdoróvyj, xoróšij, vsjákij.

c. ь → i and ъ → y before j

8.5. The most frequent change of the yers before jV is lengthening. We have already observed the same development, although in closed syllables, as the first step in the elimination of diphthongs (rules 10a, 10b, 10c). In the system of transcription used here for Proto-Slavic, the change of high vowels before j would be represented as ujC → u:jC, ijC → i:jC (see rule 10b). In Old Bulgarian the similar change would be ъjV → yjV, ьjV → ijV. For example: добръи from dobrъjь, въна from vъja, костнѫ from kostьjѫ, гостик from gostьje, болии from bolьjь, змна from zmьja (cf. modern *zmej* from zmьjь), каменик from kamenьje, and many others. The rule for this change is a generalized and simplified form of (10b):

$$(10b') \begin{bmatrix} +\text{voc} \\ +\text{high} \end{bmatrix} \rightarrow [+\text{tense}] \ // \ \underline{\quad} \begin{bmatrix} -\text{voc} \\ -\text{cons} \end{bmatrix}$$

Examples such as добръı and сильнъı for the nominative singular are quite common in the texts: силънъı SPs 65b, 26; ноцѣнъı 130a, 17; великъı і дивънъı Euch 20b, 10-11. They suggest the possibility of the change: ъjь → ъі → ъj → y, ъjь → ъj → y, or ъjь → yjь → yь → y. It is difficult to explain these examples, which are further complicated by the fact that glagolitic texts use two different systems of i-letters. In the earlier system, many traces of which are preserved in KE, SPs, Cloz, OchrF, and Ass, the letter Ⱇ is used most frequently after consonants; it corresponds to the distribution of cyrillic и. ⰻ is a diagraph representing monophthongal y. ⰺⰻ and ⰺⰹ are used for ъjь and ъji. In the younger system a new distribution of i-signs co-occurs with other features, such as ⱔ and ⱋ (Vrana 1964). ⰻ is used after consonants; Ⱇ or ⰹ occur after vowels and at the beginning of words. Monophthongal y is represented by ⰺⰻ, while ъjь, ъji are represented by ⰺⰻ, ⰺⰻ, or ⰺⰹ (Zo, Euch, Mar). In Ril ⰻ is used after consonants, and ⰺⰻ for y. Besides these basic differences, individual texts show additional distinctions, which all require explanation. Regarding the various i-vowels in glagolitic and their distributions in the texts see van Wijk 1927-28, Gâlâbov 1952 and 1974, von Arnim 1930, Tkadlčík 1956, Mareš 1956:489, 1964:14-16, 1971, 1961:17-19, Vrana 1964, and Velčeva 1977.

d. The loss of intervocalic j

8.6. In those instances where j was deleted earlier before a vowel, the change of ъ to y and the change of ь to i would not have occurred. Gâlâbov 1974:519[28] is inclined to explain forms such as *sĭlnъ*, *skъtrъ* in the dialect of the village of Suxo (Salonika) as a result of the absence of the change of ъ to y. However, he suspects that the development was ъjь → ъj → ъ.

The deletion of intervocalic j is well known in Old Bulgarian (van Wijk 1957:21). Generally the change is:

(39) j → ∅ // V —— V

This rule was implemented differently throughout the manuscripts. Glagolitic data allow us to judge the change only on the basis of its results. So, for example, in Euch we regularly find results of the change of ь to i (i → i:) before any vowel other than yer (see 8.10 for the order of rules in the system of Euch); e.g., любовиѩ 10b, 10, 10b, 16, 105b, 17-18 (любовьѩ 11a, 17 is exceptional); пѣниє 99b, 25; жѧданиє 69b, 22; созъданиє 53a, 21; велиѣ 55a, 12; дєниє 62a, 23; вьпиѩщаго 36b, 8; възьрѣниѣ 68b, 3; покааниє 66b, 5. These forms indicate the existence of j at least at the time of the change of ьjV. Exceptions occur before the high front tense vowels i and ü; e.g., црствью 66a, 12; ѡ отъданьи 98b, 7; о избытьи 98b, 7-8; шествью 18a, 24; обладанью 82b, 2. Forms with ь are probably older, and they must be explained by the early loss of j in the environment of high front tense vowels. In this regard, recall rule (10b), as well as the tendency reflected in rule D (2.2). On the basis of the outcome of the "Umlaut" of the yers (8.13), we conclude that ю was a front vowel in the system underlying Euch.

8.7. The loss of intervocalic j could lead to other changes which apply to the vowels which have now become contiguous:

1. The loss of weak yers, e.g., гостьє → гостє, гроздьє → гроздє, божьи → божи.

2. The devocalization of i: (i) and i (ь) contiguous to vowels (rule A [2.2]). Note that we do not observe the devocalization of ъ. On the other hand, when ъ comes to stand before i, we may see the change of ъj → y (e.g., вынѩ SPs 86b, 6, 87a, 14, 135a, 14, 40b, 8, 53a, 11, and such common forms as добры and сильны).

According to rule A (i(:) → j contiguous to a vowel), a form such as **kamenje** could develop from either **kamenie** or **kamenьe**. In the modern dialects, there are more indications of the change ьjV → ijV → iV → jV in the west and south; e.g., western forms such as *óden"e, kopán"e, cvék'e, lág'a*[29] (← cvetje, ladja).[30] Similar forms, e.g., *beránje, ležánje, predénje*, are cited as an archaic feature of Thracian dialects (Bojadžiev 1972).

e. The elimination of diphthongs again

8.8. The development of ъjV and ьjV is a complex process with various possible paths. In fact, rules fundamental to the development of Proto-Slavic, Old Bulgarian, and later Bulgarian intersect in this apparently minor problem. The characteristic Old Bulgarian phenomena observed in the development of these groups are the lowering of the yers, the loss of the weak yers, and the fluctuation of intervocalic j. Greater attention must be paid to the elimination of older tendencies and the appearance of newer ones. Proto-Slavic elements can be seen in the renewed application of rule (10b), which we identified as one of the components of the loss of diphthongs: the lengthening of high vowels before glides in closed syllables (4.5). During the Old Bulgarian period, the generally unstable high vowels ъ and ь began to lengthen before glides (at this time only j) followed by a vowel.

Masculine singular adjectival and participial forms with y from ъjь and plural forms with y from ъji are not so simple to explain, and it is surprising that they are considered regular. Additionally, variants such as въ инѫ, въі инѫ, and въінѫ have not been explained. What took place here: ъj → y, ъi → y, or ъj → yj? If we hold to the Proto-Slavic rule, then the change could have taken place only before j (or i which became j contiguous to a vowel). This means that the change certainly would have passed through the stage ъj → yj. The loss of j by Proto-Slavic rule (10c) followed rule (10b) — the deletion of j after a high tense vowel and before a consonant or word-boundary. We observe the identical change in numerous Old Bulgarian examples, such as дивьнъі, истиньнъі, плътьнъіхъ, въінѫ, but въіѩ and мъіѭ.

For their part, the Old Bulgarian data help us to define more precisely certain Proto-Slavic rules. Earlier, when we considered the loss of diphthongs, we did not propose a general rule for all *vowel-glide* groups, but only rules for three successive changes —

or stages — of the process. This was due to the fact that Proto-Slavic did not have diphthongs of *back vowel + j* (except a(:)j, which, as we saw, was subject to other changes or otherwise did not become a single vowel). In Old Bulgarian, however, we observe changes of ъ + j across morpheme boundaries before a vowel: dobrъ + jь, kostь + jѫ, sъtvoritъ + i. This raises the possibility of formulating a single general rule which applies to all *vowel-glide* sequences (except a(:)j), regardless of their environment, *after* the raising of vowels before high sonorants: e(:)j → i(:)j, e(:)w → i(:)w, a(:)w → u(:)w (see 4.5). For the sake of uniformity we will revert to the earlier notation of ъ as u; however, both represent yers. The general changes which we wish to capture are:

$$i(:)j \to i\colon (\text{и}) \qquad u(:)j \to u\colon (\text{ы})$$

$$\begin{matrix} 1 & 2 & & 1 \\ \begin{bmatrix} +\text{voc} \\ +\text{high} \\ -\text{back} \end{bmatrix} & \begin{bmatrix} -\text{cons} \\ -\text{lab} \end{bmatrix} & \to & \begin{bmatrix} +\text{tns} \\ -\text{back} \\ -\text{lab} \end{bmatrix} \end{matrix} \qquad \begin{matrix} 1 & 2 & & 1 \\ \begin{bmatrix} +\text{voc} \\ +\text{high} \\ +\text{back} \end{bmatrix} & \begin{bmatrix} -\text{cons} \\ -\text{lab} \end{bmatrix} & \to & \begin{bmatrix} +\text{tns} \\ +\text{back} \\ -\text{lab} \end{bmatrix} \end{matrix}$$

$$i(:)w \to \ddot{u}\colon (\text{ю}) \qquad u(:)j \to \hat{u}\colon (\text{oy})$$

$$\begin{matrix} 1 & 2 & & 1 \\ \begin{bmatrix} +\text{voc} \\ +\text{high} \\ -\text{back} \end{bmatrix} & \begin{bmatrix} -\text{cons} \\ +\text{lab} \end{bmatrix} & \to & \begin{bmatrix} +\text{tns} \\ -\text{back} \\ +\text{lab} \end{bmatrix} \end{matrix} \qquad \begin{matrix} 1 & 2 & & 1 \\ \begin{bmatrix} +\text{voc} \\ +\text{high} \\ +\text{back} \end{bmatrix} & \begin{bmatrix} -\text{cons} \\ +\text{lab} \end{bmatrix} & \to & \begin{bmatrix} +\text{tns} \\ +\text{back} \\ +\text{lab} \end{bmatrix} \end{matrix}$$

These rules may be combined as:

$$(10') \qquad \begin{matrix} 1 & 2 & & 1 \\ \begin{bmatrix} +\text{voc} \\ +\text{high} \\ \alpha\text{back} \end{bmatrix} & \begin{bmatrix} -\text{cons} \\ \beta\text{lab} \end{bmatrix} & \to & \begin{bmatrix} +\text{tns} \\ \alpha\text{back} \\ \beta\text{lab} \end{bmatrix} \end{matrix}$$

f. Devocalization of yers before vowels

According to the Proto-Slavic tendency expressed in rule A (2.2), i(:) became j contiguous to any vowel other than i(:); e.g., nasi+a:N → OB ношѫ. After the eventual loss of intervocalic j in Old Bulgarian, the conditions for this change reappeared — namely, for i and ь to become j contiguous to any vowel other than i or ь; e.g., vъ inѫ → vъjnѫ, dobrъji → dobrъj, or dobrъ+ji → dobry+ji → dobryj (j will be regularly lost after y in these forms), **denie** → **denje**. In Proto-Slavic, as well as Old Bulgarian, as long as the weak yers were retained, the devocalization of i: and i could not be conditioned by stress but only by the vocalic environment. The rule for the change of i and ь is approximately:

$$(40) \begin{bmatrix} -\text{cons} \\ +\text{high} \\ -\text{back} \\ -\text{lab} \end{bmatrix} \rightarrow [-\text{voc}] \ // \ \begin{bmatrix} +\text{voc} \\ \left\{ \begin{matrix} -\text{high} \\ +\text{back} \\ +\text{lab} \end{matrix} \right\} \end{bmatrix}$$

(High front nonlabial vowels, i and ь, become j in the environment of a vowel which is either nonhigh, or back, or labial.)

Contiguous to one another, i and ь tended to merge — rather than one or the other becoming j; compare божии → божи and forms with the contraction of other identical contiguous vowels, e.g., доброуоумоу → доброумоу, добрааго → добраго with assimilation prior to contraction: добраєго → добрааго).

g. Supr, Euch, and SPs

8.9. In order to confirm the effects of these rules, let us consider them in relation to typical, predominant cases — those which present the data systematically in several texts. The relevant rules are:

       (37) "vocalization" of the yers
       (38´) jь → ji
       (39) loss of intervocalic j
       (40) i/ь → j
       (10b) ъj → yj, ьj → ij
       (10c) the loss of j after y and i[31]

The simplest situation is found in Supr, where vowels apparently retain j in the relevant positions:

| | лютыѵихъ | съпасениѥ | сты̃ѵи |
| | 96, 3 | 148, 9 | 148, 20 |

	/ -ъjихъ	-ьjє	-ъjь/
(37)			not applied
(38′)			-ъjи
(10b)	-ъıjихъ	-иjє	-ъıjи

| | лютъıjихъ | съпасєниjє | с(ва)тъıjи[32] |

| | божии | погоубитъı и |
| | 192, 21 | 164, 4-5 |

	/ -ьjь	-ъjи/
(37)	not applied	
(38′)	-ьjи	
(10b)	-иjи	-ъıjи

| | божиjи | погоубитъı jи |

This text shows no evidence of the application of the other rules.

8.10. In Euch we find the results of the application of a greater number of rules. Euch is distinguished from Supr principally by the change of ьjь to еjь and the probable early loss of j before i. We assume the following development:

| | рекъı | дьнєи | дєниє |
| | 47a, 16 | 104a, 26 | 62a, 23 |

	/рекъjь	дьньjь	дьньjє/
(37)	not applied	дьнєjь	дєньjє
(38′)	рєкъи	дьнєи	
(40)	рєкъj	дьнєj	
(10b)	рєкъıj		дєниjє
(10c)	рєкъı		дєниє

| | рєкъı | дьнєj | дєниє |

CHAPTER FOUR

	въінѫ	отъданьи
	95a, 22	98b, 7
	/въ јинѫ	отъданьји/
(37)		
(38´)	въ инѫ	отъданьи
(40)	въјнѫ	
(10b)	въіјнѫ	
(10c)	въінѫ	
	въінѫ	отъданьи

Beyond this system we also find in the text forms such as: приємъи 13b, 8; посълавъи 24b, 2; съи 26a, 15; повєльвъи 13a, 11, 13b, 4, 40b, 2; блгвивъи 15b, 4. A particular diacritic appears over и in these forms; it probably indicates that the morpheme јь should be read separately (as ji or i?).

Additionally, the system of rules given above does not account for - ii- in declined forms of adjectives; cf. въішъниихъ and others vs. expected forms with -у-, such as плътьнъіхъ 98b, 5-6. Perhaps forms with -ii- have a morphological explanation.

The interpretation of forms in Zo and other more extensive glagolitic texts depends on our reading of the letters representing i. This problem in turn depends to a great degree on understanding the complete system of phonological features. In addition, the orthographic features of each and every text are so interrelated that uncovering the systems which they contain requires separating various orthographic layers and determining their characteristic features.

8.11. Exceptionally diverse forms make SPs perhaps the most difficult text to deal with. This manuscript is distinguished by the large number of "vocalized" yers before јь (e.g., лѫкавоі 14b, 12, съмъріто ї 10b, 1-2), and the use of ь before non-yers (e.g., одьньє 82b, 20, помъішлєньъ 97a, 4-5). Von Arnim 1930:115-25, who made a thorough statistical study of the text, determined that in those parts which he refers to as A the following types predominate: ъјь → оі and more often ъі, ъji → і and less frequently іï, ьјь → єі, ъji → ъіхъ almost twice as often as ъіихъ and ъіїхъ; examples with ьиѫ, ьь, ьє are significantly more frequent than иѫ, ıь, ıє. As a system these facts can only represent the following process:

	грѣшьнои	готовъі	грѣшьныхъ
	9a, 20	50b, 4	1a, 12-13
(37)	/грѣшьнъјь грѣшьнојь	готовъјь	грѣшьнъјихъ/
(38´)	грѣшьнои	готовъи	грѣшьнъихъ
(39)			
(40)	грѣшьној	готовъj	грѣшьнъjхъ
(10b)		готовъıj	грѣшьнъıjхъ
(10c)		готовъı	грѣшьнъıхъ
	грѣшьној	готовъı	грѣшьныхъ

	горѧщімъ	оубьєна	людєі
	7a, 1	140a, 13	66, 4
(37)	/горѧщьјимъ	оубьјєна	людьјь/
			людєјь
(38´)	горѧщьимъ		дюдєи
(39)		оубьєна	
(40)		оубјєна	людєј
(10b)			
(10c)			
	горѧщьимъ	оубјєна	людєј

h. "Reduced" i and y

8.12. There is a certain justification for the term "reduced" i, if we are dealing not with Old Bulgarian forms but with their later development. Mirčev 1958:117-18 correctly observes that Old Bulgarian forms with i and y contiguous to vowels changed as a function of stress. Consider forms such as *míja*, *píja*, *šíja*, *bíj*, *píj*, *bóžij*, *dobríjat* from OB мыѩ, пиѩ, шиѩ, бии, пии, божии, добрыј+ътъ. This i, which we view as secondary, became j when unstressed; otherwise it remained unchanged. The explanation of this fact is found in the rule that relates the feature *tense* to *stress*:

$$(35) \begin{bmatrix} +\text{vocalic} \\ \alpha\text{stress} \end{bmatrix} \rightarrow [\alpha\text{tense}]$$

The weak yers were the last remaining nontense (short) high vowels. After their loss and the introduction of mid vowels, etymological length ceased to condition the distribution of the feature *tense*. This role passed to *stress*: stressed vowels were tense, unstressed vowels were nontense. From this follows the curious conclusion that in the history of Bulgarian it was ɪ, not i, that became j in unstressed positions, for all unstressed vowels were lax. Phonetically ɪ was equivalent to Old Bulgarian ь (ĭ). In reality unstressed i was "reduced" to ɪ before it became j:

OB	камєниє	бии
	/ká:menie/	/bí:i/
(35)	ká:mɛnɪɛ	bí:ɪ
ɪ→j	ká:mɛnjɛ	bí:ɪ
modern dialect	kámɛnjɛ	bíj

3. "Umlaut" of the yers

8.13. In 1875 Jagić discovered one of the most interesting Old Bulgarian changes: the "Umlaut" of the yers. According to the so-called "Jagić Law," ь became ъ before a syllable containing a back vowel, while ъ became ь before one containing a front vowel; e.g., дъва vs. дьвѣ, вьрьнѣ vs. вьръно.

This change was subject to certain constraints reflecting the quality of the consonants preceding the yers: after velars (k, g, x) and soft consonants (including the hushers and hissers — š, ž, č, c, ʒ, and št and žd) it typically did not take place (van Wijk 1957:156, Bernštejn 1961:205). On the other hand, the change was not influenced by the consonant following the yer[33]; only the *vowel* in the following syllable was relevant. The dependence of this change on the quality of the following vowel is similar to the general conditioning factor of the lowering of the strong yers. Apparently, at a particular stage of development, the yers became unstable and subject to the regressive influence of vowels in the following syllable. For the lowering of the yers the influence was dissimilatory; for Umlaut it was assimilatory.

The Old Bulgarian Umlaut of yers can be defined specifically as a change which applied to high nontense vowels after nonhigh consonants (those neither velar nor soft) and which was conditioned by the frontness/backness of the vowel of the following syllable:

$$(41) \quad \begin{bmatrix} +\text{voc} \\ +\text{high} \\ -\text{tns} \end{bmatrix} \rightarrow [\alpha\text{back}] \; // \begin{bmatrix} +\text{cons} \\ -\text{high} \end{bmatrix} \underline{\quad\quad} C_1 \begin{bmatrix} +\text{voc} \\ \alpha\text{back} \end{bmatrix}$$

Old Bulgarian texts vary with respect to this rule principally in the chronology of the changes of the yers which they reflect. The most archaic texts show neither Umlaut nor any other change of high nontense vowels. The next stage, exemplified by Zo and Sav, shows Umlaut, but only the beginning phases of lowering. Euch and to some extent SPs (von Arnim 1930:92) show both changes. Ass[34] and Ril use ъ and ь unsystematically, and it is difficult to see any pattern which may be interpreted as Umlaut. In fact, the yers are more or less confused in all of the texts, and for this reason Umlaut can be detected only by comparisons of quantitative data.

To illustrate this point we consider Euch and Ass. We choose these texts because they have been relatively little studied from this point of view and because their comparison is particularly interesting.

In 5 samples of 1000 letters in Euch we find 434 yers, an average of 86.8/1000. Of these (putting aside examples with ръ, лъ, рь, ль — 22 in all), 350 yers (an average of 70/1000) are etymologically correct. 62 yers (12.4/1000) are incorrect. Of the latter, 45 (9/1000) are distributed according to the Umlaut rule; 17 (3.4/1000) are not.

In Ass, 10 samples of 1000 letters each were carried out — 5 in the first part, written in two columns, 5 in the second, written in one (from fol. 117a to the end). In samples from the first part, we find 425 yers (85/1000). Of them — ръ, лъ, рь, ль aside — 315 (63/1000) are used correctly, while 100 (25/1000) are not. Of those which are incorrect, 56 (11.2/1000) follow Umlaut, 44 (8.8/1000) do not. In the second part, 5 samples yielded 435 yers (86.8/1000). Of these, 344 (68.8/1000) are etymologically correct, 81 (16.2/1000) are not. Of the latter, 43 (8.6/1000) follow Umlaut, 38 (7.6/1000) do not.

These simple statistics permit the following conclusions. The frequency of the yers in Euch is greater than in the first part of Ass, and almost the same as in the second part of Ass. The etymological use of the yers is better preserved in Euch than in either part of Ass: etymologically incorrect yers make up 14.28% of all yers sampled in Euch, 23.53% in the first part of Ass, and 18.62% in the second. (In this regard, the second part of Ass is more archaic than the first.) 72.58% of the incorrect yers in Euch clearly follow Umlaut; in Ass those that follow Umlaut slightly exceed 50% — 56% in the first part and 53.08% in the second.

We may cite additional interesting data from Euch. From fol. 64a to 69b, въ(з) occurs 31 times before syllables containing back vowels and 15 times before those with front vowels. вь(з) is found 18 times before syllables with front vowels, and only twice before back vowels. Examples with ъ before front vowels can be explained to a great extent as the result of traditional orthography. In rare examples we find the preposition во besides въ and вь: во въторое 65a, 14, 87b, 5-6; во в'сько 82b, 19, in addition to examples such as вь бьдьниє 82b, 22.

Mirčev 1938:64 points out that "one of the most important tasks facing Bulgarian linguistics is determining the extent to which Old Bulgarian Umlaut has left traces in the modern language....On one hand [this] would shed light on problems related to Old Bulgarian Umlaut, and, on the other, would further strengthen the connection between Old Bulgarian and modern Bulgarian dialects." Mirčev cites contemporary dialect forms and toponyms which may be traces of this sort; e.g., *trestiga* ("a probable descendant" of OB тръст- → трьст-), *Debъr, Debrec, Debъrce, Debrъštica*, which are "distributed throughout Bulgarian lands" (Mirčev 1958:116; see also 1938:65-69).

Here we may include numerous examples of the change of ь to ъ found in nonliterary dialects as well as the literary language: *mъ́gla, mágla, mǒgla* from мьгла; *tъnъk, tъnko, tának, tánko* from тьнъкъ, тьнъко; *pъ́stro, pástro* from пьстро; *lъ́skaf* from льск-; *stъ́klo, cъkló* from стькло; *stъbló* from стьбло; *lъf, lъvove* from льв-; *pъn, pъnove* from пьн-. These forms are analogous to examples with preserved weak ъ in roots, such as *dъšter'á* (also *déšter'a, dešterka*, which result from Umlaut in certain dialects; Ščepkin 1899:177-78), *dъ́ská, dъ́no, lъ́ža, tъká, sъništa*. With respect to both old ъ and ь there was pressure for one and the same root vocalization to be generalized among all forms of a given lexeme, regardless of whether the vowel had arisen originally in weak or strong position, or whether it was etymologically correct or altered.

The fluctuation of front and back vowels in these examples gives different results throughout Bulgarian dialects. The BDA clearly records variation in forms such as *tънък/tънka* vs. *ténък/ténka* and *tъmen/tъmna* vs. *témen/témna*. In both western and eastern dialects *ténък/ténka* are less common than *témen/témna* (M. Mladenov 1966). This difference is probably due to the fact that forms with ь before back vowels in the morpheme тьм- (e.g., тьмьнъ, тьмьна, тьма)[35] are less frequent than forms with ь before back vowels in the morpheme тьн- (e.g., тьнъкъ, тьнъка).

In Bulgarian dialects there is a general tendency for back yers to replace weak yers in roots. This is especially true of Central Balkan dialects; e.g., in the dialect of Trojan: *pън', pъkъl, mъglъ̀, tънък, tъmnícъ, l'ъskъf, spънъ sъ, cъjtí, cъkló* (Kovačev 1968). In Rupa dialects the opposite tendency is observed: forms with e for ь in weak and strong syllables in root morphemes are more common; e.g., in Thracian dialects: *léskъf, penčúškъ, spéne, upéne, témen, ténък*.

In Rhodope dialects, we also observe the change of etymological ь in roots and its merger with etymological ъ, i.e., ɪ(ŋ) → ə(ŋ); e.g., *t'ônko, t'ômno, r'ôt* (рдѫъ) together with *dôš, kôšta*. What is unusual here, however, is that this development took place only in stressed syllables; that is, it is connected with the feature *tense*. (Recall the similar relevance of *tense* for the shift of front vowels to back vowels and the change of æ to á — the *jat-shift*). Additionally, in Rhodope dialects the change was preceded by the phonological softening of consonants before ь or, more precisely, by the raising of nonback consonants before high nontense nonback vowels.

Various south-western dialects reflect — to varying degrees — fluctuation between ъ and ь in weak root morphemes; in this respect they are intermediate between Balkan and Rupa dialects.

The question of the reasons for the preservation of weak yers in root morphemes (e.g., *dъno, žъne/žene, spъne/spene, mъgla*) is a difficult one. See section 6 below.

The place of the Umlaut of the yers among other changes affecting these vowels is extremely interesting. Old Bulgarian texts offer disparate data on the chronology of these changes. Before considering this particular issue, however, we must deal with the change of ь to ъ after certain consonants.

CHAPTER FOUR

4. The change of šь to šъ

8.14. A number of Old Bulgarian texts, including Euch, Mar, Sav, Cloz, and Supr, show evidence of the very important old change of high front nontense vowels to back (ь → ъ) after š, ž, and in some of them after č, žd, št, c, z (← ʒ), and r; e.g., шъли, брашъна, вьчънь, цьсаръ. Most frequently, this change has been explained as the result of the hardening of old soft consonants (van Wijk 1957:133 and 140), less often, as the result of labialization (Ščepkin 1899:335). Neither explanation is satisfactory.

The single common denominator of the consonants listed above is their softness: [+high, -back]. Why not, therefore, assume that the change was the result of their hardening? Unfortunately, the evidence of modern dialects contradicts this hypothesis. For example, in north-eastern Central Balkan dialects we find forms such as *došʼl* and *žʼne*. In the same dialects we find *mlʼáku*, *gulʼám*, but *néštu*, *réžъ*. The last two forms indicate that when ǽ became á before hard consonants, the hushing consonants were soft. We must assume that the change of šь to šъ took place before the *jat-shift*, because the former is well attested in Old Bulgarian. Consequently we must conclude that the change of šь to šъ occurred when the strident sibilants were still soft.

The change of šь to šъ is most consistent in Euch and Sav. However, these texts reflect two different dialects, for the change of ǽ to á as well as ь to ъ occur in different sets of environments.

The most limited environment for the change is observed in Euch, where we find ъ after ш, ж, and р, but ь after ч, щ, жд, ц, and з (ʒ); after л both occur. From fol. 64a to 93b, чь, щь, and ждь are regular. The ratio of жь to жъ is 13 : 18, that of шь to шъ is 4 : 32. We may conclude that the change of ь to ъ took place at a time when šč/žǯ or štʼ/ždʼ occurred before ь, not štš/ždž, that the change of ǯ to ž was only partially complete, that the change did not occur after old ǯ. Thus, the change is regular after the nonanterior continuants š, ž, and r. The spelling ръ is consistent. This fact prevents us from determining whether the change applied to rь as well as rʼь, or whether ръ was generally written according to some orthographic rule. In Euch, therefore, the relevant rule has two possible shapes:

(37a) $\begin{bmatrix} +\text{voc} \\ +\text{high} \\ -\text{tns} \end{bmatrix} \rightarrow [+\text{back}] \mathbin{/\mkern-2mu/} \begin{bmatrix} +\text{cons} \\ +\text{high} \\ -\text{ant} \\ +\text{cont} \end{bmatrix}$ ——

or

$\begin{bmatrix} +\text{voc} \\ +\text{high} \\ -\text{tns} \end{bmatrix} \rightarrow [+\text{back}] \mathbin{/\mkern-2mu/} \begin{bmatrix} +\text{cons} \\ -\text{ant} \\ +\text{cont} \end{bmatrix}$ ——

(ь becomes ъ after š, ž, r', or after š, ž, r', r.)

For example, слоужъбѣ 99b, 22; грѣшъника 101b, 7; въшъниихъ 101a, 14; ръвьнивъ 54a, 21; единачьнааго 99a, 20-21; зачьнѫ 59a, 14; блговѣцѣшааго 8a, 7; възвращьшю сѧ 70a, 10-11; рѣци 93a, 1; рождъшиѣ 84b, 11.

Sav shows a different system — or perhaps the intersection of two systems. ъ occurs after ш, ж, жд, and р'. Both ъ and ь occur after ч and щ (probably šč). ць and вьсь are regular, зь (ʒь) almost so. In Sav, the change after nonanterior high continuants is regular, and there is a clear tendency for the change to spread to other nonanterior high consonants, including šč and č. The more consistent use of ъ after жд than щ once again indicates the greater instability of voiced affricates and the cluster žǯ (4.18). The difference ждъ vs. щъ/щь shows that the change took place in some Old Bulgarian dialects at a stage when šč and ždž existed. The rule for the more general change shown by Sav is:

(37b) $\begin{bmatrix} +\text{voc} \\ +\text{high} \\ -\text{tns} \end{bmatrix} \rightarrow [+\text{back}] \mathbin{/\mkern-2mu/} \begin{bmatrix} +\text{cons} \\ -\text{ant} \\ +\text{high} \end{bmatrix}$ ——

(ь becomes ъ after š, ž, č, št', žd', and r'.)[36]

In Mar the rule is generalized in the other direction: it applies after all soft strident consonants — ш, ж, ч, жд, щ, ц, and з (ʒ):

(37c) $\begin{bmatrix} +\text{voc} \\ +\text{high} \\ -\text{tns} \end{bmatrix} \rightarrow [+\text{back}] \mathbin{/\mkern-2mu/} \begin{bmatrix} +\text{cons} \\ +\text{strd} \\ +\text{high} \end{bmatrix}$ ——

Zo does not show the change, nor is it characteristic for SPs, Ass, KF, Hil, or Ril.

There is one more important difference between Euch and Sav. In Sav the change applies to both strong and weak yers; in Euch it applies only to weak ones.: e.g., Sav вѣчъна, вѣчънъ, тлжъкъ, шъдъ, шъли vs. Euch брашъна but брашеньцє, мѫжъства but тлжєкъ. This difference reflects different orderings of the lowering of the yers with respect to the change of ь to ъ in various Old Bulgarian dialects. The retention of strong ъ and ь is typical of Sav, and the system shown in this text indicates that the change of ь to ъ after hushers took place before the lowering of the high nontense vowels. This system is reflected in New Bulgarian — mainly Balkan — dialects with forms such as *došŭl*, *žŭne* (*žné*), *šŭpna*, or *došál*, *žáne* (*žné*), *šápna*. In Euch ъ, ь, and є are distributed rather consistently in a different fashion: ъ and ь occur in weak positions, є in strong; e.g., шєпътаниє 91b, 18; брашъна 103b, 25-26; брашєн'ца 104b, 25; брашєньцє 103a, 12; мѫжєскъ 54a, 6; жєзлъ 54b, 23; слоужъбѣ 99b, 22; прѣчєстъноє 99a, 24; страшєнъ 99a, 16; тлжєкъ 97a, 25; различьно оукрашъ 8b, 9-10. Similar systems are found in modern southern, western, and Moesian dialects with forms such as *došél* (*došól*), *žéne* (*žné*), *šépna*.

The following derivations illustrate how these contrasting forms arise in the two texts:

Euch

```
         /tьmьna  šьdъ   brašьno   brašьnьсe   čьstьno   væčьnæ/
(38)      temьna  šedъ             brašenьсe   čestьno
(37a)                    brašъno
          тємъна  шєдъ   брашъно   брашєньцє   чєстъно   вѣчьнѣ
```

Sav

```
         /sъnьmъ   prišьdъ        prišьli   sѫčьсь   væčьny/
(38)                    not applicable
(37b)              prišъdъ        prišъli   sѫčъсь   væčъny
         съньмъ   пришъдъ        пришъли   сѫчъць   вѣчъны
```

THE VOCALIC SYSTEM

The results of the proposed developments are shown far more consistently in Euch than in Sav. It is difficult to say to what extent the orthographic norm of Sav and the linguistic system of its scribe are in conflict. Euch is far more promising for investigation, for it shows all of the changes of the yers in a rather consistent system. Regardless of whether this is the system of the immediate scribe of the text or the system of an earlier scribe, or whether it corresponds to the orthographic norm of some Old Bulgarian literary center, what is significant is the fact of a creative attitude towards the orthography. The free, creative, and literate attitude towards orthography shown in Euch is reminiscent of that of another remarkable Bulgarian text from a much later period, the *Trojan damaskin* of the seventeenth century.

5. Rule ordering

8.15. The phonological systems reflected in Old Bulgarian texts vary in two respects vis-à-vis the changes of the high nontense vowels:

1. the number of changes differs from text to text;

2. the order of the changes, which may be deduced from the distribution of letters in various texts, may differ.

For example, Zo and Sav show, though inconsistently, the Umlaut of the yers; however, they do not have a significant number of examples of the lowering of the yers. On the other hand, Sav shows the change of šь to šъ, which is not found in Zo. Ass and SPs very clearly show the lowering of the yers, but Umlaut and the change of šь to šъ are not characteristic of them.

Euch is particularly interesting because all three processes occur in it: lowering, Umlaut, and šь → šъ. For example, любьвь 9b, 5, 95b, 16; пльть 29b, 21; пльтъскъі 3a, 13; въпльцьша 53a, 6-7; любовиѫ 105b, 17; бедръно 58a, 3; бєздєниь 4a, 8; женєскъ 54a, 7; мѫжєскъ 54a, 6; грѣшъника 101b, 7; кръвь 103b, 16; мъздѫ 104a, 1; кротокъ 99a, 14; ток'мо 95b, 6; моудєнъ 78a, 1; тѧжєкъ 97a, 25; прѣчєстъноє 99a, 24; рѫцьмъ 97a, 2; зачьнѧ 59a, 14; страшєнъ 99a, 16; дьждь, дьждєвьнии 1b, 21-22; мыслънонѫ 7b, 3; мыслььи 7b, 5; ръвьнивъ 54a, 21; рєпътаниє 91b, 18; плодось 14a, 16-17; любовь 90b, 26, 92b, 10;

шепътаниє 91b, 18; тєлєць 15b, 6; дєниє 62a, 23; тѧжъкомь 38a, 10; д'нєсь 1b, 16.

In the first place, the forms in Euch give the impression that the lowering of strong ь is almost regular, whereas that of strong ъ is not. Next, there are examples in which ь derived from ъ by Umlaut develops into e: бєздєниь and бєдръно. Finally, in some examples ъ becomes o, while in others it is preserved before syllables containing ъ or ь. Van Wijk 1957:145 explains this feature by "the labialized or relatively forward pronunciation of reduced ъ caused by a following ь." This explanation is generally correct in so far as van Wijk's view is that the Umlaut of the yers occurred before or almost at the same time as lowering. The following approximate picture of the development of one particular Old Bulgarian dialect emerges from the analysis of Euch:

1. The change of ъ to ь before syllables containing front vowels; e.g., дъждь, пльти, любьви, възлюбитъ. There are several exceptions in the text (e.g., любовь, любовиѩ, плодось) which are outside its system and which perhaps must be explained as the influence of another dialectal or orthographic system.

2. The lowering of the high nontense yers: ь → e, ъ → o; e.g., тємьници 79b, 14; подобєствью, шєствью, вонъ, кротокъ. Fluctuations occur in strong position after r; cf., рєпътаниє 91b, 18; ръвьнивъ 54a, 21; кръвь 103b, 16.

3. ь → ъ before syllables with back vowels; e.g., правъдѫ 16a, 16; созъданиє 53a, 21; бєдръно 58a, 3; тємъна 38a, 2-3.

4. ь → ъ after certain consonants (rule 37a); e.g., въшъниихъ 101a, 14; рѫцьтє 106a, 16; слоужъбь, брашъно 70a, 24-25; горъчьє 69b, 6.

The last two rules are not ordered with respect to one another, but both must follow the first two:

	/bъdrьno	tьmьna	rьcæte	strašьnъ/
1.	bьdrьno			
2.	bedrьno	temьna		strašenъ
3.	bedrъno	temъna		
4.			rьcæte	
Euch	бєдръно	тємъна	рѫцьтє	страшєнъ

	/službьæ	vъnъ	ovьnъ /
1.			
2.		vonъ	ovenъ
3.			
4.	službъæ		

Euch слоужъбѣ вонъ овенъ

The new and unexpected insight which this generative analysis offers is that the Umlaut rule, discovered by Jagić in Zo, is only the most general formulation of this Old Bulgarian change. Euch shows an Old Bulgarian system in which both yers do not shift simultaneously: ъ → ь first, and applies in both strong and weak positions. The change of ь to ъ follows the lowering of ь and ъ, and applies only to weak ь. This fact is more than a detail in this development; it has considerable importance for explaining the substantial traces of the change of weak ь to ъ in root morphemes in Bulgarian dialects (e.g., mъglá, tъnъk, stъbló), and the generalization of the back vowel in examples such as pъnove — pъn, tъnъk — tъnka, lъvove — lъv.

On the basis of data from Euch, rule (41) must be divided into two separate rules for two nonsimultaneous regressive assimilations with respect to *back*, where (41a) comes necessarily before and (41b) after (37).

$$(41a) \begin{bmatrix} +\text{voc} \\ +\text{high} \\ -\text{tns} \end{bmatrix} \rightarrow [-\text{back}] \; // \; \begin{bmatrix} -\text{voc} \\ -\text{back} \end{bmatrix} \text{———} C_1 \begin{bmatrix} +\text{voc} \\ -\text{back} \end{bmatrix}$$

(ъ becomes ь after nonvelar consonants and before front vowels.)

$$(41b) \begin{bmatrix} +\text{voc} \\ +\text{high} \\ -\text{tns} \end{bmatrix} \rightarrow [+\text{back}] \; // \; \begin{bmatrix} -\text{voc} \\ -\text{high} \end{bmatrix} \text{———} C_1 \begin{bmatrix} +\text{voc} \\ +\text{back} \end{bmatrix}$$

(ь becomes ъ after hard consonants and before back vowels.)

Both of these rules must apply before šь → šъ. This fact has long been known, but has been described erroneously as a consequence of the two changes applying with different strength. Note, e.g., that according to van Wijk 1957:155, "the hushing consonants (š, etc.) have a stronger influence on the change than other factors."

6. Weak yers

a. Weak yers in roots

8.16. The last change which applied to the yers was their deletion in weak positions. This well-described development must be formulated more precisely. After the lowering of strong yers — that is, in environments where they were subject to regressive dissimilation — the only remaining high nontense vowels were the weak yers. Calling these vowels "weak" is purely conventional. In fact, the weak yers actually were high nontense (short) vowels which had remained unchanged, became unstable, and then disappeared.

The instability of nontense (short) high vowels is observed in many languages. Essentially the same change recurs in the later development of the modern dialects where unstressed u, i, and ə disappear. For example, it is described in dialects along the lower Vardar (Romanski 1932), in the Banat (Stojkov 1959), and in south-eastern Bulgaria in the areas of Xaskovo and Xarmanli (Xoliolčev 1969). There are parallel developments in neighboring Balkan languages and elsewhere. In an interesting study, Xoliolčev 1969 explains the loss of unstressed high vowels as a consequence of two phonetic properties: the small angle of the jaw during the articulation of high vowels and their comparatively short absolute duration — which is naturally even shorter in unstressed syllables. Thus for example, bánicə → báncə, rábutə → ráptə, žénətə → žéntə. Essentially the same process is observed in Old Bulgarian examples such as вьсько → всько, мъногъ → многъ.

With the loss of the remaining Old Bulgarian high nontense vowels, the reorganization of oppositions among the high vowels was completed, and the feature *tense* ceased to function distinctively in the system.

The loss of the weak yers has been the subject of many descriptions and investigations. The texts show that their loss was a gradual process. Some manuscripts, such as SPs (eleventh century) and DE, show indisputable examples of the deletion of weak yers along with examples where word-final yers were preserved and underwent other changes; e.g., творитъı и, смърито ı. These facts indicate that there was a long period during which the use of high nontense vowels in weak syllables was facultative. In this regard see Xoliolčev 1959:35-36 for statistical data describing the retention and loss of unstressed vowels in the modern dialects.

8.17. We still face the question of why weak yers were preserved in certain roots; e.g., in modern dialect forms such as *lъže, laže*; *mъgla, mъngla, magla*; *dъno* (and *dno*); *žъne, žene* (and *žne*); *tъče* (and *tkae*); *dъšter'a, dašterka* (and *šterka, ščerka, čerka, kerka*); *dъščica* (and *ščica, štica*); *tъnъk, tъnka, tanok, tanka, tenak, tenka* (and *knok, knoka*).

Probably the retention of the vowel was preceded by its lowering: ь → e, ъ → ʌ (→ ě or á). Lowering in such instances is most common in north-eastern dialects. It is lexically limited in western and Rupa dialects (see BDA). Dialects with preserved weak yers in roots formed the basis of the modern literary language (e.g., *dъno, tъče, dъšter'a*).[37]

From the historical point of view, the retention of weak yers in roots presents a difficult problem. Some believe that "it usually occurred when [the yers] were in initial syllables and their loss would have led to the creation of consonant clusters difficult to pronounce" (Mirčev 1958:112). This explanation is hardly sufficient: it is not equally valid for all dialects, all lexemes, or all Slavic languages.

It is crucial to note that in dialects in which the reflexes of ъ and ѫ are not the same, in root morphemes the retained weak yer has the quality of the reflex of ѫ, not ъ; e.g., in the dialect of Prilep: *son, doš*, but *laže, tanok* as *zap, pat*; in the dialect of Kostur: *son, doš*, but *mъgla, mъngla* as *krъnk, krъngo, lъnk, lъngo*. This fact indicates that in Bulgarian dialects the lowering of weak yers and their merger with the reflexes of the nasals took place *after* the lowering of the strong yers: ъ → ʌ (→ o), ь → e. In turn, this process shows that the labialization of the mid back vowel (ʌ → o) was secondary in all dialects and that it was opposed — particularly in roots — by another tendency, the merger of the mid back vowel with the back nasal, which *possibly* may have taken place as ʌ → ǫ or ʌŋ. Very valuable data on the interaction of the yers and the nasals is provided by dialects with eastern characteristics which show ъ in roots while at the same time preserving nasalization (9.7).

Thus, before formulating the rule which deletes the remaining weak yers, we need to account for two other changes:

1. the lowering of weak yers in roots (with various lexical constraints throughout the dialects);

2. the merger of the mid back nonlabial vowel with ѫ.

The optimal formalization of the first is:

(42) $\begin{bmatrix} +\text{voc} \\ -\text{low} \\ -\text{tns} \end{bmatrix} \rightarrow [-\text{high}] \;//\; \begin{bmatrix} \underline{\hspace{2cm}} \\ \text{root morpheme} \end{bmatrix}$

Regarding the possibility that ь → ъ and ъ → ь preceded this rule, see 8.13 and 8.14. Informally the second change is:

(43) ʌ and ǫ (ʌŋ) merge.[38]

For details of the development of the nasals see 9.12.

b. The loss of weak yers

The final change which applies to high nontense vowels is the loss of weak yers. After all other changes affecting the yers have taken place, their loss can be expressed simply by the deletion of all high nontense vowels. In Old Bulgarian the high nontense vowels are ə (ъ) and ɪ (ь); in modern Bulgarian dialects they are unstressed reduced vowels:

(44) $\begin{bmatrix} +\text{vocalic} \\ +\text{high} \\ -\text{tense} \end{bmatrix} \rightarrow \emptyset$

This rule must apply after the lowering of strong yers and the lowering of weak yers in roots.

B. Nasal vowels

1. Early vocalization

9.0. We have referred many times above to nasalization and the so-called nasal vowels. On the basis of our analysis it follows that before the reshaping of the vocalic system and before the creation of the glagolitic alphabet, Bulgarian Slavic dialects were characterized by groups of high vowels plus the nasal velar consonant ŋ. The high vowels here were i and u (ь and ъ, resp.); the labialization of the second member of the pair remains an open question. In addition, glagolitic shows that archaic dialects preserved groups of front low tense vowel plus nasal, (j)æ + ŋ, written ѩ and reflecting IE *ja:N in first person singular present tense verbal endings, accusative and instrumental singular forms of a-stem nouns, and third person plural present tense endings of je-stem verbs; e.g., знаѭ, землѭ, знаѭтъ. This low front vowel was subject to the early change jæ(ŋ) → ja(ŋ) (see the discussion of the distribution of ѧ, ѩ, ѥ, and ѭ in glagolitic texts in 7.1-7.4 above), which led to its merger with the back nasal vowel. Early glagolitic preserves traces of an archaic dialect without the change of æ to a and traces of a front vocalization of ѫ (cf. the same name for ѩ in abecedariums: *hie* in Abcd and γέα in the Banduri abecedarium; Vrana 1963). In Middle Bulgarian texts ѩ is written with the letter for the front nasal; e.g., волѧ, боурѧ, вонѧ (acc sg), frequently ѧ (= ѭ acc sg), знаѧ (1st pers sg pres). Groups of vowels and nasal consonants before another consonant or word-boundary were unstable and subject to change.

2. ѫ → оу

9.1. One of the earliest changes is uŋ → uw (оу; see rule 12). As already pointed out (4.6), this change appears in Bulgarian in doublets with ѫ and оу along with the opposite change, uw → uŋ; e.g., ноужда vs. нѫжда. In some archaic Bulgarian dialects groups of *back high vowel* + *nasal consonant* were probably preserved to a fairly late point.[39] This created possibilities for the direct development of uŋ to uw (оу) without an intermediate stage with a nasal vowel. Among other things, such a development explains individual examples of оу instead of ѫ which are found in many Old Bulgarian texts, including Mar, SPs, and Cloz; e.g., Cloz моу(ка) 3b, 16, 10b, 20, 12a, 35 vs. мѫ(ка) 6a, 39, 8b, 1, 10a, 38, 10b, 16, 10b, 17, 13a, 34, 13b, 6.

3. Vocalic nasalization

9.2. In general, a stage of development with nasal vowels is characteristic for Bulgarian dialects. It must be emphasized, however, that vocalic nasalization was a late and uneven process. Various stages of the process are attested in the graphic systems themselves of Old Bulgarian. At the time of its introduction, glagolitic reflected a phonological system prior to the appearance of nasal vowels, a system which still preserved Vŋ: ⱻ, ⱻ, and ⱻ. Cyrillic reflects a dialect with nasal vowels (Ү): ѫ, ѧ, ѧ, and ѧ. However, one can observe some differences in the glagolitic texts. Texts with early angular glagolitic, like KF, SPs and OchrFol, preserve traces of an archaic feature: the second part of the letters for the nasals, ⱻ, is often not only written separately but often above the line of characters. In Zo, Mar, Cloz, Ril, Ass, and Euch, we can distinguish a tendency to join the two components of the letters and to write them both on the same line.[40] Thus, new letters — authentic nasal vowels — evolved. In the same texts, ⱻ does not signify a nasal consonant but a front nasal vowel.

Differences in the old texts probably reflect different chronological systems and, perhaps, processes which spread geographically in an uneven fashion. For this reason variations in the modern dialects require tracing concrete changes in separate types of systems. This remains the task of the historical dialectology of Middle and early New Bulgarian. Here we follow some of the approximate changes in a single dialect, that of Salonika, using well-known data from the villages of Suxo and Visoka.

Let us begin by considering a number of general regularities in the development of nasalization in Slavic and other languages. The nasalization of vowels contiguous to nasal consonants — usually before a nasal consonant followed by a word-boundary or another nasal consonant — occurs in many languages. In Bulgarian dialects it has its own characteristic features. According to Schane 1973:64 and 66-67, nasalization and denasalization occur in the following order:

1. Nasalization of vowels before a nasal consonant followed by a word-boundary or another consonant:

(45) $\begin{bmatrix} +\text{voc} \\ -\text{cons} \end{bmatrix} \rightarrow [+\text{nasal}] \;//\; \underline{} \; \begin{bmatrix} +\text{cons} \\ +\text{nas} \end{bmatrix}$ (CX) #

(A vowel is nasalized before a nasal consonant followed by another consonant or word-boundary.)

2. The loss of nasal consonants after nasal vowels:

(46) $\begin{bmatrix} +\text{cons} \\ +\text{nas} \end{bmatrix} \rightarrow \emptyset \;//\; \begin{bmatrix} +\text{voc} \\ +\text{nas} \end{bmatrix} \underline{}$

(Nasal consonants are lost after nasal vowels.)

3. The denasalization of the nasal vowel:

(47) [+vocalic] → [-nasal]

In the course of this process we can distinguish a number of particular features which must be taken into account:

1. Nasalization often does not apply simultaneously to all vowels. Front vowels tend to nasalize first, and among them low front vowels before others. Denasalization generally begins among high vowels (Chen 1974:913, Chen and Wang 1975:275-78).

2. Nasalization depends on the environment in which VN occurs. In various languages it is possible to observe the following descending order in the tendency towards nasalization:
   a. before another nasal consonant (in the group VNN)
   b. before word-boundary
   c. before continuant consonants
   d. before voiceless noncontinuants (stops and affricates)
   e. before voiced noncontinuants

(See Koschmieder 1951, Georgiev 1957 and 1957a, Nikolov 1970, Illič-Svityč 1962, Tolstaja 1966, Ruhlen 1972).

At the point when vowel nasalization begins, the nasal consonant which invokes it is ŋ, [+high, +back, -coronal, -labial]. The nasalization of the vowel and the deletion of the nasal consonant are related to the loss of the closure in the nasal consonant, ŋ:

(48) $\begin{bmatrix} +\text{cons} \\ +\text{back} \\ +\text{nas} \end{bmatrix} \rightarrow [+\text{continuant}]$

4. Nasal vowels

Nasal vowels have a tendency to become low (Mirčev 1958:101, Chen 1974). In Bulgarian, at a given point, the nasal vowels became mid; e.g., e, ъ, o) or low (æ, a, ô). How can the details of these changes be represented?

Probably at a point when VN still existed, the high nontense (short) vowels became mid; i.e., ъŋ → ʌŋ, ıŋ → ɛŋ. This took place after the Umlaut of the yers and certainly before the loss of weak yers — and approximately at the same time as the lowering of the strong yers. The fact that the nasals lowered at the same time as the yers led to the merger of ъ and ѫ, on one hand, and ь and ѧ, on the other, in many Bulgarian dialects. We should pay particular attention to the fact that this merger tended to be strongest in root morphemes, particularly in the case of weak yers. For example, in the Kostur dialect we find *dóš*, but *pắnt* and *mắngla*; in Salonika *bắnc* (← бъзъ), *bắnčfa*, *pắnt*, but *dánuk*, *bъnzó*. Becoming mid, the high nontense vowels naturally missed the application of the rule that deleted weak yers. Later, the mid vowels developed in various ways in Bulgarian dialects. In other words, the so-called "secondary yers" refer to ʌ or ʌ(ŋ) for back vowels, ɛ or ɛ(ŋ) for front vowels (mid nontense vowels). Different dialect developments were due to different changes connected with the intersection of a number of tendencies.

The mid vowels lengthened, becoming identical in this respect to other vowels after the loss of the distinctive contrast of the feature *tense*. The lengthening of back mid vowels could have entailed their labialization. The tendency to lengthen is strongest for yers in strong positions, probably due to the dissimilative nature of the change. The lowering of ъ to o is consequently the result of several successive changes:

1. the lowering of high nontense vowels (ъ → ʌ, ь → ɛ)
2. the lengthening of mid vowels (ʌ → ʌː, ɛ → e)
3. the labialization of back mid tense vowels (ʌː → o; see 8.1 and 6.1)

a. The labialization of back nasal vowels

9.3. In some dialects ʌ and ѧ lengthened at the same time, which led to the labialization of the nasal as well: ъ → o and ѫ → ǫ. The results of such a change are found in archaic dialects such as those of Debar and the lower Prespa. In the latter, the labial nasal was lowered further, leading to a contrast: ъ → o, but ѫ → ǫ → ô.

Slavic toponyms in Greece preserve traces of archaic Old Bulgarian dialects in which lengthening and labialization of the nasal vowels preceded changes of the yers, e.g., Δόμνιτσα (дѫбьница), ογγά (лѫгъ) (Mirčev 1958:46). Reading the back nasal letter as ǫ is justified, of course, only on the assumption that the mid vowel was represented faithfully and that it actually reflects an old change.

It is necessary to be extremely cautious in interpreting the data in the oldest texts: the confusion of the letters for о and ѫ in the oldest period could reflect the confusion of ѧ (ä) and ѫ (ą̈), as well as that of о and ǫ.[41] In my view, there is no reason to assert categorically that the letter for the back nasal in glagolitic must be read as ǫ, rather than ѫ (a short back mid nonlabial vowel). We may suppose, however, that the confusion of ѥ (о) and ѭ (ѫ) on the basis of their shared labiality is reflected in some copies dating from the eleventh century. The majority of examples of this sort are found in SPs, Euch, and Ass.

Examples of ѥ for ѭ and vice versa are most common in SPs. Together with the frequent use of ѥ for ѥ (ъ), they are of unquestionable significance for the linguistic characterization of the text. Examples of the confusion of ѥ and ѭ: подѭ мноѭ 20b, 16; правъдѭѥѭ твоеѭѥ 35b, 3; ѭтрѭба 36a, 13-14; гѥслѣх (addition in the margin) 39a, 6; твѭѥѭ 44b, 8, 65b, 6-7; тобѭѥѭ 54b, 17; мнѭѥѭ 57b, 5; о деснѥѭ 59a, 9; отъринѭѥвы (ѥ corrected to ѭ) 74a, 6; правъдѭѥѭ 77b, 12; възѥсвѭстъ 78b, 2; живѭтъ (for живѥтъ) 81a, 15, глоумлѣхѥ сѭ 83a, 2; дѥбровѣ 93a, 14; лѥкъ 96a, 21, 104a, 19, помѣнѥшѭ 102a, 18; пѭть 108a, 2; поидѭтъ 109b, 15; въ пѭтı 109b, 19; сътѥжаѭѥштѥѭ 110a, 3; сѭбоѭѥ 115a, 12; омѥтıхъ 116b, 13; оскѥдьшѭ 120a, 11; рѥкамı 128a, 3; законопрѣстѥплѥниѥ 129b, 1; молıтвѥ 130b, 21, 144b, 11, 140b, 9; мѥдрıтъ 136a, 14; помѭѥнѥ 140b, 10; заблѥдшѭ 141a, 9; прѥзı (ἀκρίδες) 145b, 15. From fol. 146 to the end there are no instances of ѥ for ѭ or vice versa, but ѥ is found for ѥ.

Unlike ѭ, the letter ѹ (оу) in SPs is always fully written, and it is difficult to find cases of ѥ for ѹ. In Ass there are examples of ѥ for ѭ as well as ѹ.

The confusion of ѥ and ѭ in Old Bulgarian texts occurs together with the confusion of ѭ (ѧ) and ѥ (є). Consider, for example, SPs оуслышашѥ 21a, 9; ѥзъщı 1b, 17; отѥготьшѭ 49b, 3; възложѥтъ 65b, 20; їмѭѥнı 78b, 6; наслѣдѥтъ 85a, 9; поштѥдıтъ 89b, 3; съпѥштı 115b, 27; ѡдръжашѥ 116b, 18.

In SPs various Old Bulgarian orthographic systems and various chronological and dialectal layers intersect — leading to the absence of consistency and orthographic authority. Euch, on the other hand, is one of the most orthographically consistent Old Bulgarian texts. Against this background of orthographic stability, examples of the confusion of ѥ and ѭ are relatively frequent; e.g., ѥзѥѭ 10b, 14; ѭрѭжıъ 29a, 4; бѭѥдѭѥщıєı for бѥдѭѥщıєı, нѭѥжѭ

(=ножд) 96a, 17. In Cloz we find similar examples: не могѫште 5a, 20.

The explanation for the labialization of mid back vowels, as already pointed out, can be connected with the lengthening of old short vowels at a given point. From this it follows that at a certain time, stress, as the new conditioning factor of length, could become the conditioning factor of labiality as well. Perhaps we can find here an explanation for certain aspects of the vocalization of Rhodope dialects; compare: *góba, zóp, dóš, dóska, takóf,* but *zabót, rakáve, daskí, laíca* in the dialect of the village of Trigrad (Devin; Stojkov 1962a:21). The tendency for the mid back vowel to be labialized was probably strong and widespread in the early period of the development of Bulgarian.

b. The back nasal as ъ

9.4. We need to pay special attention to the fluctuation in the Latin letters rendering the reflexes of ъ and ѫ in the Čerged prayers, dating from the sixteenth century and presumably representing the dialect of settlers from the area of Svištov, who had come to this area three centuries earlier (Miletič 1896). For example: *rantze, poncsenye, trombenieto, peaskot, ogniot, go βlyakoha, βoberi, zvon, bandi, prandt, ne stapam, manka, zandi, tunuvam, kaʃta, βartze, dobor, parvo, βkampa, tesniot, peant*. It is noteworthy that examples of o are less frequent for the back nasal than for ъ. In modern north-eastern dialects o occurs for ъ principally in the masculine singular definite article: *nusó, zəbó*, for example.

The tendency for the mid back vowel to labialize is clearly opposed by another tendency. In the environment of a consonantal nasal element, the back mid vowel tends to retain (or to take on) the vocalization of ъ. Under stress it is ɤ́ (e.g., pɤ́(n)t); unstressed it is ʌ or ə. Compare the literary forms *zʌbɤ́* and *ɤ́gəl*.[42] The contiguous nasal consonant, when closely bound to the preceding vowel in the syllable structure C_0VNC and $C_0VN\#$, played an undeniable role in the phonologization of the nonlabial quality of the mid back vowel. The connection of ъ and contiguous sonorant consonants can be seen in other phonological developments in Bulgarian, namely:

1. the development of ꞃ and ḹ to ъr/rъ and ъl/lъ, which can also be observed in central and western dialects in which a and o are the reflexes of ѫ and ъ;

2. in the dialect of the village of Smolsko (Pirdop region), for example, where the process additionally requires a following sonorant consonant; cf. sʌrná, gъ́rlo, vъ́rlo, but gŕnci, grbn'áč, vŕx (Kânčev 1968:14);

3. in the existence of so-called ъ-*reduction*, found predominantly in the environment of soft sonorant consonants or j; e.g., ból'ən, nʌdír'ə (literary bólen, nadíre).

This process may be represented as VN → *nonlabial vowel* + *nasal consonant*. Its general formalization is:

$$(49) \quad \begin{bmatrix} +\text{voc} \\ -\text{high} \\ -\text{low} \end{bmatrix} \rightarrow [-\text{lab}] \ // \ \underline{\quad} \begin{bmatrix} -\text{voc} \\ +\text{nas} \end{bmatrix} (CX) \ \#$$

This rule explains, for example, why in the dialect of Oxrid the reflex of ѫ is ъ, while the reflex of ѧ is o: dóš, vón, but pъ́t, zъ́p; likewise in other, more southern dialects: dóš, vón, but pъ́nt, zъ́mp. Additionally, the rule allows us to draw the following conclusions:

1. In dialects with ъ as the reflex of ѫ, the accompanying nasal element was retained longer. This holds for a large number of eastern dialects and for the southern-most western dialects.

2. For dialects with ъ as the reflex of ѫ and ѧ, we may assume the confusion of ǫ (ʌN) and ʌ from ъ, with a nonlabial vocalization appearing in all positions or at least in roots. Consider, for example, the reflexes of ѧ and ѫ in the dialects of emigrants from the areas of Gümüldjina (Komotiní) and Salonika, in Moesian dialects, and elsewhere.

c. The reflexes a, æ, ô

9.5. The change of ѫ to a results from the change of ǫ to ą because of the tendency of nasal vowels to lower. This tendency also led to the lowering of the front nasal: ę → æ̨ (Mirčev 1958:102). It is even possible that the front nasal changed first due to the fact that front vowels are more apt to be nasalized (Chen 1974:913). The low vocalization of the reflex of ѧ is preserved in some contemporary Rhodope dialects and in the area of Korçë; e.g., under stress in Korçë *m'ǽso, l'ǽšča, p'ǽtok, dá͡mp, golá͡mp, sá͡nt* (сѫдъ) (Mirčev 1958:100-102).

The vocalization of a as the reflex of ѫ and ъ in central a-dialects is due to the merger of ѧ and ѧ, perhaps simultaneously with the lowering of the nasal. The merger of ѫ and ъ is once more observed mainly in roots.[43] As typical examples see dialects in the areas of Botevgrad and Pirdop.

The vocalizations ô or ôN for ѫ indicate the lengthening and labialization of ѧ prior to lowering.

d. "Secondary yer"

Commonly used in Bulgarian linguistics, the term "secondary yer," can be accepted conventionally *only* for ъ and ѫ with the provision that it refers to a mid back nonlabial nontense vowel, i.e., ѧ, as opposed to OB ъ, which was back, high, and nontense. This mid vowel was a stage in the development of all reflexes of the Old Bulgarian back vowels ъ and ѫ (except where ѫ → u), during which nasalization, lengthening, labialization, and lowering took place unevenly throughout the dialects and thereby led to the great diversity which we observe. Short e (ɛ) was the intermediate stage in the development of the front vowels.

5. Nasal assimilation

9.6. The process of nasalization and denasalization could be interrupted if the nasal consonant is assimilated to the consonant which follows it. Before velars ŋ would remain unchanged, while becoming m before labials, n before coronals (dentals and alveopalatals), and so on.[44] Before continuants ŋ would lose its closure, leading to the nasalization of the preceding vowel. On the basis of data from the dialects of Salonika and the contemporary literary language (Georgiev 1957, 1957a, Nikolov 1970), nasal assimilation in Bulgarian would affect the features *back, coronal,* and *continuant*:

$$(50) \quad [+\text{nas}] \rightarrow \begin{bmatrix} \alpha\text{cont} \\ \beta\text{cor} \\ \gamma\text{back} \end{bmatrix} \; // \; [+\text{voc}] \; \underline{\quad} \; \begin{bmatrix} \alpha\text{cont} \\ \beta\text{cor} \\ \gamma\text{back} \end{bmatrix}$$

(See the next section for examples from Salonika.) After nasal assimilation the nasality of the vowel before noncontinuous nasal consonants becomes phonologically irrelevant; e.g., *pént*, *pъnt*, *dъmbó*, *krъnk*.

6. Nasalization in Suxo and Visoko (Salonika)

9.7. In Bulgarian dialects which preserve nasalization we observe the results of some of the above tendencies in the development of ѫ and ѧ before completion of the cycle of nasalization. For example, according to published material from the villages of Suxo and Visoko, nasalization and denasalization took place only in certain positions:

1. *Before nasal consonants*; e.g., *uv'ánuva* (S, V).[45] In this instance, nasalization, accompanied by lowering, is an early change; cf. OB оувьнѧти (with the change of -Ndn- to -Nn-), but оувѧдати. The same is observed in OB помьнѧти (-iNn- → æNn- → -æn-) vs. помѧнѧти, and пѣнѧзь (from Germanic *phenning*) (Georgiev 1969:122).

2. *Word-finally*; e.g., *ím'a*, but *ím'anta*, *s'ǽm'a — s'ǽm'anta*, *vъ́m'a — vъ́m'anta*. Additionally, the nasal consonant was generalized as an element of the plural morpheme: *mur'ǽnta* (plural of *móri* 'sea'), *pismónta* (plural of *pismó*); also *b'alílunta*, *červílunta*. From the modern data we cannot determine if nasalization of the final vowel was connected with its lowering: ę → æ → a (→ ѧ in unstressed syllables, transcribed as a or ą), or with late *ъ-reduction* of front vowels in unstressed syllables: C'ɛ → C'ı → C'ə.[46]

3. *Before continuants*: s, z, š, ž, f, v, x; e.g., *m'ǽsu* (S), *gazó* (S), *mъ́šku* (S), *mésu* (V), *gъ́ska* (S, V), *pumínax* (S, V). Sometimes (e.g., *m'ǽsu* (S)) the nasalization of the vowel was accompanied by lowering; this is observed again in front vowels, where nasalization may have taken place earlier.[47]

4. *Before voiceless stops in lexically limited examples where nasalization presumably occurred relatively late*: *sǎ us'ǽknuvam* (S, V), *m'ánka* (мѧкъка; V). It is interesting that the few examples of this sort occur before k.

Before noncontinuants (stops and affricates) the nasal consonant remained, while assimilating to the following consonant and thereby blocking the application of nasalization and denasalization; e.g., žéntfa, žintfárin (S, V), péntuk (S, V), rъ́nkata (S, V), dъ́mp, dъmbót (S, V), gъ́mba (S, V), mъ́ndra (S, V), misinčína (S, V), purъ́nčinu (S), pájanǯina (S). The assimilation affects *back* and *coronal*. Before continuant consonants, the feature *continuant* was also probably assimilated, but the loss of the closure led to early nasalization. Before noncontinuants, assimilation took the following path: before back noncoronals (k, g) the nasal consonant remained noncoronal and back ŋ; before nonback noncoronals (m, b), it became nonback and noncoronal m; before nonback coronals (t, d, c, ʒ, č, ǯ), it became nonback coronal n. The transcribed dialect data do not indicate softness in the nasal consonant, but we may suppose that in some dialects it possibly became high before nonback high consonants, such as n' and č'.

Until the exact nature of the nasal assimilation is understood, the chronology of other changes involved in the development of the nasals cannot be clarified. This issue is extremely complex in the dialects of Suxo and Visoko, related here, as it is, to explanations of two other regionally characteristic developments: the confusion of ъ and ѫ in roots and the affricatization of fricatives after VN.

In all probability the first of these two changes represents the merger of ъ and ъN at a given point. The fact that the direction of this process — at least in roots — is ъ → ъN is extremely important for the history of Bulgarian. In Suxo and Visoko it is observed only before noncontinuants: bъ́nčfa (S, V), bъ́nc, bъnʒó (бъзъ; S, V), lanǯá (S, V), lanǯíca (S, V), lanǯlíif (literary lъžlív; S), dlъ́nga, dlъ́ngu, dlъ́nuk, mъ́ngla, stъ́nglu. Before continuants ъN is not observed: dъ́х, (S, V), rъ́š, rъštá (S, V), dъ́š (S, V), dъ́štira (S), snъ́xa, snaxáta (S, V), pъ́xkam, pъ́xnuvam (S, V), dъ́ska, daskáta (S, V). It is strange that the nasal consonants occur only after back vowels; ь is not confused with ѧ. Apparently there is no symmetry in the evolutions of front and back vowels in this case. Once again, an explanation may be found in the tendency for front vowels to nasalize more readily than back vowels. Examples with lowering point perhaps to the early nasalization of front vowels; recall the examples given above such as: m'ǽsu (S), sǎ us'ǽknuvam (S, V), m'ánka (V). These cases lead to the confusion not of ѧ and ь, but ѧ and ѣ. The form *pentél/pintél* is also widely found in south-eastern dialects; it is attested rather early: DE from the beginning of the twelfth century has пѧтєль (John 13:38, 18:27) for пьтєль.

Another possible explanation for this fact may be the early change of ь to ъ in certain roots (8.17); e.g., *mъ́ngla, stъ́nglu*. These forms show that the appearance of secondary nasality follows the change of ь to ъ. On the other hand, we need to consider that secondary nasality is not observed after rъ and lъ (excluding *dlъ́nga, dlъ́ngu*). Consequently the process took place before changes of r̥ and l̥.

In general, the loss of the weak yers either put an end to or limited processes of nasalization. This seems to have been caused by some pressure to limit the extent of variation among alternative forms of a given morpheme. That is, had nasalization not been interrupted when the weak yers disappeared, it would have applied to morphemes containing VN in forms such as *ténko* (←tenъko), altering them to such an extent that their connection to related forms, e.g., *ténuk* (←tenъkъ), would have been lost. The possibility of levelings in underlying forms of this sort is established by examples such as *dlъ́nga/dlъ́nuk* alongside *ténka/ténuk*.

Roots show a clear tendency to retain *vowel + nasal consonant*; that is, they tend not to undergo the nasalization of vowels and the subsequent loss of the nasal consonants. Theoretically speaking, this process is an interesting example of the stability of morphophonemic structure: the change in question is avoided through alteration of the conditioning factors which invoke its application. In this particular case the continuant consonant after VN becomes noncontinuant: s → c, z → ʒ, š → č, ž → ǯ. For example, *bъ́nc* (бѫзъ; S, V), *banʒó* (S, V), *inʒík* (ѩзꙑкъ; S), *ganʒót* (V), but *gъ́s, gazó* (S), *vъ́nzil* (S, V), *mъ́nč* (мѫжь; S, V), *tánǯim* (тѫжити; S) *vъ́nǯi* (S), *lъnǯá* (S, V). These examples include forms with continuants after etymological ъN as well as ъ. Forms such as *mъ́ngla* and *bъ́nčfa* are usually explained as "secondary nasalization" before stops and affricates, i.e., as a generalization of the rule for the distribution of ъ and ъN before certain consonants. This, however, does not explain examples with affricates, such as *banʒó*, and *lanʒá*. Additionally, we must not forget that forms with *front vowel + nonetymological N + nonetymological affricate* do not occur. The development can be explained only by assuming that the change of ъ to ъN was earlier than nasal assimilation and affricatization. In this case, affricatization turns out to be a result of nasal assimilation and the creation of a new environment of two contiguous continuants, not the result of the split of nasal vowels into *vowel + nasal consonant*. The order of these changes is approximately:

1. ъ, ъN → ъN in roots. Illič-Svytič 1962:86 speaks of "a period in which [ъ] (← ǫ) and [ъⁿ], [ъn], [æ] (← ę) and [æⁿ], [æn] were allophones of one phoneme." An approximate formalization of this rule, leaving aside the question of vowel quality for the time being, would be:

(43′) ъ → ъN // $\left[\overline{root\ morpheme} \right]$

2. *Nasal assimilation*, with n before noncontinuant dentals and alveopalatals, ŋ before noncontinuant velars, and m before noncontinuant labials, and the loss of closure before noncontinuants; see rule (50) above.

3. After the nasal consonant lost its closure before continuants (Nikolov 1970), the vowel was nasalized and the consonant lost; later the vowel itself lost its nasality; e.g., meNso → meⁿso → męso (or mæ̨so) → meso (or mæso).

4. As a result of pressure to preserve nasal consonants in morphophonemic structure, continuants become noncontinuants: s → c, z → ʒ, š → č, ž → ǯ. Affricatization blocks the subsequent regular processes of nasalization and denasalization of the vowel. Compare *mъ́nč, inʒík, bъ́nc, vъnʒíl*, but *mъ́šku, m'ǽsu* (S), *mésu* (V). The rule is:

(52) [+cons] → [−cont] // [+voc][+nas] ——

5. At a later stage, the vowel is nasalized before voiceless noncontinuants — although in Suxo and Visoko we find isolated examples of denasalization before k. The preservation of the nasal consonant in these examples leads to the voicing of the consonant; e.g., *stъ́nglu* for *stъ́nklu, pájangi* for *pájanki*. Voicing after nasal consonants is found in other languages (Dell 1973:111). It is well known in Greek, from which Bulgarian borrowed several forms with nd for nt; e.g., in the Bojana inscription from the middle of the thirteenth century: при...цр҃и Костаньдинь Асьни.[48]

The history of nasality in Salonika combines a variety of phenomena, the analysis of which is interesting for general linguistic theory as well as for the history of Bulgarian. Particularly important for Bulgarian historical dialectology is the fact that the merger of the vocalization of ѫ and ъ proceeded in the direction of ѫ, rather than ъ.

7. Evolutionary tendencies

9.8. Thus, the various reflexes of the nasals ѫ and ѧ in Bulgarian dialects derive from general underlying forms with ъN and ьN, resp. Different reflexes are due to the complex interaction of a number of phonetic tendencies, the most important of which are:

1. *The merger of ŋ and w after back high u (ъ)*. The change of ŋ to w leads to the reflex u (oy) for the back nasal in certain forms and certain dialects.

2. *The change of ъ and ь to mid nontense vowels, which are unstable.*

3. *The nasalization of vowels before N*. Nasalization applies unevenly to front and back vowels and in different ways in different positions.

4. *The tendency of the mid back vowel to become ъ in the environment of nasal consonants*. The new nonlabial mid vowel was close to ʌ — nonhigh, nonlow, back, nonlabial, and nontense; when stressed, it becomes ɨ́.

5. *The lengthening of mid short vowels*, which in many dialects leads to labialization — most frequently for the back vowel. This change is connected in some dialects with stress, the new conditioning factor of the *tense* (length) in vowels.

6. *The tendency of nasal vowels to lower*. This process leads to the reflexes æ, a, ô from ę̈, ą, and ǫ.

7. *Nasal assimilation*, which stops or impedes the process of nasalization.

8. *The denasalization of nasal vowels.*

Notes

1. Shevelov 1963:249 provides the example врътоградъ from *urtigard- (Got *aurtigards*). However, this form can be explained as wr̥togard- → vr̥togard-, not urt- → wurt- → vurt-. Fortunatov 1919:250 adds another example, vuj(čo) 'mother's brother', but he himself gives the variants vuj- and uj- (cf. Bulgarian dialects) and contrasts a Polish form uj- in old texts with new vuj-.
2. Mirčev 1958:106 gives another explanation: "With the gradual change of ѫ to ъ the labial element characteristic of the articulation of ѫ first separated as ṷ, which then became *v*. In this way Old Bulgarian initial ѫ became vѫ."
3. Cloz 9c, 11-12: дш҃ѫ къ себѣ съвѫзомь любовьнъıмь совъкоуплѣѭще.
4. Traces of prothetic w before ѫ in East Slavic and Serbo-Croatian are few, but real. They include examples with g (e.g., Russ, SC *gusenica*, SC *guž(va)*; for w → g see below) and the well-known Russian form *vjazat'*, which most investigators explain as analogy to *vѫz- (Meillet 1934: §93). This suggests the development uŋz- → wuŋz- → wuwz- → û:z- (cf. Russ *uzy, uzel*).
5. This rule helps clarify a number of points related to the character and chronology of changes of ѫ in Slovenian, e.g., *vogel* vs. *ògel*. In Ukrainian later labializations prevent the clear reconstruction of the old development.
6. Changes (7), (10b), (10c), and (7a) can be looked upon conventionally as a single, general process: w becomes a vowel before a glide or consonant (cf. the elimination of diphthongs), and a consonant before a vowel. This can be formalized as:

$$(7'') \quad \begin{bmatrix} +\text{son} \\ +\text{lab} \end{bmatrix} \rightarrow \begin{bmatrix} \alpha\text{voc} \\ \beta\text{cons} \end{bmatrix} \bigg/\!\!\bigg/ \underline{} \begin{bmatrix} -\alpha\text{voc} \\ -\beta\text{cons} \end{bmatrix}$$

We know very little about this new v: we do not know if it was a sonorant, or if it was labiodental or bilabial. In all likelihood these features alternated in various positions and various dialects, which ultimately accounts for the very complicated modern state of affairs. See vols. 1 and 2 of the BDA; Tilkov 1974.

7. See Bernštejn 1968 on the loss of intervocalic j. His chronology of the change raises many questions which we will consider elsewhere.
8. The ü found in modern south-eastern dialects is a new feature, which again encounters systematic resistance.
9. See, e.g., Fortunatov 1919:12, Trubetzkoj 1954:64-69 and 72, and Stieber 1969:24 on the old vocalization of ю as ü:. Diels 1932:44 cites the consistent spelling of отьца vs. отъцю in glagolitic records as proof that ю was pronounced as ju or ü.
10. Vestiges of the use of оу for оу and ȣ for ю are found in another thirteenth-century Middle Bulgarian manuscript, Stam (Velčeva 1968).
11. This is related to Fortunatov's claim (1919:12) that — contrary to the situation in other manuscripts — ю represents ju in OstE.
12. Only the changes of the yers and nasals in Rhodope dialects have any special interest in this respect; they are the subject of a separate study.
13. Scatton 1975:14 uses the same notation to describe this change in modern Bulgarian.
14. The same tendency is observed in the development of English.
15. Forms with ря are exceptionally rare in Old Bulgarian. They occur only in Supr. In 120 pages of the manuscript, the ratio of рь : ра : ря is 9 : 7: 1; compare ль/л' : ля :: 32 : 33, and нь/н'ь : ня :: 33 : 43.
16. Forms with ща and жда in a system of this type may mean that the change took place at the point when štš, ždž existed (4.18), while those with щь and ждь—when šč, žǯ or št', žd' existed.
17. Or even more generally: æ → a after every soft consonant *if* it were possible to prove that l, n, r could not be soft at the time of the change, and that æ after vowels was not iotated. There is insufficient evidence for these claims.
18. Reconstruction of the old dialects is further complicated in this case by another development: the later shift of (j)a to e before soft consonants; e.g., *Marijána* vs. *Marijénke, jexníjъ*. These relatively new words followed models for the distribution of (j)a already existing in the dialects.

19. The pages refer to the Ščepkin edition of 1903.
20. The cliff inscription at Krepča (district of Târgovište) contains the archaic form отьць: въ има отьць и сна....
21. Jakobson 1963:24 refers to a nasal "without a specific feature." In our treatment this is not a nasal "in general," but ŋ (4.3).
22. According to Ščepkin the vocalization of ѫє was ÿ.
23. є for ѫ and ѭ for ѧ (Velčeva 1966a).
24. It is necessary to clearly distinguish between Old Bulgarian ъ, high nontense [ə], and New Bulgarian ъ, tense central [ъ] when stressed, [ʌ] or [ə] when unstressed.
25. The development of forms with ръ, ър, лъ, ъл from ŗ, ḷ probably also contributed to the wide distribution of the nonlabial central vocalization of ъ. Forms of this sort are extremely frequent and are encountered without exception in root morphemes; e.g., *prъ̀ſ, dъrvó*.
26. In his edition of the SPs, for every example of э or э for ѫє or ѭє, Sever'janov adds a footnote: "The scribe does not write the second half of the glagolitic letter for ѫ, which results in the reading o" (1922:141, 144, 145, e.g.).
27. A similar lowering of stressed vowels before a glide ([-consonantal, -syllabic, +high...]) is observed in the history of English. During and after the fifteenth century, the vowel shift of the diphthongs **ij → ej, uw → ow** resembles in many respects the "vocalization" of stressed yers before **j** in the Slavic languages. Note the notation proposed by Chomsky and Halle 1968:256 and 258:

$$\begin{bmatrix} -\text{low} \\ +\text{tns} \\ +\text{strs} \end{bmatrix} \rightarrow [-\text{high}] \;//\; \underline{\qquad} \; \begin{bmatrix} -\text{voc} \\ -\text{cons} \end{bmatrix}$$

28. Dobrev 1974 offers a different explanation: in forms such as *sĭlnъ* and *prædnъ* he sees traces of Old Bulgarian vocalizations such as вcь, днь, старць, зимнъ.
29. Mirčev 1958:136 is right in calling the soft consonants in these forms "true palatals." Particularly important are forms with **k'** and **g'** from new clusters of **tj** and **dj**, resp. These are characteristic of dialects in Strandja and many western dialects, including those in the areas of Mixajlovgrad, Sofia, Botevgrad, Samokov, Stankedimitrov, and Blagoevgrad. The softness appears only before **j**. Mirčev is not correct, however, when he speaks of "the strong softening of the consonants *n*

and *l* before the vowels *e* and *i* in western dialects." Compare *zéle* (participle) and *zél"e* (← zelьje).

30. The soft consonants that develop before j in western dialects are palatal: [−coronal, −anterior, −strident]. They show that at a given stage of development, the old rule (C) (2.2) was replaced in part of the Bulgarian linguistic territory by a new rule applying to soft consonants:

$$\begin{bmatrix} +\text{high} \\ -\text{back} \\ -\text{strd} \end{bmatrix} \rightarrow \begin{bmatrix} -\text{ant} \\ -\text{cor} \end{bmatrix}$$

31. Here Cyrillic is predominantly used to maintain proximity with Old Bulgarian.

32. There are rare examples, such as единьи 21, 27, шестьи, which are perhaps archaic forms with a separate and emphasized definite morpheme jь.

33. According to van Wijk 1957:157, "The Zograph Gospel uses въ л'юб- consistently (6 times), and възл'юб- and въ н'ѭ(же) relatively frequently, while l' and n' before front vowels are more often preceded by ь from ъ. This can be explained as the direct influence of the vowels. However, in other dialects the influence of the consonants was more significant. Thus, Sav consistently has вь лю- and almost always възлюб-." However, the data from Sav is not decisive in this case because ю may be read also as the front vowel ü (5.3).

34. According to van Wijk 1957:158, "Codex Assemanianus must be left aside."

35. Cf. Euch тъмѫ 55a, 8, 33a, 2, тъмы 15a, 14, 33a, 24, 93a, 24-93b, 1, тъмами 93b, 1, as well as тъмѣ 39b, 8, but вь темьници 79b, 14, темьнымь 32b, 7. Some scholars (e.g., van Wijk 1957:158-59) are inclined to explain forms such as тъмѣ by the shift of ь to ъ before labial consonants. Cf. forms such as възъми, сънъмиште, сънъмѣ. This explanation is not entirely convincing because: (1) similar forms are found together with forms in which the yer is followed by a syllable with a back vowel (e.g., възъмѫ, тъма) and with forms such as темьница (see the examples from Euch); (2) a similar labialization is found only before m, which raises the possibility that the nasality of the consonant plays some role. This problem will be open to solution only after full statistical analysis of the data.

36. The specification [+consonantal] is perhaps superfluous. We do not know whether the change also applied to *glide* + ь (jь → jъ) in some dialects.
37. This has led to a theoretically interesting reordering of rules: in the grammar of modern Bulgarian the deletion of the yers now comes before their lowering (Scatton 1975:12-26).
38. This change did not take place in some morphemes (e.g., ноужда) and in ъ-dialects (e.g., in the areas of Trân and Belogradčik), where the back nasal remained high (uŋ → uw → oy). See 4.6 and 9.1, which describe the elimination of diphthongs, including the mutual confusion between uŋ and uw, and the next section, describing the development of the nasals.
39. Contrary to combinations with front high vowels, which become nonhigh nasal vowels relatively early in the Slavic languages. In this regard, consider the more consistent preservation of the front nasal letter in Old Russian texts (Kolesov 1971:99), as well as the fact that nasalization in many languages begins with the front vowels (Chen 1974:913).
40. In some texts (Euch, RF, Ass) we even find spellings with a reduced first element. Sometimes the letter carries a diacritic which does not go beyond the height of the letter.
41. According to Mirčev 1958:50, "at an early point in the development of Old Bulgarian (the ninth century) a number of features typical for Bulgarian during the pre-literate period still existed....The vowel *o* was still open."
42. Consider the formulae: ə-ʌ-ɨ-ə and ə-ʌ-á-ə in the conversational literary language (Tilkov and Bojadžiev 1977:71 and 199); e.g., [dəšter'á, zʌbɨ́, məžestvó, p'ásək, ɨ́gəl, məgʌzín, zəkʌčálkə].
43. It is well known that in the dialects of Erkeč and Teteven ъ̣ and ѫ give æ when stressed and a̠ (ʌ) when unstressed. This change does not apply to ь and ѧ; they are mid front e even when stressed. Several exceptions are found in roots, where we may suppose the early change of ь to ъ; cf. *lǽskav, sǽn, dǽš, gǽba, kǽšta*, but *daždéc, zabí* (Stojkov 1968:78). This system supposes the lowering of the lengthened mid vowel under stress and its change to low æ sometime after the *jat-shift* in eastern Bulgarian dialects. Why stressed ъ and ѫ developed to front æ rather than back a remains an interesting problem.

44. A number of languages (e.g., Cuban Spanish) show very refined assimilations of nasal consonants to following consonants (Harris 1969, Dell 1973:120).
45. S=Suxo, V=Visoka; examples given follow Gołąb 1960-63, which systematizes the materials of Małecki 1934-36.
46. The Salonika dialects of Suxo and Visoka share characteristic features of eastern Bulgarian dialects with respect to the development of ѣ, changes of unstressed vowels, softening of consonants before front vowels, and the reflexes of ъ and ѫ in roots, for example.
47. OB мѣсѧць may be an example of old nasalization and lowering; according to Shevelov 1964:320 the form also shows dissimilation for nasality.
48. See Gâlâbov 1963:32 regarding fluctuation in the proper nouns Константинъ and Констандинъ, Антоние and Андоние.

Conclusion

Generative analysis of the phonological development of Proto-Slavic and Old Bulgarian makes it possible to establish the tentative order and the form of many changes which they were subject to. A number of these changes turn out to be assimilatory or dissimilatory in nature and can be seen to represent several general tendencies. In addition to the elimination of closed syllables, the tendencies of the early period include: assimilation of vowels and consonants with respect to *back*, regressive assimilations of vowels and consonants (including the dental palatalizations and the first stage of the elimination of diphthongs), the change of soft ([+high, -back]) consonants to [+strident], and characteristic changes which apply to consonants that are [+delayed release] (affricates, long stops).

The softening of consonants turns out to be a series of changes which apply first to velars, then dentals, and finally labials. Velars are softened in the environment of nonconsonantal nonback segments (front vowels and j); dentals are softened before nonvocalic high segments (j, soft consonants, or high back stops—k and g—followed immediately by a front vowel). Data from before the eleventh century provide no evidence for the softening of nonvelars before front vowels.

Forms with шт/жд arise from the change of delayed-release consonants t'ː/d'ː to št'/žd'. This process shares certain features with the change of tt (tː) to st. In accordance with a rule which remained in effect over an extended period of Proto-Slavic, t' and d' became č and ǯ, resp.; in this way the reflexes of *tj, *dj, and *kt' were identical to the results of the first palatalization of velars (cf. *sk' → šč). The changes of šč to štš and št', and žǯ to ždž and žd' have parallels in changes such as sc to sts and st (cf. OB людьсцѣи ~ людьстѣи. By the same rule the final strident consonants of certain clusters were lost in a number of examples which until now have remained unexplained: skv → sk, stv → st (OB сквозѣ ~ скозѣ, листвиє ~ листиє); later vdv → vd (e.g., New Bulgarian *vdigna* from **vdvigna**).

Voiced affricates appear to be less stable than unvoiced affricates. This accounts for the weak traces of žǯ in Old Bulgarian records, the early change of ǯ to ž, and the fluctuation of Old Bulgarian ꙃ and з. The glagolitic letter ⱛ may be interpreted as original šč, and the fluctuation of ѱ and шѹ has a parallel in the fluctuation of ци and ст (from the second regressive palatalization of velars).

The consonantalization of the back glide w after nonlabial consonants (e.g., tw → tv) is parallel to the consonantalization of j after labial consonants (e.g., mj → ml'—"epenthetic l"). On the other hand, the loss of w after labial consonants (e.g., bw → b) is matched by the loss of j, the nonback glide, after nonlabials.

The term "semi-soft consonants" corresponds to what in this study are anterior high consonants. We observe the tendency for high anterior consonants—c', ʒ', s'—to harden. This could take place also after the change of æ to a after soft consonants and j.

In general, the Proto-Slavic palatalizations introduce new consonants and lead to symmetry with respect to the features *strident, continuant,* and *voiced*. Changes following the dental palatalizations are related to limiting the number of strident consonants in the system and their frequency of occurrence.

As a consequence of the tendency of vowels to be raised under certain circumstances, short vowels occurring before nasal consonants in closed syllables changed. Thus, in this environment, before the elimination of diphthongs, short vowels merged with ĭ and ŭ. On the basis of this hypothesis, the fluctuation of ѫ and oy is viewed here as the result of the fluctuation of ŋ and w.

The nasal that derives from *ja:N (represented by glagolitic ҩє) is assumed to be a front vowel, close to æ. The symbol є in early glagolitic is taken as the symbol for the back nasal consonant ŋ; it is called *en*. In the glagolitic of the second Old Bulgarian type (Zo, Cloz, Euch), the letter comes to represent the non-iotated front nasal vowel.

Nasalization is treated as a late process, the stages of which can be observed in the Old Bulgarian graphic system and in the modern dialects. Individual steps in the process of nasalization are accompanied by additional changes which lead to the considerable diversity of the modern reflexes.

Labiality is not taken as phonologically relevant in the analysis of the changes of Proto-Slavic vowels. After the loss of diphthongs, which gives rise to the two labials vowels ü (ю) and u (оу), new oppositions with respect to *labial* appear, resulting in the complete reorganization of the vocalic system. In this complex process we observe the following phenomena:

CONCLUSION

1. *the tendency to strengthen the oppositions of high vowels, now more frequent*; the development of prothetic w and j is related to this tendency.

2. *reduction in the number of high vowels*, which is related to the tendency for high back vowels to be labialized and high nonback vowels to be nonlabialized; this tendency appears in changes which affect ю and ъɪ.

3. *the lowering of nontense (short) high vowels—the yers—* which involved regressive dissimilation; yers that were not lowered disappeared.

4. *introduction of a contrast with respect to the feature* low *among vowels*; mid vowels appear.

5. *the tendency for mid back vowels to be labialized:* ʌ → o; this change is related to changes with respect to *tense* (length).

6. *the loss of the old contrast with respect to the feature* tense, *which becomes dependent on stress.*

7. *the tendency of* ъ *and* ѫ *to merge in the latter*, a process which is opposed to the tendency of mid back vowels to become labial; the former occurs predominantly in roots and in dialects with later nasalization; the preservation of the nonlabial vocalization of ѫ is influenced by a contiguous sonorant, in this case a nasal consonant in a closed syllable.

8. *the tendency of vowels to become back after soft consonants and* j: ѥ → ѭ, ѣ → a, ю → oy, ь → ъ; we have assumed that the "confusion of nasals" is part of this process, though it is not reflected in the orthographic norms of Old Bulgarian; the later change known as the *jat-shift* appears to be an extension of the tendency of æ to become a after soft consonants under new circumstances.

9. *the imprecision of the term "secondary yer"*; regular early changes include e, ь, ьN → ε, εN or ę, and ъ, ъN → ʌ, ʌN or ǫ; there is no evidence for the existence of a stage when a general yer-like vowel was the reflex of ъ, ѫ, ь, ѧ in all positions; the change of ь to ъ in forms such as *mъgla, pъn* is taken to be early and is explained in connection with the "Umlaut" of the yers; according to data from Euch, "Umlaut" did not affect both two yers simultaneously: ъ → ь preceded ь → ъ.

CONCLUSION

10. rejection of the notions "tense yers" and "reduced и and ы"; the facts which these terms refer to are treated as a series of changes which apply to ьj and ъj before vowels.

* * *

The sound changes of Proto-Slavic lead to reorganization of morphophonemic (abstract phonemic) structure. So, for example, the early fronting of vowels, the change of a(:)j → e:, the loss of consonants in certain positions, and other changes, lexicalize new environments and create morphemes lacking earlier automatic alternations which would have preserved traces of underlying forms. Consider, for example, c and æ in цѣлъ (as opposed to c in рѫцѣхъ), š in нощть, and c, v, æ in цвѣтъ. No trace of the old alternations in these morphemes remains in Bulgarian dialects.

Underlying morphophonemic (abstract phonemic) structure, the common basis for all Bulgarian dialects, contains the following segments and important clusters: b, p, m, v, d, t, g, k, x, l, n, r, probably ļ and ŗ, l', n', r', s, s', c', ʒ', z; *soft* š, ž, ǯ, and č; prothetic j and w before high vowels and etymological j before nonhigh vowels; bj, pj, mj, vj, sc, šč, žǯ; ьj and ъj before vowels. There are no phonologically palatalized consonants before front vowels.

The underlying vocalic system was the following:

			nonback		back	
high	nontense		ь	ı	ъ	ə
	tense	nonlabial	и	i	ы	y
		labial	ю	ü	oy	u
nonhigh	nontense		є	ɛ	o	ʌ
	tense		ѣ	æ	a	a

At this point the "nasal vowels" were sequences of ь, ъ, æ, or a plus nasal consonant in closed syllables.

The glagolitic alphabet reflects a somewhat later stage, when the nasals were ʌŋ, ɛŋ, and æŋ. In this system ɔ is a constituent of the shapes of letters representing nontense vowels: ɘ, ə, ⱻ, ᴈ; cf. also ⱻɛ, ᴈɛ. A triangle, △ or ▽, is a component of those

CONCLUSION

representing tense nonback vowels: Ⱂ, Ⱇ, Ⰻ for i, Ⱓ for ü, Ⰰ for æ, Ⱔ for jæŋ. Back tense vowels comprise two elements: Ⱆ for monophthongal y in original glagolitic and Ⱆ or Ⱛ for u. The letter for a is outside this system: it is represented by a cross +; it does, however, join Δ in Ⰰ (æ, ѣ).

ɪ	Ⰻ	ə	Ⰻ
i	Ⱇ, Ⱂ, Ⰻ	y	Ⱆ, Ⱇ
ü	Ⱓ	u	Ⱛ
ɛ	Ⱃ	ʌ	Ⱁ
ɛŋ	Ⱔ	ʌŋ	Ⱔ
æ	Δ	a	+
æŋ	Ⱔ		

Glagolitic is a convenient point of departure for the study of later changes. The analysis of glagolitic in conjunction with data from the Bulgarian dialects of Suxo and Visoka (Salonika) reveals a number of important features in the development of vowels. These data are significant, in the first place, for explaining changes in dialects where ъ and ѫ merge in root morphemes.

Early dialect differences reflected in Old Bulgarian records can be grouped as in the following fashion:

1. *Differences which represent different stages of one and the same process and which are caused by chronologically uneven changes*; e.g., the contrast between ⱋ (šč) and шт (št) in glagolitic texts; sc and st from *sk; differences with respect to the nasals, which are represented as sequences of vowel plus nasal consonant in early glagolitic, but as nasal vowels in cyrillic; variations reflected in the distribution of ζ and з; the fluctuation of ü and u, shown orthographically by the confusion of ю and oy. Some changes, like the presence or absence of prothetic j before initial a or the first examples of the change of æ to a after soft consonants and j, are perhaps inherited from an earlier period.

2. *Differences due to various ranges of application*, i.e., different degrees of generality; e.g., differences in the extent to which vowels change with respect to the feature *back* after various consonants; see, for example, the change of æ to a in Old Bulgarian.

3. *Differences due to the simultaneous action of different tendencies*, which may lead to different outcomes; the most characteristic examples involve variation in the reflexes of the yers and the nasal vowels. Here we also include differences due to various rule orderings; e.g., forms such as дошълъ vs. дошелъ, differences in the development of ъj and ьj before vowels (8.5), changes of prothetic w, and cæ vs. ca.

The above-listed differences do not constitute systems and, as a whole, do not characterize distinct areas.

The analysis presented in this study must be carried further and applied to the concrete reconstruction of the histories of individual Bulgarian dialect systems.

Works Cited

Auty, R. 1963. "Glagolitic Ⱄ and Ⱍ: Facts, conjectures, and probabilities." *Zbornik u čast Stjepana Ivšića*, 5-11. Zagreb: Hrvatsko filološko društvo.
Avanesov, R.I. 1947. "Iz istorii russkogo vokalizma. Zvuki i i y." *Vestnik MGU* 1, 41-57.
Avanesov, R.I. 1948. "O dolgix šipjaščix v russkom jazyke." *Doklady i soobščenija filologičeskogo fakul'teta MGU* 6, 23-30.
Avanesov, R.I. 1968. "K istorii čeredovanija soglasnyx pri obrazovanii umen'šitel'nyx suščestvitel'nyx v praslavjanskom." *Slavjanskoe jazykoznanie. VI meždunarodnyj s"ezd slavistov*, 3-18. M.: Nauka.
Avanesov, R.I. 1971. "Zametki po russkoj fonetiki." *Fonetika. Fonologija. Grammatika*, 82-84. M.: Nauka.
Avanesov, R.I. 1974. *Russkaja literaturnaja i dialektnaja fonetika.* M.: Prosveščenie.
Bernšstejn, S.B. 1948. *Razyskanija v oblasti bolgarskoj istoričeskoj dialektologii.* M.: AN SSSR.
Bernštejn, S.B. 1961. *Očerk sravnitel'noj grammatiki slavjanskix jazykov.* Vol. 1. Vvedenie, fonetika. M.: AN SSSR.
Bernštejn, S.B. 1968. "Kontrakcija i struktura sloga v slavjanskix jazykax." *Slavjanskoe jazykoznanie. VI meždunarodnyj s"ezd slavistov*, 19-31. M.: Nauka.
Bernštejn, S.B. 1974. *Očerk sravnitel'noj grammatiki slavjanskix jazykov.* Vol. 2. Čeredovanija, imennye osnovy. M.: AN SSSR.
Birnbaum, H. 1963. "Reinterpretacje fonologiczne nosówek słowiańskich." *American Contributions to the Fifth International Congress of Slavists*, vol. 1, 27-48. The Hague: Mouton.
Birnbaum, H. 1966. "The dialects of Common Slavic." *Ancient Indo-European Dialects*, ed. H. Birnbaum and J. Puhvel, 153-97. Berkeley: Univ. of California Press.
Bojadžiev, T. 1972. *Govorât na s. Sâčanli, Gjumjurdžinsko.* Trudove po bâlgarska dialektologija 7. S.: BAN.
Bojadžiev, T. 1973. "Promjanata t', $d' > k'$, g' v strandžanskija govor." *Ezik i literatura* 28, no. 4, 34-44.
Brückner, A. 1931. "$\c{A}$ and u Dubletten im Slavischen." *Zeitschrift für slavische Philologie* 8, no. 3-4, 436-41.

Brückner, A. 1957. *Słownik etymologiczny języka polskiego*. 2nd ed. Warsaw: Wiedza Powszechna.
Bulygina, T.V. 1971. "O russkix dolgix šipjaščix." *Fonetika. Fonologija. Grammatika*, 84-91. M.: Nauka.
Čalâkov, M. 1968. "Načalnoto konsonantno reduvane g : v v slavjanskite ezici." *Slavističen sbornik*, 19-29. S.: BAN.
Channon, R. 1972. *On the Place of the Progressive Palatalization of Velars in the Relative Chronology of Slavic*. The Hague: Mouton.
Chen, M. 1973. "Predicative Power in Phonological Description." *Lingua* 32, no. 3, 173-91.
Chen, M. 1974. "Metarules and Universal Constraints in Phonological Theory." *Proceedings of the Eleventh International Congress of Linguists*, vol. 2, 909-24. Bologna: Società editrice il Mulino Bologna.
Chen, M. and W.S.-Y. Wang. 1975. "Sound Change: Actuation and Implementation." *Language* 51, no. 2, 255-81.
Chomsky, N. and M. Halle. 1968. *The Sound Pattern of English*. N.Y.: Harper and Row.
Conev, B. 1905. "Kjustendilsko četveroevangelie: srednebâlgarski prototip na VI pravopisna škola." *Periodičesko spisanie* 6, 536-61.
Conev, B. 1906. *Dobrejšovo četveroevangelie. Srednobâlgarski pametnik ot XIII v*. Bâlgarski starini 1. S.: Dâržavna pečatnica.
Conev, B. 1914. *Vračansko evangelie*. Bâlgarski starini 4. S.: Dâržavna pečatnica.
Conev, B. 1919. *Istorija na bâlgarskij ezik*. Vol. 1. S.: Dâržavna pečatnica.
Dell, F. 1973. *Les règles et les sons. Introduction à la phonologie générative*. Paris: Hermann.
Diels, P. 1932. *Altkirchenslawische Grammatik*. Heidelberg: C. Winter.
Diver, W. 1955. "The Problem of Old Bulgarian *št*." *Word* 11, no. 2, 228-36.
Dobrev, Iv. 1969. "V zaštita na glagoličeskite pismena." *Bâlgarski ezik* 19, no. 3, 241-46.
Dobrev, Iv. 1974. "Starinna čerta na edin južen bâlgarski govor." *V pamet na prof. St. Stojkov*, 163-66. S.: BAN.

Ekblom, R. 1935. *Die Palatalisierung von k, g, ch im Slavischen.* Skrifter utgivna av K. Humanistiska Vetenskaps-Samfundet i Uppsala 29, no. 5. Uppsala: Almqvist and Wiksells.

Ekblom, R. 1937. "Le slave **koldęd'z̆ъ.*" *Acta Jutlandica* 9, no. 1, 414-19.

Ekblom, R. 1951. *Die frühe dorsale Palatalisierung im Slavischen.* Skrifter utgivna av K. Humanistiska Vetenskaps-Samfundet i Uppsala 39, no. 2. Uppsala: Almqvist and Wiksells.

Filin, F.P. 1962. *Obrazovanie jazyka vostočnyx slavjan.* M.-L.: AN SSSR.

Filin, F.P. 1973. *Proisxoždenie russkogo, ukrainskogo i belorusskogo jazykov.* L.: Nauka.

Fortunatov, F.F. 1919. *Lekcii po fonetike staroslavjanskogo (cerkovnoslavjanskogo) jazyka.* P.: Otdelenie russkogo jazyka i slovesnosti.

Furdal, A. 1961. *Rozpad języka prasłowiańskiego w świetle rozwoju głosowego.* Prace Wrocławskiego Towarzystwa Naukowego, Series A, no. 70.

Gâlâbov, Iv. 1952. "Kâm razvoja na *y* v imenitelen padež na složnite prilagatelnite v bâlgarski ezik." *Izvestija na Instituta za bâlgarski ezik* 1, 169-80.

Gâlâbov, Iv. 1963. *Nadpisite kâm Bojanskite stenopisi.* S.: BAN.

Gâlâbov, Iv. 1963a. "Vâprosi na starobâlgarskata fonetika i pismo." *Bâlgarski ezik* 13, no. 3, 204-10.

Gâlâbov, Iv. [Galabov, I.] 1973. "Urslavische Auslautprobleme." *Wiener slavistisches Jahrbuch* 18, 5-17.

Gâlâbov, Iv. 1974. "Glagoličeskoto ъı, načalnata istorija na glagoličeskata azbuka i edna osobenost na dialektnata mikrostruktura na južnite bâlgarski govorni oblasti." *V pamet na prof. St. Stojkov,* 515-21. S.: BAN.

Georgiev, V.I. 1957. "Edna osobenost v proiznošenieto na sâglasnata *n* v bâlgarski." *Bâlgarski ezik* 7, no. 2, 154-55.

Georgiev, V.I. 1957a. "Po vâprosa za nosovite glasni v sâvremennija bâlgarski ezik." *Bâlgarski ezik* 7, no. 4, 353.

Georgiev, V.I. 1960. *Bâlgarska etimologija i onomastika.* S.: BAN.

Georgiev, V.I. 1961. "Dâšte, brate — starinni preživelici v bâlgarskija ezik." *Bâlgarski ezik* 11, no. 2, 97-101.

Georgiev, V.I. 1964. *Vokalnata sistema v razvoja na slavjanskite ezici.* S.: BAN.

Georgiev, V.I. 1969. *Osnovni problemi na slavjanskata diaxronna morfologija.* S.: BAN.

Georgiev, V.I. 1971. "Proisxoždenie okončanij tret'ego lica množestvennogo čisla nastojaščego vremeni v bolgarskom jazyke." *Issledovanija po slavjanskomu jazykoznaniju*, 42-44. M.: Nauka.
Georgiev, V.I. et al. 1968. *Obščeslavjanskoe značenie problemy akan'ja*. S.: BAN.
Giannelli, C. and A. Vaillant. 1958. *Un Lexique macédonien du XVIe siècle*. Paris: Institut d'études slaves.
Gołǫb, Zb. [Golomb, Zb.] 1960-63. "Dva makedonski govora (Na Suxo i Visoka vo Solunsko)." *Makedonski jazik* 11-12, nos. 1-2 (1960-61), 113-82 and 13-14, nos. 1-2 (1962-63), 173-276.
Gorškova, K.V. 1972. *Istoričeskaja dialektologija russkogo jazyka*. M.: Prosveščenie.
Guxman, M.M. 1962. "Sistema glasnyx fonem v germanskix jazykax." Chapter 2 of *Sravnitel'naja grammatika germanskix jazykov*, vol. 2, ed. M.M. Guxman et al., 72-140. M.: AN SSSR.
Halle, M. 1962. "Phonology in Generative Grammar." *Word* 18, nos. 1-2, 54-72.
Halle, M. and K.N. Stevens. 1969. "On the Feature 'Advanced Tongue Root.'" *Quarterly Progress Report No. 94, Research Lab of Electronics, M.I.T.*, 209-15.
Hamm, J. [Xamm, J.] 1965. "Nekotorye zamečanija k diaxroničeskim issledovanijam." *Voprosy jazykoznanija* 14, no. 1, 22-36.
Hamm, J. 1970. *Staroslavenska gramatika*. Zagreb: Školska knjiga.
Harris, J.W. 1969. *Spanish Phonology*. Cambridge: M.I.T. Press.
Ilčev, P. 1969. "Kâm pârvonačalnoto sâstojanie na glagoličeskata grafična sistema." *Ezik i literatura* 24, no. 5, 29-39.
Ilčev, P. 1972. "Znakova motiviranost v glagolicata." *Ezik i literatura* 27, no. 1, 16-24.
Ilčev, P. 1973. "Aspekti v izučavaneto na glagolicata." *Slavistični izsledvanija* 3, 52-63. S.: Nauka i izkustvo.
Il'inskij, G.A. 1912. *Slepčenskij apostol XII veka*. M.: Tip. G. Lissnera i D. Sobko.
Illič-Svityč, V.M. 1962. "O stadijax utrati rinezma v jugo-zapadnyx makedonskix govorax." *Voprosy slavjanskogo jazykoznanija* 6, 76-88.
Illič-Svityč, V.M. 1967. "Sravnitel'naja grammatika slavjanskix jazykov." *Sovetskoe jazykoznanie za 50 let*, 73-87. M.: Nauka.

Ivanov, J.N. 1972. *Bâlgarski dialekten atlas. Bâlgarskite govori ot Egejska Makedonija.* Vol. 1. S.: BAN.
Ivanova, V. 1955. "Nadpisât na Mostič i preslavskijat epigrafski material." In Stančev 1955:43-144. Also *Bâlgarski ezik* 5, no. 2 (1955), 44-117.
Jakobson, R.O. 1963. "Opyt fonologičeskogo podxoda k istoričeskim voprosam slavjanskoj akcentologii. Pozdnij period slavjanskoj jazykovoj praistorii." *American Contributions to the Fifth International Congress of Slavists,* vol. 1, 153-78. The Hague: Mouton.
Jakobson, R.O. 1971. "Remarques sur l'évolution phonolgique du russe comparée à celle des autres langues slaves." In his *Selected Writings,* vol. 1, 7-116. The Hague: Mouton.
Jakobson, R.O., ed. 1975. *N.S. Trubetzkoy's Letters and Notes.* The Hague: Mouton.
Jakobson, R.O. and M. Halle. 1971. "Tenseness and Laxness." In R.O. Jakobson, *Selected Writings,* vol. 1, 550-55. The Hague: Mouton.
Jakobson, R., C.G.M. Fant, and M. Halle. 1955. *Preliminaries to Speech Analysis. The Distinctive Features and Their Correlates.* Cambridge: M.I.T. Press.
Jakobson, R.O. et al. 1928. "Quelles sont les méthodes les mieux appropriées à un exposé complet et pratique de la grammaire d'une langue quelconque?" *Actes du Premier Congrès International de Linguists,* 33-36. Leiden: A.W. Sijthoff.
Jeżowa, M. 1968. *Z problemów tak zwanej trzeciej palatalizacji tylnojęzykowych w językach słowiańskich.* Wrocław: Zaklad. Narod. im. Ossolińskich.
Kalnyn, L.E. 1961. *Razvitie korreljacii tverdyx i mjagkix soglasnyx fonem v slavjanskix jazykax.* M.: AN SSSR.
Kânčev, Iv. 1968. "Govorât na s. Smolsko, Pirdopsko." *Bâlgarska dialektologija: proučvanija i materiali* 4, 5-159. S.: BAN.
Keyser, S.J. 1963. Review of H. Kurath and R.I. McDavid, Jr., *The Pronunciation of English in the Atlantic States. Language* 39, no. 2, 303-16.
Keyser, S.J. 1973. "Tense/Lax Alternations among the Low Vowels." *A Festschrift for Morris Halle,* 77-92. N.Y.: Holt, Rinehart, and Winston.
King, R.D. 1969. *Historical Linguistics and Generative Grammar.* Englewood Cliffs, NJ: Prentice-Hall.

King, R.D. 1973. "Rule Insertion." *Language* 49, no. 3, 551-78.
Kiparsky, P. 1965. "Phonological Change." Ph.D. dissertation, M.I.T.
Kiparsky, P. 1972. "Linguistic Universals and Linguistic Change." *Universals in Linguistic Theory*, 171-202. N.Y.: Holt, Rinehart, and Winston.
Kiparsky, P. 1973. "Phonological Representations." *Three Dimensions of Linguistic Theory*, 1-136. Tokyo: TEC.
Kiparsky, P. 1974. "A Note on Vowel Features." *NELS V: Papers from the Fifth Annual Meeting of the North Eastern Linguistic Society*, 162-71.
Kiparsky, V. [Kiparskij, V.] 1958. "O xronologii slavjano-finskix leksičeskix otnošenij." *Scando-Slavica* 4, 127-36.
Kočev, Iv. 1968. "O balkanskom xaraktere mjagkix soglasnyx v pozicii konca slova v bolgarskom jazyke." *Actes du Premier Congrès International des Études Balkaniques et Sud-Est Européennes*, vol. 6, 447-61. S.: BAN.
Kolesov, V.V. 1971. "Izmenenie nosovyx glasnyx po materialam russkix rukopisej XI veka." *Studia Rossica Posnaniensia* 2, 97-115.
Kolesov, V.V. 1973. "Praslavjanskaja fonema ǫ v rannix preobrazovanijax slavjanskix vokal'nyx sistem." *VII Międzynarodowy kongres slawistów: Streszczenia referatów i komunikatów*, 39-40. Warsaw: Państwowe Wydawnictwo Naukowe.
Koschmieder, E. 1951. "Bemerkungen zur Aussprache des Bulgarischen." *Zeitschrift für vergleichenden Sprachforschung* 69, nos. 3-4, 216-24.
Kotova, N.V. 1963. "Zvukovaja sistema govora rajona Gorno pole." *Slavjanskaja filologija* 4, 32-63.
Kotova, N.V. 1974. "Za konsonanta *l* pred *e* i *i* v bâlgarskija knižoven izgovor." *V pamet na prof. St. Stojkov*, 91-92. S.: BAN.
Kovačev, St. 1968. "Trojanskijat govor." *Bâlgarska dialektologija: proučvanija i materiali* 4, 161-242. S.: BAN.
Kul'bakin, S.M. 1907. *Oxridskaja rukopis' Apostola konca XII veka*. Bâlgarski starini 3. S.: Dâržavna pečatnica.
Kul'bakin, S.M. 1929. *Le vieux slave*. Paris: H. Champion.
Lang, P. 1910. "Náslovné *u* a jeho prothese v slovanštině." *Sborník filologický* 1, 175-89.

Lehmann, W.P. 1955. "The Proto-Indo-European Resonants in Germanic." *Language* 31, no. 3, 355-66.
Lekomceva, M.I. 1966. "K opisaniju fonologičeskoj sistemy staroslavjanskogo jazyka na osnove ternarnogo principa." *Lingvističeskie issledovanija po obščej i slavjanskoj tipologii*, 117-23. M.: Nauka.
Lekov, Iv. 1960. *Nasoki v razvoja na fonologičnite sistemi na slavjanskite ezici.* S.: BAN.
Lekov, Iv. 1968. *Kratka sravnitelno-istoričeska i tipologičeska gramatika na slavjanskite ezici.* S.: BAN.
Leskien, A. 1919. *Grammatik der altbulgarischen (altkirchenslavischen) Sprache.* Heidelberg: C. Winter.
Lightner, T. 1966. "On Descriptions of Common Slavic Phonology." *Slavic Review* 25, no. 4, 679-86.
Lunt, H.G. 1957. "Ligatures in Old Church Slavonic Glagolitic Manuscripts." *Slavistična revija* [Ljubljana] 10, nos. 1-4, 253-67.
Lunt, H.G. 1959. "Contributions to the Study of Old Church Slavonic." *International Journal of Slavic Linguistics and Poetics* 1-2, 9-37.
Lunt, H.G. 1974. *Old Church Slavonic Grammar.* 6th ed., rev. and ext. with an epilogue "Toward a Generative Phonology of Old Church Slavonic." The Hague: Mouton.
Lunt, H.G. [Lant, G.G.] 1977. "Praslavjanskaja progressivnaja palatalizacija." *Nahtigalov zbornik*, 167-81. Ljubljana: n.p.
Machek, V. 1958. "Zur Erklärung der sog. Baudouinischen Palatalisierung im Slavischen und im Baltischen." *Mélanges linguistiques offerts à Emil Petrovici*, 327-35. Cercetări de lingvistică 3, supplement. Bucharest: Academia Republicii Populare Romîne.
Małecki, M. 1934-36. *Dwie gwary makedońskie. Sucho i Wysoka w Słouńskiem. Cz 1: Teksty.* Biblioteka ludu słowiańskiego (Cracow), 1934, dział A, no. 2, 1-20. *Cz. 2: Słownik.* Ibid., 1936, dział A, no. 3, 1-135.
Mareš, F.V. 1956. "Vznik slovanského fonologického systému a jeho vývoj do konce období slovanské jazykové jednoty." *Slavia* 25, no. 4, 443-95.
Mareš, F.V. 1959. "Střídnice i̯-ových a u̯-ových diftongů v období slovanské jazykové jednoty." *Slavia* 28, no. 3, 347-49.

Mareš, F.V. [Mareš, V.F.] 1961. "Drevneslavjanskij literaturnyj jazyk v Velikomoravskom gosudarstve." *Voprosy jazykoznanija* 10, no. 2, 12-23.
Mareš, F.V. [Mareš, V.F.] 1962. "Rannij period morfologičeskogo razvitija slavjanskogo sklonenija." *Voprosy jazykoznanija* 11, no. 6, 13-21.
Mareš, F.V. [Mareš, V.F.] 1963. "Proisxoždenie slavjanskogo nosovogo ǫ (jǫ)." *Voprosy slavjanskogo jazykoznanija* 7, 7-11.
Mareš, F.V. 1963a. "Vznik a raný vývoj slovanské deklinace." *Československé přednášky pro V. mezinárodní sjezd slavistů v Sofii*, 51-69. Prague: Československá akad. věd.
Mareš, F.V. 1964. "Azbučna báseň z rukopisu Státní veřejné knihovny Saltykova-Ščedrina v Leningradě." *Slovo* [Zagreb] 14, 5-24.
Mareš, F.V. 1965. *The Origin of the Slavic Phonological System and Its Development up to the End of Slavic Language Unity*. Michigan Slavic Materials 6. Ann Arbor: Dept. of Slavic Languages and Literatures, Univ. of Michigan.
Mareš, F.V. 1971. "Hlaholice na Moravě a v Čechách." *Slovo* [Zagreb] 21, 133-200.
Mažiulis, V. 1973. "Proisxoždenie balto-slavjanskix tematičeskix form instr. pl." *Rocznik slawistyczny* 34, no. 1, 17-21.
Mazon, A. 1936. *Documents, contes et chansons slaves de l'Albanie du sud*. Paris: Librarie Droz.
Meillet, A. 1906. "Sur l'initiale des mots vieux slaves єcє et a." *Stat'ji po slavjanovedeniju pod redakcieju V.I. Lamanskogo*, vol. 2, 387-91. SPb.: Imp. akademija nauk.
Meillet, A. 1934. *Le slave commun*. 2nd ed. Paris: H. Champion.
Meillet, A. 1964. *Introduction à l'étude comparative des langues indo-européennes*. University: Univ. of Alabama Press.
Meyer, K.H. 1928. "Die Wechsel von ě und ja im Codex Suprasliensis." *Symbolae Grammaticae in Honorem Ioannis Rozwadowski*, vol. 2, 193-203. Cracow: Gebethner and Wolff.
Mikkola, J.J. 1894. *Berührungen zwischen den westfinnischen und slavischen Sprachen*. Helsingfors: Druckerei der Finnischen Litteraturgesellschaft.
Miletič, L. 1886. "Osobenostite na ezika v Marijnskija pametnik." *Periodičesko spisanie* 19-20, 219-52.

Miletič, L. 1896. "Sedmigradskite bâlgari." *Sbornik za narodni umotvorenija, nauki i knižnina* 13, 153-256.
Mirčev, K. 1938. "Kâm makedonskata dialektologija." *Makedonski pregled* 11, nos. 1-2, 64-70.
Mirčev, K. 1958. *Istoričeska gramatika na bâlgarskija ezik.* S.: BAN. [2nd ed., 1963; 3rd ed., 1978.]
Mirčev, K. and Xr. Kodov. 1965. *Eninski apostol: starobâlgarski pametnik ot XI v.* S.: BAN.
Mixailè, G. 1964. "Staroslavjanskie nadpisi, otkrytye v s. Basarab' (Obl. Dobrodža)." *Revue roumaine de linguistique* 9, no. 2, 149-69.
Mladenov, M.S. 1966. *Ixtimanskijat govor.* Trudove po bâlgarska dialektologija 2. S.: BAN.
Mladenov, St. 1929. *Geschichte der bulgarischen Sprache.* Berlin: W. de Gruyter.
Mladenov, St. 1941. *Etimologičeski i pravopisen rečnik na bâlgarskija knižoven ezik.* S.: X.G. Danov.
Mošin, Vl. 1973. "Još o Hrabru, slavenskim azbukama i azbučnim molitavama." *Slovo* [Zagreb] 23, 5-71.
Nedeljković, O. 1965. "Još jednom o hronološkom primatu glagoljice." *Slovo* [Zagreb] 15-16, 19-58.
Nedeljković, O. 1971. "Neke inovacije u fonološkom sistemu prvobitne glagoljice." *Slovo* [Zagreb] 21, 79-93.
Nieminen, E. 1956. "Slavisch *(j)ustro, (j)utro* und Verwandte." *Scando-Slavica* 2, 13-28.
Nikolov, B. 1970. "Po vâprosa za nosovite glasni v bâlgarskija knižoven ezik." *Bâlgarski ezik* 20, nos. 2-3, 163-74.
Paul, H. 1960. *Prinzipien der Sprachgeschichte.* 9th ed. Tübingen: Niemeyer.
Pavlović, M. 1957. "Znak Ѫ i njegove glasovne vrednosti." *Slovo* [Zagreb] 6-8, 278-91.
Perkell, J.S. 1969. *Physiology of Speech Production: Results and Implications of a Quantitative Cineradiographic Study.* Cambridge: M.I.T. Press.
Perkell, J.S. 1971. "Physiology of Speech Production: A Preliminary Study of Two Suggested Revisions of the Features Specifying Vowels." *Quarterly Progress Report No. 102, Research Lab of Electronics, M.I.T.*, 123-39.
Popova, T.V. 1962. "Korreljacija tverdyx i mjagkix soglasnyx fonem v bolgarskom jazyke." *Slavjanskoe jazykoznanie. Kratkie soob. Instituta slavjanovedenija AN SSSR* 35, 3-28.

Reformatskij, A.A. 1963. "Jazyk, struktura, i fonologija." *Prace filologiczne* 18, no. 1, 105-11.
Reiter, N. 1964. *Der Dialekt von Titov-Veles*. Berlin: Harrassowitz.
Revzin, I.I. 1964. "K logičeskomu obosnovaniju teorii fonologičeskix priznakov." *Voprosy jazykoznanija* 13, no. 5, 59-65.
Richter, E. 1940. "Die italienischen č und ŝ Laute." *Archives néerlandaises de phonétique expérimentale* 16, 1-38.
Romanski, St. 1932. "Dolnovardarskijat govor." *Makedonski pregled* 8, no. 1, 99-140.
Ruhlen, M. 1972. "Nasal Vowels." *Working Papers on Language Universals* [Stanford Univ.] 12, 1-36.
Samilov, M. 1968. "Problems in the Historical Dialectology of Macedonian." *The Slavonic and East European Review* 46, no. 107, 277-81.
Saporta, S. 1965. "Ordered Rules, Dialect Differences and Historical Processes." *Langauge* 41, no. 2, 218-24.
Scargill, M.H. 1951. *Notes on the Development of the Principal Sounds of Indo-European through Proto-Germanic into Old English.* Toronto: Toronto Univ. Press.
Scatton, E. 1975. *Bulgarian Phonology.* Cambridge: Slavica.
Scatton, E. 1976. "Forms Such as [cál]/[cáli] in Dialects of East Balkan Slavic." *Slavic Linguistics and Language Teaching*, ed. T.F. Magner, 249-58. Cambridge: Slavica.
Scatton, E. 1978. "Old Church Slavonic tj/dj ~ št/žd." *Linguistics* 208, 13-21.
Ščepkin, V.N. 1899. *Razsuždenie o jazyke Savvinoj knigi.* SPb.: Otdelenie russkogo jazyka i slovesnosti.
Ščepkin, V.N. 1903. *Savvina kniga.* Pamjatniki staroslavjanskogo jazyka 1, no. 2. SPb.: Imp. akademija nauk.
Ščepkin, V.N. 1906. *Bolonskaja psaltyr'.* SPb.: Otdelenie russkogo jazyka i slovesnosti.
Seliščev, A.M. 1929. *Polog i ego bolgarskoe naselenie.* S.: Izd-vo Makedonskogo naučnogo instituta.
Seliščev, A.M. 1951. *Staroslavjanskij jazyk.* Part 1. M.: Učpedgiz.
Schane, S.A. 1973. *Generative Phonology.* Englewood Cliffs, NJ: Prentice-Hall.
Shevelov, G.Y. 1963. "Prothetic Consonants in Slavic." *American Contributions to the Fifth International Congress of Slavists, Sofia*, vol. 1, 243-62. The Hague: Mouton.

WORKS CITED

Shevelov, G.Y. 1964. *A Prehistory of Slavic.* Heidelberg: C. Winter.
Shibatani, M. 1973. "The Role of Surface Phonetic Constraints in Generative Phonology." *Language* 49, no. 1, 87-106.
Sławski, Fr. 1947. "Oboczność ǫ : u w językach słoviańskych." *Slavia Occidentalis* [Poznań] 18, 246-90.
Stančev, St. et al. 1955. *Nadpisât na Čârgobilja Mostič.* S.: BAN.
Stang, C.S. 1966. *Vergleichende Grammatik der Baltischen Sprachen.* Oslo: Universitetsforlaget.
Stankov, V. 1974. "Promeni na lateralnite sâglasni v govora na s. Gorna Bešovica, Vračansko." *V pamet na prof. St. Stojkov,* 189-93. S.: BAN.
Stieber, Zd. 1969. *Zarys gramatyki porównawczej języków słowiańskich.* Part 1. Warsaw: Państwowe Wydawnictwo Naukowe.
Stojkov, St. 1956. "Edna nova promjana na sâglasnata *l* v bâlgarski ezik." *Bâlgarski ezik* 6, no. 3, 239-44.
Stojkov, St. 1959. "Edno novo javlenie v bâlgarskija vokalizâm." *Bâlgarski ezik* 9, no. 1, 12-19.
Stojkov, St. 1962. "Kâm dialektnija konsonantizâm v bâlgarskija ezik." *Bâlgarski ezik,* nos. 1-2, 13-19.
Stojkov, St. 1962a. "Kâm vokalizma na smoljanskija govor (Preglas na glasna *a* v *ê, e* v govora na Trigrad, Devinsko)." *Ezik i literatura* 17, no. 1, 19-24.
Stojkov, St. 1968. *Bâlgarska dialektologija.* 2nd ed. S.: BAN.
Stojkov, St. 1968a. "Kâm vokalnata tipologija na rodopskite govori." *Slavističen sbornik,* 229-43. S.: BAN.
Stojkov, St. 1971. "Novaja pervaja palatalizacija v bolgarskom jazyke." *Issledovanija po slavjanskomu jazykoznaniju,* 375-80. M.: Nauka.
Šylo, H. 1949. "Javyšče protezy v slov'ans'kyx movax." *Voprosy slavjanskogo jazykoznanija* [L'vov] 2, 229-47.
Tilkov, D. 1974. "Funkcionirane na fonemata /v/ v knižovnija bâlgarski ezik." *Bâlgarski ezik* 24, no. 2, 166-69.
Tilkov, D. and T. Bojadžiev. 1977. *Bâlgarska fonetika.* S.: Nauka i izkustvo.
Tkadlčík, V. 1956. "Trojí hlaholské *i* v Kijevských listech." *Slavia* 25, no. 2, 200-16.
Tkadlčík, V. 1964. "Dvojí ch v hlaholici." *Slavia* 33, no. 2, 182-93.
Tkadlčík, V. 1971. "Systém hlaholské abecedy." *Studia palaeoslovenica,* 357-77. Prague: Academia.

Tolstaja, S.M. 1966. "K fonologičeskoj interpretacii pol'skogo rinezma." *Lingvističeskie issledovanija po obščej i slavjanskoj tipologii*, 124-40. M.: Nauka.
Toporov, V.N. 1959. "Nekotorye soobraženija otnositel'no izučenija istorii praslavjanskogo jazyka." *Slavjanskoe jazykoznanie. Sbornik statej*, 3-27. M.: AN SSSR.
Trávníček, F. 1928. "Prothese či hiát?" *Symbolae grammaticae in honorem Ioannis Rozwadowski*, vol. 2, 139-51. Cracow: Gebethner and Wolff.
Trubetzkoy, N.S. 1930. "Über die Entstehung der gemeinwestslawischen Eigentümlichkeiten auf dem Gebiete des Konsonantismus." *Zeitschrift für slavische Philologie* 7, nos. 3-4, 383-406.
Trubetzkoy, N.S. 1954. *Altkirchenslavische Grammatik*. Vienna: Rudolf Jagoditsch.
Ugrinova, R. 1951. "Govorite vo Skopsko." Diplomski raboti, 2. Skopje: Katedra za južnoslovenski jazici, Filosofski fakultet na univerzitetot.
Vaillant, A. 1950. *Grammaire comparée des langues slaves*. Vol. 1. Lyon: I.A.C.
van Wijk, N. [van Vejk, N.] 1927-28. "O naprjažennom ъ (ь) v Sbornike Kloca." *Slavia* 6, nos. 2-3, 239-45.
van Wijk, N. 1931. *Geschichte der altkirchenslavischen Sprache*. Berlin: W. de Gruyter.
van Wijk, N. [van Vejk, N.] 1950. "K istorii fonologičeskoj sistemy v obščeslavjanskom jazyke pozdnego perioda." *Slavia* 19, nos. 3-4, 293-313.
van Wijk, N. [van Vejk, N.] 1957. *Istorija staroslavjanskogo jazyka*. M.: Izd-vo inostrannoj lit-ry.
Vasmer, M. 1941. *Die Slaven in Griechenland*. Berlin: W. de Gruyter.
Večerka, R. 1972. "K praslovanským palatalizacím velár." *Sborník prací filosofické fakulty Brněnské University*, Series A, no. 20, 53-61.
Velčeva, B. 1964. "Pokazatelni mestoimenija i narečija v novobâlgarskite pametnici ot XVII i XVIII v." *Izvestija na Instituta za bâlgarski ezik* 10, 159-234.
Velčeva, B. 1966. "Glagolicata i školata na Kliment Oxridski." *Kliment Oxridski*, 133-41. S.: BAN.

Velčeva, B. 1966a. "Vâprosi na kâsnata glagolica (Nosovkite v pârvija počerk na Oxridskija apostol)." *Bâlgarski ezik* 26, no. 1, 3-9.
Velčeva, B. 1969. "Eine Besonderheit der Glagolica." *Zeitschrift für Slavistik* 14, no. 4, 501-505.
Velčeva, B. 1969a. "Kâm ustanovjavaneto na srednobâlgarskite pravopisni tipove (Stamatovo evangelie ot XIII vek)." *Izvestija na Instituta za bâlgarski ezik* 17, 233-86.
Velčeva, B. 1973. "Vâprosât na Ѡ v glagoličeskata azbuka." *Izvestija na Instituta za bâlgarski ezik* 22, 105-24.
Velčeva, B. 1973a. "Pravila, poraždašti izmenenijata na [r], [l] v tri bâlgarski govora." *Slavjanska filologija* 12, 221-36.
Velčeva, B. 1977. "Glagoličeskijat *i*-problem i Rilskite listove." *Bâlgarski ezik* 27, no. 6, 456-60.
Vennemann, T. 1971. "The Phonology of Gothic Vowels." *Language* 47, no. 1, 90-132.
Vennemann, T. 1974. "Restructuring." *Lingua* 33, no. 2, 137-56.
Vidoevski, B. 1962. *Kumanovskiot govor.* Skopje: Institut za makedonski jazik.
von Arnim, B. 1930. *Studien zum altbulgarischen Psalterium Sinaiticum.* Leipzig: Markert and Petters.
Voyles, B. 1967. "Simplicity, Ordered Rules, and the First Sound Shift." *Language* 43, no. 3, 636-60.
Vrana, J. 1963. "O postanku i karakteru staroslovjenskih azbukvara i azbučnich molitava." *Filologija* [Zagreb] 4, 191-204.
Vrana, J. 1964. "Glagoljski grafemi Ⱋ — Ⱌ, ⰞⰕ — ⰞⰝ i njihova ćirilska transkripcija." *Slavia* 33, no. 2, 171-81.
Wukasch, C. 1976. "A Rule Reordering in Late Proto-Slavic." *International Review of Slavic Linguistics* 1, no. 1, 119-27.
Xoliolčev, Xr. 1969. "Kâm vâprosa za izpadaneto na kraeslovni *i* i *u* v bâlgarskite govori." *Bâlgarski ezik* 19, no. 1, 27-37.
Zinder, L.R. 1963. "Fonematičeskaja suščnost' dolgogo palatalizovannogo [š:] v russkom jazyke." *Naučnye doklady vysšej školy. Filologičeskie nauki* 2, 137-42.
Zinkjavičjus, Z. 1972. "O razvitii baltijskogo vokalizma." *Baltoslavjanskij sbornik,* 5-14. M.: Nauka.
Žuravlev, V.K. 1961. "Formirovanie gruppovogo singarmonizma v praslavjanskom jazyke." *Voprosy jazykoznanija* 10, no. 4, 33-45.

Žuravlev, V.K. 1965. "Genezis protezov v slavjanskix jazykax." *Voprosy jazykoznanija* 14, no. 4, 32-43.
Žuravlev, V.K. 1965a. "Genezis gruppovogo singarmonizma v praslavjanskom jazyke." Avtoreferat doktorskoj dissertacii. M.: Filologičeskij fakul'tet, MGU.
Žuravlev, V.K. 1966. "Gruppofonema kak osnovnaja fonolologičeskaja edinica praslavjanskogo jazyka." *Issledovanija po fonologii*, 79-96. M.: Nauka.
Žuravlev, V.K. 1968. See Georgiev et al., 1968.

OTHER SLAVICA BOOKS

Catherine V. Chvany and Richard D. Brecht, eds.: *Morphosyntax in Slavic*, 1980

Jozef Cíger-Hronský: *Jozef Mak* (a novel), translated from Slovak by Andrew Cincura, Afterword by Peter Petro, 1985

Frederick Columbus: *Introductory Workbook in Historical Phonology*, 1974

Julian W. Connolly & Sonia I. Ketchian, eds.: *Studies in Honor of Vsevolod Setchkarev*, 1987

Gary Cox: *Tyrant and Victim in Dostoevsky*, 1984

Anna Lisa Crone & Catherine V. Chvany, eds.: *New Studies in Russian Language and Literature*, 1987

R. G. A. de Bray: *Guide to the South Slavonic Languages (Guide to the Slavonic Languages, Third Edition, Revised and Expanded, Part 1);*, 1980

Carolina De Maegd Soep: *Chekhov and Women: Women in the Life and Work of Chekhov*, 1987

Bruce L. Derwing and Tom M. S. Priestly: *Reading Rules for Russian: A Systematic Approach to Russian Spelling and Pronunciation, with Notes on Dialectal and Stylistic Variation*, 1980

Dorothy Disterheft: *The Syntactic Development of the Infinitive in Indo-European*, 1980

Thomas Eekman and Dean S. Worth, eds.: *Russian Poetics* Proceedings of the International Colloquium at UCLA, September 22-26, 1975, 1983

James S. Elliott: *Russian for Trade Negotiations with the USSR*, 1981

Ralph Carter Elwood, ed.: *Reconsiderations on the Russian Revolution*, 1976

Michael S. Flier and Richard D. Brecht, eds.: *Issues in Russian Morphosyntax*, 1985

Michael S. Flier and Alan Timberlake, eds: *The Scope of Slavic Aspect*, 1985

John Miles Foley, ed.: *Comparative Research on Oral Traditions: A Memorial for Milman Parry*, 1987

John M. Foley, ed.: *Oral Traditional Literature A Festschrift for Albert Bates Lord*, 1981

Diana Greene: *Insidious Intent: An Interpretation of Fedor Sologub's* The Petty Demon, 1986

Charles E. Gribble, ed.: *Medieval Slavic Texts, Vol. 1, Old and Middle Russian Texts*, 1973

OTHER SLAVICA BOOKS

Charles E. Gribble: *Reading Bulgarian Through Russian*, 1987
Charles E. Gribble: *Russian Root List with a Sketch of Word Formation, Second Edition*, 1982
Charles E. Gribble: *A Short Dictionary of 18th-Century Russian*/Словарик Русского Языка 18-го Века, 1976
Charles E. Gribble, ed.: *Studies Presented to Professor Roman Jakobson by His Students*, 1968
George J. Gutsche and Lauren G. Leighton, eds., 1982
Morris Halle, ed.: *Roman Jakobson: What He Taught Us*, 1983
Charles J. Halperin: *The Tatar Yoke*, 1986
William S. Hamilton: *Introduction to Russian Phonology and Word Structure*, 1980
Pierre R. Hart: *G. R. Derzhavin: A Poet's Progress*, 1978
Michael Heim: *Contemporary Czech*, 1982
Michael Heim, Zlata Meyerstein, and Dean Worth: *Readings in Czech*, 1985
M. Hubenova & others: *A Course in Modern Bulgarian, Parts 1 and 2*, 1983
Martin E. Huld: *Basic Albanian Etymologies*, 1984
Charles Isenberg: *Substantial Proofs of Being: Osip Mandelstam's Literary Prose*, 1987
Roman Jakobson, with the assistance of Kathy Santilli: *Brain and Language Cerebral Hemispheres and Linguistic Structure in Mutual Light*, 1980
Donald K. Jarvis and Elena D. Lifshitz: *Viewpoints: A Listening and Conversation Course in Russian, Third Edition*, 1985; plus *Instructor's Manual*
Leslie A. Johnson: *The Experience of Time in Crime and Punishment*, 1985
Raina Katzarova-Kukudova and Kiril Djenev: *Bulgarian Folk Dances*, 1976
Emily R. Klenin: *Animacy in Russian: A New Interpretation, 1983*
Andrej Kodjak, Krystyna Pomorska, and Kiril Taranovsky, eds.: *Alexander Puškin Symposium II*, 1980
Andrej Kodjak, Krystyna Pomorska, Stephen Rudy, eds.: *Myth in Literature*, 1985
Andrej Kodjak: *Pushkin's I. P. Belkin*, 1979
Andrej Kodjak, Michael J. Connolly, Krystyna Pomorska, eds.: *Structural Analysis of Narrative Texts (Conference Papers)*, 1980
Demetrius J. Koubourlis, ed.: *Topics in Slavic Phonology*, 1974

OTHER SLAVICA BOOKS

Ronald D. LeBlanc: *The Russianization of Gil Blas: A Study in Literary Appropriation*, 1986

Richard L. Leed and Slava Paperno: *5000 Russian Words With All Their Inflected Forms: A Russian-English Dictionary*, 1987

Richard L. Leed, Alexander D. Nakhimovsky, and Alice S. Nakhimovsky: *Beginning Russian*, Vol. *1*, 1981; Vol. *2*, 1982

Edgar H. Lehrman: *A Handbook to Eighty-Six of Chekhov's Stories in Russian*, 1985

Lauren Leighton, ed.: *Studies in Honor of Xenia Gąsiorowska*, 1983

Rado L. Lencek: *The Structure and History of the Slovene Language*, 1982

Jules F. Levin and Peter D. Haikalis, with Anatole A. Forostenko: *Reading Modern Russian*, 1979

Maurice I. Levin: *Russian Declension and Conjugation: A Structural Description with Exercises*, 1978

Alexander Lipson: *A Russian Course.* Part *1*, Part *2*, and Part *3*, 1981; *Teacher's Manual* by Stephen J. Molinsky 1981

Yvonne R. Lockwood: *Text and Context Folksong in a Bosnian Muslim Village*, 1983

Sophia Lubensky & Donald K. Jarvis, eds.: *Teaching, Learning, Acquiring Russian*, 1984

Horace G. Lunt: *Fundamentals of Russian*, 1982

Paul Macura: *Russian-English Botanical Dictionary*, 1982

Thomas G. Magner, ed.: *Slavic Linguistics and Language Teaching*, 1976

Vladimir Markov and Dean S. Worth, eds.: *From Los Angeles to Kiev Papers on the Occasion of the Ninth International Congress of Slavists*, 1983

Mateja Matejić and Dragan Milivojević: *An Anthology of Medieval Serbian Literature in English*, 1978

Peter J. Mayo: *The Morphology of Aspect in Seventeenth-Century Russian (Based on Texts of the Smutnoe Vremja)*, 1985

Vasa D. Mihailovich and Mateja Matejić: *A Comprehensive Bibliography of Yugoslav Literature in English, 1593-1980*, 1984

Edward Możejko, ed.: *Vasiliy Pavlovich Aksënov: A Writer in Quest of Himself*, 1986

Edward Możejko: *Yordan Yovkov*, 1984

Alexander D. Nakhimovsky and Richard L. Leed: *Advanced Russian, Second Edition, Revised*, 1987

OTHER SLAVICA BOOKS

The Comprehensive Russian Grammar of A. A. Barsov/ Обстоятельная грамматика А. А. Барсова, Critical Edition by Lawrence W. Newman, 1980

Felix J. Oinas: *Essays on Russian Folklore and Mythology,* 1985

Hongor Oulanoff: *The Prose Fiction of Veniamin Kaverin,* 1976

Lora Paperno: *Getting Around Town in Russian: Situational Dialogs,* English translation and photographs by Richard D. Sylvester, 1987

Slava Paperno, Alexander D. Nakhimovsky, Alice S. Nakhimovsky, and Richard L. Leed: *Intermediate Russian: The Twelve Chairs,* 1985

Ruth L. Pearce: *Russian For Expository Prose, Vol. 1 Introductory Course,* 1983

Gerald Pirog: *Aleksandr Blok's* Итальянские Стихи *Confrontation and Disillusionment,* 1983

Stanley J. Rabinowitz: *Sologub's Literary Children: Keys to a Symbolist's Prose,* 1980

Gilbert C. Rappaport: *Grammatical Function and Syntactic Structure: The Adverbial Participle of Russian,* 1984

Lester A. Rice: *Hungarian Morphological Irregularities,* 1970

David F. Robinson: *Lithuanian Reverse Dictionary,* 1976

Don K. Rowney & G. Edward Orchard, eds.: *Russian and Slavic History,* 1977

Catherine Rudin: *Aspects of Bulgarian Syntax: Complementizers and WH Constructions,* 1986

Ernest A. Scatton: *Bulgarian Phonology,* 1975

Ernest A. Scatton: *A Reference Grammar of Modern Bulgarian,* 1984

William R. Schmalstieg: *Introduction to Old Church Slavic, second edition, revised and expanded,* 1983

R. D. Schupbach: *Lexical Specialization in Russian,* 1984

Peter Seyffert: *Soviet Literary Structuralism: Background Debate Issues,* 1985

Kot K. Shangriladze and Erica W. Townsend, eds.: Papers for the V. Congress of Southeast European Studies (Belgrade, September 1984), 1984

Michael Shapiro: *Aspects of Russian Morphology, A Semiotic Investigation,* 1969

J. Thomas Shaw: *Pushkin A Concordance to the Poetry,* 1985

Efraim Sicher: *Style and Structure in the Prose of Isaak Babel',* 1986

OTHER SLAVICA BOOKS

Mark S. Simpson: *The Russian Gothic Novel and its British Antecedents*, 1986

Greta N. Slobin, ed.: *Aleksej Remizov: Approaches to a Protean Writer*, 1987

Theofanis G. Stavrou and Peter R. Weisensel: *Russian Travelers to the Christian East from the Twelfth to the Twentieth Century*, 1985

Gerald Stone and Dean S. Worth, eds.: *The Formation of the Slavonic Literary Languages, Proceedings of a Conference Held in Memory of Robert Auty and Anne Pennington at Oxford 6-11 July 1981*, 1985

Roland Sussex and J. C. Eade, eds.: *Culture and Nationalism in Nineteenth-Century Eastern Europe*, 1985

Oscar E. Swan: *First Year Polish, second edition, revised and expanded*, 1983

Oscar E. Swan: *Intermediate Polish*, 1986

Charles E. Townsend: *Continuing With Russian*, 1981

Charles E. Townsend: *Czech Through Russian*, 1981

Charles E. Townsend: *The Memoirs of Princess Natal'ja Borisovna Dolgorukaja*, 1977

Charles E. Townsend: *Russian Word Formation, corrected reprint*, 1975 (1980)

Charles E. Townsend & Veronica N. Dolenko: *Instructor's Manual to Accompany Continuing With Russian*, 1987

Janet G. Tucker: *Innokentij Annenskij and the Acmeist Doctrine*, 1987

Walter N. Vickery, ed.: *Aleksandr Blok Centennial Conference*, 1984

Daniel C. Waugh, ed.: *Essays in Honor of A. A. Zimin*, 1985

Daniel C. Waugh: *The Great Turkes Defiance On the History of the Apocryphal Correspondence of the Ottoman Sultan in its Muscovite and Russian Variants*, 1978

Susan Wobst: *Russian Readings and Grammatical Terminology*, 1978

James B. Woodward: *The Symbolic Art of Gogol: Essays on His Short Fiction*, 1982

Dean S. Worth: *Origins of Russian Grammar Notes on the state of Russian philology before the advent of printed grammars*, 1983